THE COMPLETE IDIOT'S GUIDE® TO

Computer Illustration

by Marc Campbell

ALPHA
A Pearson Education Company

International Standard Book Number: 0-02-864319-4
Library of Congress Catalog Card Number: Available upon request.

04 03 02   8 7 6 5 4 3 2 1

Interpretation of the printing code: The rightmost number of the first series of numbers is the year of the book's printing; the rightmost number of the second series of numbers is the number of the book's printing. For example, a printing code of 02-1 shows that the first printing occurred in 2002.

Printed in the United States of America

Note: This publication contains the opinions and ideas of its author. It is intended to provide helpful and informative material on the subject matter covered. It is sold with the understanding that the author and publisher are not engaged in rendering professional services in the book. If the reader requires personal assistance or advice, a competent professional should be consulted.

The author and publisher specifically disclaim any responsibility for any liability, loss, or risk, personal or otherwise, which is incurred as a consequence, directly or indirectly, of the use and application of any of the contents of this book.

For marketing and publicity, please call: 317-581-3722

The publisher offers discounts on this book when ordered in quantity for bulk purchases and special sales.

For sales within the United States, please contact: Corporate and Government Sales, 1-800-382-3419 or corpsales@pearsontechgroup.com

Outside the United States, please contact: International Sales, 317-581-3793 or international@pearsontechgroup.com

Publisher: *Marie Butler-Knight*
Product Manager: *Phil Kitchel*
Managing Editor: *Jennifer Chisholm*
Acquisitions Editor: *Eric Heagy*
Development Editor: *Michael Koch*
Production Editor: *Katherin Bidwell*
Copy Editor: *Fran Blauw*
Cover/Book Designer: *Trina Wurst*
Indexer: *Angie Bess*
Layout/Proofreading: *Angela Calvert, Svetlana Dominguez*

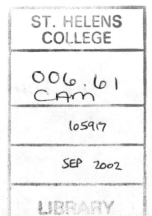

Contents at a Glance

Contents

Appendixes

Foreword

Par•a•digm/n.

1. example or pattern
2. simplified description of a system
3. two 1/10th units of the American dollar—"I have a pair-a-dimes"

It's been 12 years since I plugged in my first home computer and fired up my copy of Photoshop 3—what a blast! It had little brushes and neat-o palettes and mysterious tools with pictures that made no sense, but it was easy to see right away that the crisp white canvas staring back at me was going to be an ally—a valuable tool that I'd better learn how to harness and use for good, not evil.

Since then I've logged hundreds of hours inside illustration programs like Adobe Illustrator, Macromedia Freehand, CorelDRAW, and Canvas. I've discovered most of what I know by accident or trial by fire, either by selecting tools that I wasn't familiar with and seeing how they worked or facing impossible deadlines for impossible clients that wanted impossible results under impossible conditions .... Necessity is still very much the mother of invention—and ulcers! I wish I knew then that resources like Marc Campbell's well-designed and logically laid-out book would exist for idiots like me. Reading this book now, I envy today's novice computer illustrator standing before the vast sea of the computer graphic vista. Armed with this book and a modest amount of effort anyone should be able to decipher the mystifying and stupefying world of computer illustration.

Vectors? Paths? Color Modes? Pixels? Lassos? Eyedropper Tools!? Swatches?!?

The learning curve is steep, the nomenclature cumbersome, and the technology can be expensive. But the rewards are enormous. The diligent student and the ardent enthusiast will be wise to find clear, easily defined paradigms. And this book is just that: an easily defined, well-conceived paradigm that helps you, the disciple, make relationships between the mundane world around us and the abstract world of 1s and 0s inside your CPU (Central Processing Unit). Marc has taken an entire discipline and created a primer that anyone can follow and everyone will benefit from.

Whether you are an idiot, a dummy, or a reasonably intelligent human being, you'll explore the foundations of computer imaging through each chapter of this smartly designed and elegant book. By following the structure of this book, you'll see that each chapter is a foundation for the one that follows it—with blocks of information that yield a solid, practical understanding of how things work the way they do in a computer illustration package.

The digital tools that have become part of the graphic illustrator's skill set over the last dozen years should be viewed as extensions of the concepts and techniques that visual artists have been using for thousands of years. A well-rounded awareness of form and design theory will certainly help anyone embracing the digital side of visual art for the first time. Many balk at the idea of creating imagery purely in virtual space, given that all your time and effort in a digital illustration can ultimately be summed up in a few lines of code—the 1s and 0s I've already referred to. But I would encourage the computer illustrator to consider that, regardless of your training, experience, and personal aesthetic, computer illustration still has its roots in your imagination and is as informed by the history of art through the ages as any visual arts discipline.

The connections between heart, hand, mouse, CPU interface, monitor; all these things should nourish your ability and passion in creating art not just on paper or a napkin with lipstick or crayons, but also on the computer. That blank white canvas on your monitor that stares back at you should inspire and challenge you. There really are no mistakes to be made in creating art on the computer. It will forgive an infinite number of awkward steps you may take as you explore your particular aspirations.

Let Marc show you how to realize some of these aspirations with *The Complete Idiot's Guide to Computer Illustration!*

Cheers!

James Dean Conklin, 4/2002
Art Director, Total Training
Creative Director, Greenhead Media

Introduction

The philosopher Nietzsche said, and I'm paraphrasing here, that image is everything. Not surprisingly, he contends that life without art is unendurable. If this is true, then learning to create art on the computer is the unendurable part for many artists today.

Computer illustration in particular gets singled out as one of life's great hardships. Critics use words such as *unfathomable*, *unintuitive*, *clumsy*, and *tedious*. There is some truth to this. Computer illustration isn't like its traditional, pen-and-paper counterpart. Approaching it as if it were is a sure recipe for frustration.

But if you approach it as it is—a brand-new set of techniques using a brand-new set of tools—the hardship disappears. The unfathomable becomes sensible, the unintuitive becomes clear, the clumsy becomes precise, and the tedious becomes fun. This book shows you how easy and straightforward computer illustration can be.

Whether you're a nonillustrator with artistic leanings or an accomplished master of pen and paper, my advice to you is the same: Start at the beginning of the book, work through all the examples in order, and repeat them as many times as you need to feel comfortable. Feel free to come up with exercises of your own as you go. The idea here is to practice. The more you practice, the better you get, and the easier computer illustration becomes.

There are no grades and no final exam. Take as much time as you need for each chapter. Stop when you feel like you need a break. Every now and then, go back to previous chapters and review the material, just to keep it fresh in your mind. You never know when a seemingly pointless tool or technique will suddenly make perfect sense.

The bottom line is that you can do it. I have every confidence. I've worked with all kinds of people with all kinds of experience levels, all of them with one thing in common: They thought for sure that they could not, cannot, and would never. A few kept this attitude and completed self-fulfilling prophecies. Most maintained an open mind and discovered that there was more inside them than they realized.

Who Should Read This Book

This book is for anyone who wants to create illustrations with a computer. It assumes no knowledge of computer graphics and no experience in illustration. It explains all the jargon and clarifies the underlying concepts. It operates on the proven principle that if you want to learn computer illustration, you can and you will. Go through this book with patience, practice, and persistence, and you will come out the other side a computer illustrator.

How This Book Is Organized

This book is divided into six parts.

Part 1, "Computer Illustration at a Glance," provides an overview of the field of computer illustration and introduces you to Adobe Illustrator, the industry-standard drawing software.

Part 2, "Creating Line Art," shows you how to use the various drawing tools to produce an illustration.

Part 3, "Adding Color, Style, and Type," brings your line art to life and helps you to flesh out your artistic vision.

Part 4, "Now You're Cooking," shows you how to get the most out of the digital drawing environment with menu commands and transformation tools.

Part 5, "Getting Fancy," provides guidelines and techniques for making the best use of special effects.

Part 6, "Applying Finishing Touches," takes your illustration project to completion and shows you how to publish your work in a variety of forms.

Use the appendixes at the end of the book as quick reference. Compare different software packages for computer illustration in Appendix A, "An Illustrator's Guide to Software." Install the trial software and explore the CD-ROM in Appendix B, "What's on the CD-ROM." Find clear explanations of technical jargon in Appendix C, "Glossary."

The focus of the book is learning by doing. Parts 2 through 6 feature a running practice exercise: creating a full-blown comic strip from scratch. Check the first two pages of the color insert in this book for a preview. The CD-ROM contains all the art files you need to create this comic, but you can also supply 100 percent of the art yourself by following the step-by-step instructions at the end of each chapter. Completing the project involves just about every technique that I describe in the book, so it's a thorough (and hopefully entertaining) way to learn about computer illustration.

Hardware Requirements

To use the illustration and graphics software on the CD-ROM, your computer needs to meet the following minimum requirements:

- Intel Pentium II processor (Windows) or PowerPC Processor (Macintosh)
- Windows 98 or Mac OS 8.5
- 128MB RAM

- 460MB (Windows) or 500MB (Macintosh) free hard disk space
- Screen resolution of 800 by 600 pixels and 256 colors

If your operating system is Mac OS X, run the applications in Classic mode.

Extras

Along the way, I throw in extra bits and miscellaneous tasty morsels in the form of sidebars. I use four kinds for your informational pleasure:

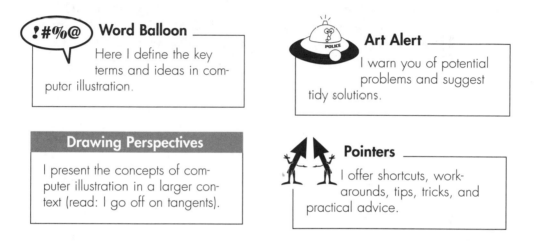

Word Balloon
Here I define the key terms and ideas in computer illustration.

Art Alert
I warn you of potential problems and suggest tidy solutions.

Drawing Perspectives
I present the concepts of computer illustration in a larger context (read: I go off on tangents).

Pointers
I offer shortcuts, workarounds, tips, tricks, and practical advice.

Acknowledgments

The writer of a book gets his name on the cover, but as a certain senator from New York once said, "It takes a village." There would be no book for me to write without the talent, sweat, and dedication of some very fine people I now have the honor of publicly thanking.

So thank you, Neil Salkind, agent and adviser. Thank you, Craig Wiley, Stacey Barone, Kristin Pickens, Jessica Richards, and the team of professionals at Studio B. Thank you, Eric Heagy, standard-bearer, tape cutter, and inside man. Thank you, Michael Koch, for knowing when to take the wheel. Thank you, Katherin Bidwell, for smooth sailing on the sea of production. Thank you, Fran Blauw, for knowing what I meant to say. Thank you, Michael Hunter, for your care and feeding of the CD-ROM. And a big thank you to all the people at Pearson whom I didn't have the pleasure of meeting, but whose late nights and hard work are directly responsible for this book.

Most especially, thank you, Bobbi Jo, for your vast patience and constant support.

Special Thanks to the Technical Reviewer

The Complete Idiot's Guide to Computer Illustration was reviewed by an expert who double-checked the accuracy of what you will learn here to help us ensure that this book gives you everything you need to know about the basics of computer illustration. Special thanks are extended to Cheryl Roy.

Trademarks

All terms mentioned in this book that are known to be or are suspected of being trademarks or service marks have been appropriately capitalized. Alpha Books and Pearson Education, Inc., cannot attest to the accuracy of this information. Use of a term in this book should not be regarded as affecting the validity of any trademark or service mark.

Part 1

Computer Illustration at a Glance

What is this thing called computer illustration? How does it work? How do you do it? Here is where you find out. This part explains the field of computer illustration, introduces you to the two kinds of computer graphics, and demonstrates the user interface of the software. Kindly check any lingering self-doubts at the door. I promise you, all you need is your desire to learn, and you will succeed at computer illustration.

Ready? Great! Just turn the page to begin your adventure.

So You Want to Be a Computer Illustrator

In This Chapter

◆ Defining computer illustration

◆ Exploring other areas of interest

◆ Equipping yourself as a computer illustrator

"What if," somebody must have said, long ago, at the dawn of the digital age, "we convert visual information like lines, shapes, and colors into binary information for use with computers?"

"Of course!" would have been the obvious reply. "That would mean precise control! Clean editing! Easy storage! Why, if this idea catches on, it will give creative people the ultimate illustration studio right inside their personal computers!"

The idea has indeed caught on. Computer illustration is everywhere. As computers become an even greater part of our everyday lives, they become an even greater part of our creative lives. Computers play such a prominent role in publishing, broadcasting, entertainment, and advertising, it is hard to imagine these fields without them. Look at any commercial media product— a book, a magazine, a television newscast—and you're bound to find an illustration of one kind or another. That illustration appears there because of a

The Platform Myth

According to the Platform myth, you need a Mac to do computer illustration.

There's no doubt about it. Creative professionals usually prefer Macintosh computers, and computer illustrators are no exception. Ask them why, and they'll tell you that the Mac is more intuitive and easier to use. They'll tell you that it looks better than a Windows PC. They'll relate the tangled history of Steve Jobs and Bill Gates for as long as you can stand to listen.

But the fact of the matter is this: You don't need a Macintosh to do computer illustration, and you especially don't need one to get started in the field. All the major software packages such as Adobe Illustrator and Macromedia FreeHand come in both Windows and Macintosh varieties. You can get special hardware such as graphics tablets and giant monitors for both Mac and Windows systems. Perhaps there was a time when Mac beat Windows in creative applications, but that time is no more.

It all comes down to which platform makes you the most comfortable. If you like Mac, choose Mac. If you like Windows, choose Windows.

Let me add one proviso to my recommendation. If you would like to earn a living as a computer illustrator, get acquainted with the Mac. Don't necessarily run out and buy one. Just borrow some time with a friend's G4 or sit with the iMac at the local public library. The idea is to become comfortable enough with the operating system so that you can open and close the software, which works virtually the same no matter the platform. Log a few solid Macintosh hours, and you can take that job in the all-Mac studio with confidence.

> **Drawing Perspectives**
>
> The first version of Adobe Photoshop that ran on the Windows platform was version 2.5.1, which shipped in 1993.

The Authenticity Myth

The Authenticity myth declares that computer illustration isn't real illustration.

Au contraire! Computer illustration is as real as it gets. Or at least it can be.

There's no doubt that illustration software comes with all kinds of goodies like effects and filters that you can use to process your work. Some software can correct or improve the quality of your lines as you go. Purists complain that these features are the death of human creativity. "Who has done this work?" they cry. "The machine or the person?"

Computer illustration that relies too much on special effects often falls short of the mark. However, I would remind the critics that the computer is a tool, in spite of all its sophistication. It doesn't do anything that the artist doesn't tell it to do first. Knowing how best to use the computer is an important part of computer illustration, and in this regard, it is no less creative than choosing the right paper, pen, ink, or brush.

The Difficulty Myth

If you subscribe to the Difficulty myth, you believe that computer illustration is harder than traditional illustration.

Computer illustration is different, at least. It's different enough that some experienced traditional illustrators find it hard to make the switch. Then again, some writers prefer banging out pages on their Smith Corona instead of using a word processor.

An open mind and an adventurous spirit make all the difference here. Computer illustration, like traditional illustration, is a skill that anyone can learn. And the more you work at it, the easier it becomes.

Exploring the Family Tree

Computer illustration is just one part of the wonderful world of computer graphics. There are many others.

There's also *computer animation*, which of course, lets you bring static drawings to life. Traditional animation and traditional illustration are really two different things, but computer animation and computer illustration are much closer in spirit. In fact, you can use many of the techniques from this book in computer animation, especially when you create computer animation for the web. Much of the animation you see on the web is in the Flash or Shockwave format. These formats give you small file sizes, which make the animations easy to download. In most cases, you can bring your computer drawings directly into the Flash or Shockwave animation as you create it, which means that you don't have to redraw your art.

Art Alert

Add special effects to your computer art like you would add hot peppers to chili. You only need a few to get the point across. Use too many effects, and they overpower the flavor of your work.

Word Balloon

Computer animation enables you to bring static drawings to life. Flash and Shockwave are two formats for computer animation that work especially well on the web, because Flash and Shockwave files can download quickly. **Digital photography** lets you capture and manipulate photographic information. Desktop publishing gives you the capability to create page layouts on the computer.

Digital photography is another close cousin. With hardware accessories such as a digital camera or scanner and some graphics software, you can use your computer to capture, restore, crop, touch up, send, save, and print photographic information. You can move portions of one photograph into another, and you can make objects (and people) disappear without a trace, as you can see in the doctored UFO photo shown in Figure 1.3. Doing these things with digital photographs is trickier than doing them with computer illustrations for reasons that I discuss in Chapter 2, "Of Pixels and Paths."

Figure 1.3

Flying saucer? What flying saucer? Thanks to photo-editing software, the truth is no longer out there.

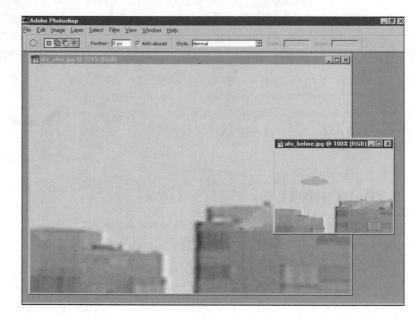

One of my favorite graphics applications is *desktop publishing*, which enables you to create page layouts on the computer. You can combine illustrations, photographs, and text from many different sources, and you can print your finished pages as a newsletter or booklet. You don't even need a printer to do this! Many page layout programs enable you to distribute your work in electronic formats such as Adobe Acrobat.

Pointers

Many designers and artists create electronic portfolios of their work in Adobe Acrobat format. Acrobat is a good choice, because just about everyone has the Acrobat Reader software. To make the Acrobat file, all you need is desktop publishing software such as Adobe PageMaker. Then sending out your portfolio to prospective employers or clients is as simple as attaching it to an e-mail message.

This book is about computer illustration. But I'll throw in a little information about these other areas as we go along. Just don't tell my editor!

Building an Illustration Studio

I won't lie to you: Outfitting yourself as a professional computer illustrator can mean a substantial financial commitment. Fortunately, the cost of computer illustration as a rewarding hobby isn't nearly as steep. In either case, the trial software on the CD-ROM can help to get you started.

Gathering the Essentials

To do computer illustration, you need the following equipment:

◆ A computer

◆ A monitor

◆ A mouse (or equivalent)

◆ Graphics software

For the computer, pick your poison: Windows or Mac. In a perfect world, you would choose a machine that has lots of memory and lots of processing speed. But you can get the job done as long as you have lots of memory. Industry-standard software such as Adobe Illustrator requires at least 128MB of RAM. You will do better if you can swing 256MB, especially if you want to run programs such as Adobe Photoshop simultaneously. Plenty of hard drive space makes another good investment. Print-quality graphics files tend to take up room.

For the monitor, larger is better. You're drawing illustrations, so it's helpful to have plenty of screen space. The average monitor screen size is 17 inches, which provides a workable amount of visual real estate. If you find room in your budget, consider a high-end 21-inch display. No truer friend does a computer illustrator have.

Monitors these days come in two sizes: fat and thin. Fat monitors, or CRT (cathode ray tube) monitors, look like TV sets. These monitors give you the best image quality for computer illustration, but they leave a considerable *footprint*. That is, they take up a significant portion of your desk space. They also flicker, and they can cause eyestrain or headaches if you stare at them too closely for too long. It goes without saying that CRT monitors are heavy, ugly, dusty, and cumbersome, and they have thick power cords and cables coming out of them. The newer LCD (liquid quartz display) monitors are quite thin, so they alleviate problems with desk space, and they flicker less for fewer head pains. As *objets d'art*, they are cool by anyone's definition. However, LCD monitors can be

But the real usefulness of a graphics tablet lies in its pressure sensitivity. Press down harder or lighten your touch, and you can change the quality of your line as you draw. Pressure sensitivity helps to make your work more expressive.

Wacom produces the most popular and consistently praised graphics tablets with pressure sensitivity. Wacom's Graphire2 is budget-priced and feature-packed, although the drawing surface of this tablet is a bit small for professional tastes. The Intuos2, also by Wacom, makes a better choice for the working computer illustrator. The Intuos2 boasts 1,024 levels of pressure sensitivity and comes in a variety of sizes to suit your desk space and personal preferences. Larger tablets aren't necessarily better tablets when it comes to illustration, but if you also do drafting, size is essential.

Art Alert

Not all graphics tablets support pressure sensitivity, so make sure you check for it before you open your wallet. Also, some pieces of software might not respond to pressure information, but all the major graphics applications do, including Illustrator and Photoshop.

Pointers

You've heard it before, but I'll say it again anyway: Back up your work. The last thing you need is to lose your art in a hard drive crash. So always, always, always back up your work. You should also back up your work, back up your work, and don't forget to back up your work. When you finish, be sure to back up your work.

Because graphics files can get very, very large, you will find it helpful to invest in some sort of external storage. This way, you can *archive*, or store, your finished work, which frees up your hard drive for your current projects. External storage also comes in handy for backing up your files. (You do make backups, right?) Large graphics files rarely fit on a standard 3.5-inch floppy disk, which holds 1.44MB.

Zip drives and Jaz drives, both from Iomega, require special kinds of disks that look something like floppies, only thicker. Zip disks hold up to 100MB or 250MB of data, depending on the type of drive, whereas Jaz disks can pack in a massive 2GB. You can erase and reuse both kinds of disks.

CD-R and CD-RW drives *burn*, or write data to, compact discs. CD-R is a write-once format, which means that once you burn the data onto the disc, you cannot erase it or change it. And don't bother leaving room on a CD-R for future use. As soon as you write something to a CD-R, even if it's just a single byte of information, the rest of the disc *closes*, or becomes unusable.

Some CD-burning software enables you to create multisession CDs, which keeps the remaining space on a CD-R open for new data. However, you still cannot reclaim space on the CD-R if you delete from it, and you can only transfer a multisession CD to another computer that has the same CD-burning software.

CD-RW and CD-RW drivesdoesn't have this limitation. CD-RW discs are rewritable, but you need a special CD-RW drive to use them. They don't work in ordinary CD-R drives. Likewise, you cannot rewrite or reopen a regular CD-R just by popping it into a CD-RW drive.

DVD-R, DVD-RW, and DVD-RAM drives show incredible promise, even if their price tags cause premature graying. All three of these drives write data to DVDs, which have many times the capacity of compact discs. DVD-R discs aren't rewritable, but DVD-RW discs are.

DVD-RAM is an interesting format. A DVD-RAM disc works like your computer's hard disk, only not as fast. These discs are rewritable, and they come as single- or double-sided. One double-sided DVD-RAM can hold 9.4GB. That's twice as much as my laptop computer! Imagine dumping your entire hard drive onto a couple of DVD-RAMs. Even if you lost everything in a hardware crash, you could restore it all, exactly as it was. Now that's what I call a backup. Table 1.1 provides an at-a-glance overview of your external storage options.

Table 1.1 Common External Storage Media

External Storage Medium	Capacity	Rewritable?
3.5-inch floppy disk	1.44MB	Yes
Zip disk	100MB or 250MB	Yes
CD-R	650MB or 700MB	No
CD-RW	650MB or 700MB	Yes
Jaz disk	2GB	Yes
DVD-R	3.95GB or 4.7GB	No
DVD-RW	4.7GB	Yes
DVD-RAM	4.7GB or 9.4GB	Yes

Scanners and digital cameras are useful for bringing external images into your illustrations. The computer gives you exceptional freedom in mixing different kinds of images in interesting ways. This is a freedom you will want to explore.

Finally, third-party plug-ins can improve and expand the capabilities of your graphics programs. A *plug-in* adds new tools, functions, or menu commands to an existing piece of software. For instance, if you get the Macromedia Flash plug-in for your web browser, your browser gains the capability to play Flash animations. Without the plug-in, Flash movies will not play.

Most of the time, the company that develops a plug-in isn't the same company that develops the original software. In fact, plug-in developers are often very small companies or sole proprietors. Third-party authorship is generally a good thing, because it gives smaller software houses a way to compete in a marketplace dominated by giants. But it can also lead to problems. Third parties don't always document or test their plug-ins as thoroughly as they should, so their products can be unreliable or incompatible with your system. And if you do need technical support, the plug-in vendor may not provide 24-hour customer service or even a phone number for you to call.

!#%@) Word Balloon

A **plug-in** is a piece of software that adds new tools, functions, or menu commands to another piece of software.

Drawing Perspectives

The most popular plug-in for the Netscape web browser is Macromedia Flash Player, which means that now is an exceptional time for computer illustrators to experiment with computer animation on the web.

How can you tell a good plug-in from a bad one? A good old-fashioned web search will uncover much that is useful. Computer people like to complain about things, and computer artists are noisier than most (except maybe programmers). If one of your colleagues has experienced trouble with a plug-in, you can bet that this person has made a public declaration about it somewhere on the web. Just point your browser to www.google.com and search for the plug-in you want to research.

You might start your search at the original software publisher's site. Adobe officially endorses several of the best plug-ins for its products, including Illustrator and Photoshop. To find out what's available, check out www.adobe.com, or pop the CD-ROM from this book into your computer. The CD-ROM contains trial versions of some very choice plug-ins, all bearing the Adobe seal of approval.

The Least You Need to Know

- ◆ Computer illustration is a method for creating art.
- ◆ Traditional illustration and computer illustration have many similarities but just as many differences.
- ◆ When you need clean, clear, non-noisy line art, computer illustration works best.
- ◆ Computer illustration extends into the worlds of computer animation, digital photography, and desktop publishing.
- ◆ At the bare minimum, you need a computer, a monitor, a mouse, and graphics software to create computer illustrations.

Of Pixels and Paths

In This Chapter

◆ Comparing raster graphics and vector graphics

◆ Using an image editor with raster graphics

◆ Using an illustration program with vector graphics

◆ Rasterizing vector graphics

Night and day. Summer and winter. Black and white. Yin and yang. If philosophers know anything, it's that this world is full of opposites.

Computer illustration is no exception. As an illustrator, you will work with two types of computer images: raster (or bitmap) graphics and vector graphics. Raster graphics are all about pixels. Vector graphics are all about paths.

These two types of graphics are as different as they can possibly be. Each has its advantages and drawbacks. You will find different uses for them in your projects, and you will create them on different pieces of software. In this chapter, I introduce you to the differences between rasters and vectors and pixels and paths.

What Is a Pixel?

A *pixel* is nothing more than a very small, colored rectangle. By itself, it isn't terribly impressive, as you can see in Figure 2.1. But if you put enough of them together, organizing them on a grid and varying their colors, you can create the appearance of an image.

Many methods of image compression exist. If you know something about computer graphics already, you'll recognize these methods as graphics file formats. For those not in the know, raster images come in many different formats. Three of the most common are BMP (Windows Bitmap), JPEG (Joint Picture Experts Group), and GIF (Graphical Interchange Format). The BMP format is uncompressed. It's like the unproductive employee. BMP images can take up lots of disk space, but they also retain all their image information, so there is no risk to the picture quality. The JPEG and GIF formats are compressed, and they work best with specific types of raster images. The JPEG format offers exceptional compression for photos and color-rich images, whereas the GIF does justice to many kinds of line art.

Good image editors such as Photoshop give you many compression formats and enable you to choose the right amount of *loss*, or how much picture information gets discarded in the compression process. The JPEG format is *lossy*, which means that some picture information gets discarded when you save your image as a JPEG. By contrast, the GIF format is *lossless*. Saving your image as a GIF simply makes the graphics file more efficient. However, the GIF format also limits the number of colors in an image to a maximum of 256. This is why JPEGs are better for photos, which can have tens of thousands of colors, even though JPEG compression is lossy.

Understanding the Pros and Cons

Raster graphics are convenient and versatile. Many common pieces of software can work with them: web browsers, image editors, desktop publishing programs, word processors, spreadsheets, e-mail programs, and so on. And rasters translate well across platforms—a JPEG image looks the same on Windows and Mac machines. Raster graphics are truly graphics for the masses.

On the downside, raster graphics are a pain to edit.

Raster graphics create images with pixels. So to edit a raster graphic, you have to edit the pixels within the graphic. With my original cat photo weighing in at more than two million pixels, that's quite an editing job.

Pointers

Photoshop's Magic Wand tool takes some of the sting out of photo editing. The Magic Wand examines your raster image, looking for pixels of similar color. The idea here is that similarly colored pixels in close proximity probably belong to the same shape or object. This method isn't 100 percent accurate, but it can help you to extract large groups of cat or chair pixels in a short amount of time. More on that in Chapter 20, "Putting the Pieces Together."

To make matters worse, the computer doesn't see a raster graphic the same way that we humans do. We look at the photo and see a cat on a chair. But to the computer, there is no cat, and there is no chair. There are only columns and rows of differently colored rectangles. The computer cannot tell where the chair ends and the cat begins. The computer doesn't perceive the shapes of these objects, in other words.

So, if you want to move the cat off the chair so you can sit and relax, you can't just click the cat and drag. You have to get down to the nitty-gritty and transfer the cat pixels to their new location, which leaves a cat-shaped hole in your image, because the computer cannot tell the difference between the foreground and the background, as Figure 2.5 demonstrates. You then have to fill in the hole with chair pixels that you borrow from some other area of the photo. In Chapter 1, "So You Want to Be a Computer Illustrator," I mention that photo editing is tricky. This is what I was talking about.

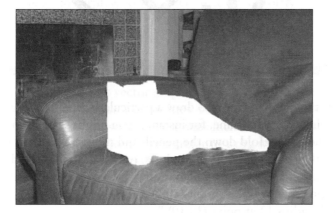

Figure 2.5

In a raster image, the computer cannot distinguish between the foreground and the background. When you move the cat pixels, they leave behind a cat-shaped hole.

Rasters are also resolution-dependent, which can cause problems with resizing. If you blow up a raster image, you effectively change its resolution. Increase the size too much, and you lose image quality. The same holds true for stretching a portion of a raster image. The more you stretch, the more you effectively change the resolution in that portion of the image. Lack of clarity is sure to follow.

Still, raster graphics make a good final format for your images. Everyone with a computer can view them and print them. But because of their limitations in editing, rasters aren't the best choice for creating computer art from scratch. You need a different kind of graphic—one that makes image creation and editing a breeze. Does it exist? Read on!

What Is a Path?

A *path* is a description of a shape. Unlike a pixel, which is always rectangular, a path can be a straight line, a curve, a circle, a box, a star, a letter, or just about anything else, and it can be of any conceivable size. Figure 2.6 shows just a few of the shapes that a path can describe.

!#%@ Word Balloon

A **path** is a description of a shape.

You will notice immediately some differences between the raster and vector versions of this image. The raster image is a photograph, obviously, and the vector image is an illustration. The vector doesn't contain the same level of nuance in shading and detail. Then again, it isn't supposed to. It's an illustration.

What you might not notice immediately is that the vector image is much, much smaller in terms of file size than the raster image. The raster weighs in at 6.19MB, compared to the vector's slender-by-comparison 112KB. Part of the reason for this is that the vector image isn't as visually sophisticated as the raster, but this isn't the main reason. The main reason is that paths are better at describing this image than pixels. In other words, it takes more of the computer's resources to express this image in pixels than it does in paths.

In a raster, the number of pixels determines the file size of the image. In a vector, it's the number (and complexity) of the paths. If I take a picture of the chair without the cat (assuming that I can get the cat off the chair long enough to use the camera), I find that the catless photo has exactly the same file size as the original. Why? Because there are exactly 2,160,000 pixels in each photo. Additional chair pixels may replace the missing cat pixels, but it's the same number of pixels in both cases, and the same number of pixels equals the same file size. However, if I draw a vector image of the chair without the cat, the file size drops. Why? Because the cat paths aren't there. The catless image has fewer paths. The fewer the paths, the smaller the file.

Drawing Perspectives
Vector graphics hold their own on the raster-dominated web. Flash and Shockwave animation is vector-based. And emerging web technologies such as SVG (Scalable Vector Graphics) promise to bring vector graphics front and center.

When you work with vector graphics, you don't have to worry about resolution or compression. Period. There are no pixels to resolve or compress. The computer displays your vector image in perfect clarity and sharpness, no matter where you choose to present it—whether on screen or on paper.

Understanding the Pros and Cons

Vector graphics are ridiculously resilient, which makes them easy to edit. You can blow them up, shrink them down, twist them, stretch them, and otherwise transform them as much as you want with absolutely no loss of image quality. Remember that a path isn't a shape but a description of a shape. It's a set of drawing instructions. So, in vector graphics, if you adjust the shape of a path, what you're really doing is refining your instructions. The computer is amazingly flexible in this regard. You can change your mind an infinite number of times, and the computer never gets irritated. It simply redraws the shape according to your new specifications, maintaining razor-sharp image quality.

Working with multiple paths is just as easy. Remember when I tried to move the cat pixels in my photograph? It left a cat-shaped hole in the background. But with vector graphics, the computer understands the various shapes that make up an image, and it knows the difference between the foreground and the background. With my vector image of the cat on the chair, I can simply drag the cat paths wherever I choose without disrupting the chair paths in any way, as Figure 2.8 shows. The computer-savvy among you will say that these vector graphics are *object-oriented graphics*, because each path is an object, or its own separate element.

!#%@) **Word Balloon**

In **object-oriented graphics,** each path is its own independent object that you can change without affecting any other object in the drawing.

Figure 2.8

With vector graphics, the cat and the chair are two separate things. You can move one without affecting the other.

The major drawback to vector graphics is their lack of versatility. Vectors truly shine when it comes to line-art illustrations, but they don't make sense for other types of images, especially photos. In principle, you could describe a photograph in terms of paths. But in practice, this just isn't feasible. A vector photograph would contain so many paths that its file size would be immense. And the paths would be so small that they might as well be pixels.

Because vectors aren't as versatile as their pixel-based cousins, they don't get the same level of support in typical computer applications. They creep into desktop publishing software and word processors in the form of clip art, but the majority of consumer software is raster-oriented. Perhaps the most important piece of consumer software of all, the web browser, leaves vectors out cold. None of the major browsers display vector images without special plug-ins, such as the Macromedia Flash Player. If you go out in search of broad software support for vectors, you will find it only in the more expensive graphics packages designed for creative professionals. This is fine if you want to share your work with your fellow graphics people, but what if you want to give your art to the world?

Still, vectors provide a huge advantage over raster graphics when it comes to creating and editing line art. But the elite status of vector graphics is troubling. You don't want to create art that people will not be able to enjoy because they don't have the right equipment. If only you could change a vector image into a raster image after you finish editing it! Hmmm ….

Rasterizing Vectors and Vectorizing Rasters

I have some good news, and the good news is this: Changing a vector into a raster is a piece of cake. As I mentioned before, you can represent any conceivable image as a series of pixels. All you need is the right software. Both Illustrator and Photoshop can *rasterize* vector images in a few simple steps. I discuss this in more detail in Chapter 20.

Does the process work the other way around? Can you take a raster image, such as a photograph, vectorize it, edit the heck out of it, and then rasterize it again? The answer is yes and no. Changing a raster image into a vector image is not what you would call an exact science. Some illustration programs purport to do this with a process called *tracing*, but the results are unreliable and abstract, as you can see in Figure 2.9. Rasters with simple foregrounds and backgrounds have the best chance at becoming vectors. But even with the most faithful traces, the computer has a hard time figuring out which pixels belong with which shapes, and this makes editing these vector graphics tedious. It is often easier to redraw the raster as a vector from scratch.

At least you can go from vector to raster without trouble. Therefore, your approach will be this: You will create illustrations with vector graphics, giving you the most flexibility with drawing and editing. Then you will convert your vector graphics to rasters for ease of distribution.

Figure 2.9

You can change a raster image into a vector image with software such as Macromedia Flash, but the results aren't picture perfect.

The Least You Need to Know

◆ Raster graphics create images from pixels.

◆ Raster graphics work best with photographs.

◆ Raster graphics can be troublesome to edit, but they are easy to distribute.

◆ Vector graphics create images from paths.

◆ Vector graphics work best with line art.

◆ Vector graphics are easy to edit, but they can be hard to distribute.

◆ Rasterizing finished vector graphics gives you the best features of both.

Chapter 3

Illustrating Illustrator

In This Chapter

- Exploring the Illustrator interface
- Using the toolbox
- Working with palettes
- Using the Zoom and Hand tools
- Saving your work

Enough talk and theory—time to get down to business. This chapter gives you a quick introduction to Adobe Illustrator, which is the software you will be using for most of the examples in this book, which means that now is the time to install the trial software on the CD-ROM. See Appendix B, "What's on the CD-ROM," for more details on how to do this. Remember, once you install the Illustrator trial, you have 30 days to use it. The Photoshop trial doesn't expire, but it also doesn't allow you to save or print your work.

If you are new to the computer illustration game, feel free to go through this chapter at your own pace. And when you finish, I encourage you to schedule some play-around time with Illustrator before you go on to Chapter 4, "Delivering Straight Lines." You can repeat the short drawing exercise that I tackle in this chapter, or you can fiddle around with some of the other tools. Don't worry about creating a masterpiece at this point. Don't even sweat it if you feel like you don't know what you're doing. Just take the software for a test drive. Have some fun! The more comfortable you get with Illustrator, the easier it will become to use.

With that, I now cordially invite you to launch the program.

Introducing the Interface

When you start Adobe Illustrator, a colorful title card greets you while the application boots up. By the way, the lovely lady on Illustrator's title card is, of course, Venus from Botticelli's *The Birth of Venus*. To see her in a slightly less recognizable form, hold down Alt (Windows) or Option (Mac) and choose Help → About Illustrator.

After a moment or two, the title card goes away, and the Illustrator interface appears, shown in Figure 3.1. What you see on your screen may not exactly match the picture of the interface in this book. This is because the Illustrator interface is highly customizable. You can set it up to accommodate the way you prefer to work. I'll explain how to do this as I go.

Figure 3.1

Here it is: the Adobe Illustrator interface.

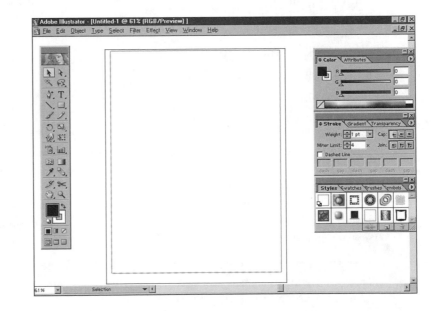

Meet the Toolbox

The heart of Adobe Illustrator is the toolbox, shown in Figure 3.2. The toolbox is the tall, narrow, floating window with the icons. If you don't see the toolbox anywhere on your screen, choose Window → Tools.

Figure 3.2

The toolbox is the tall, nar-row, floating window with the icons.

As you might expect, the toolbox contains the tools you will use to create illustrations. Here's how it works: Click the icon of the tool that you want. The icon button appears pressed in, and the tool activates. At this point, none of the tools will actually do anything, because you haven't opened a new document window, but you can practice selecting tools to get a feel for the process.

Some of the tool buttons have a tiny triangle in the lower right corner, as you can see in Figure 3.3. This triangle is your signal that related tools are hiding underneath. To show these tools, click the tool icon and hold down the left mouse button. In a moment, the hidden tools appear. While keeping the mouse button pressed down, select one of these tools and release the mouse button. This icon replaces the original icon in the toolbox. To revert to the original tool, hold down the mouse button again, and pick the first icon on the left from the set of hidden tools. The default tool is always the first tool on the left.

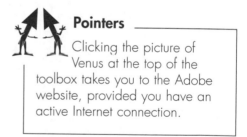

Pointers

Clicking the picture of Venus at the top of the toolbox takes you to the Adobe website, provided you have an active Internet connection.

If you find that this business of hidden tools is trying your patience, you can tear off any set of tools so that they appear as a miniature floating window, as shown in Figure 3.4. To do this, call up the hidden tools again by holding down the left mouse button. Then choose the triangle icon at the far right, and release. You now have easy access to all the tools of the set. Click the X (or Close) button to close the tear-off window.

Figure 3.3

Some tool icons have a small triangle in the lower right corner. Holding down the mouse button on these icons reveals a set of hidden tools.

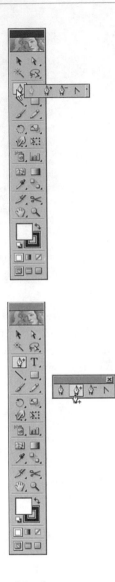

Figure 3.4

Tear off a set of hidden tools for easy access.

I explore some of the other toolbox functions later in this chapter.

Meet the Palettes

The toolbox isn't the only floating window in Illustrator. There are many, many others, as shown in Figure 3.5. You probably see a few of them on the screen right now. These floating windows, or *palettes*, work like miniature control panels. They give you access to many useful commands and options.

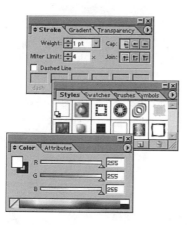

Figure 3.5

Illustrator's many palettes contain commands and options for working with your art.

You can move a palette to any convenient location on the screen by clicking the blue bar at the top of the palette, holding down the mouse button, and dragging. Release the mouse button to drop the palette.

Too many palettes can clutter your work area in a hurry, so Illustrator gives you a number of ways to organize them.

The easiest way to deal with palettes is to close them all. Close a palette by clicking the X button in the upper-right corner. Then, when you need to use a particular palette, you can call it up again by choosing it from the Window menu. For instance, to open the Align palette, which enables you to line up and distribute the objects in your drawing, choose Window → Show Align. When you finish, choose Window → Align Again or just click the X button.

Notice that Illustrator arranges palettes into groups. For instance, the Layers, Actions, and Links palettes appear in the same floating window. Click the tabs to call up the different palettes in this group. Clicking the Links tab, for instance, brings the Links palette front and center.

You can rearrange the groups to your liking. To separate a palette from its current group, click the palette's name tab and hold down the mouse button. Then drag the palette outside the floating window. When you release the mouse button, the palette becomes its own floating window. To add this palette to a different group, drag the name tab into the tabs of the other palettes. Another

Art Alert

Illustrator has four palettes that let you work with text: Character, Paragraph, MM Design, and Tab Ruler. In Illustrator 9, these don't appear in the Window menu with all the other palettes for some reason. They turn up in the Type menu instead. Illustrator 10, the version of the software that comes on the CD-ROM, addresses this inconsistency by placing the text palettes under Window → Type, where they belong.

way to group palettes is to dock them. Docking connects two or more palettes so that you can move them around the screen as a single unit. To dock a palette, drag its name tab to the bottom of another palette. To disconnect a docked palette, drag its name tab away.

Please note that once you rearrange or dock a palette, that's where the palette stays, so the configuration of your palettes may not match the ones in this book. This can be confusing at first, but part of the beauty of palettes is that you can organize them however you want. Don't be alarmed, then, if your screen looks slightly different. As long as you see the right palette somewhere, you're doing everything correctly.

To conserve space, you can minimize a palette by clicking the minus (-) button in the upper-right corner. When you minimize a palette, only the name tabs show. Clicking one of the tabs causes the palette to return to its previous size.

If you look at the lower right corner of the Layers group, for instance, you will see three diagonal lines (see Figure 3.6). These lines indicate that you can resize the palette. To resize a palette, move the mouse pointer to one of the palette's corners. When the mouse pointer changes into a two-way arrow, hold down the mouse button and drag the palette to the size you prefer. Not all palettes have this feature, so make sure you check for the three diagonal lines before you try to resize the palette.

Figure 3.6

You can resize palettes that have three diagonal lines in the lower-right corner.

Each palette contains a menu of commands and options. To access a palette's menu, click the triangle button at the top right of the palette, just under the X button. The menu slides out, as in Figure 3.7. You can double-click the name tab of a palette to cycle through the various palette sizes, from minimized to all options showing.

Figure 3.7

A palette's menu opens after you click the triangle icon at the top right.

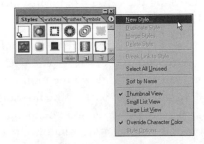

Remember those hidden tools from the toolbox? Some palettes also have extra options that you don't see unless you go looking for them (see Figure 3.8). Take the Stroke palette, for instance. When you activate the Stroke palette, two triangles appear in the left corner of the tab. These triangles tell you that the Stroke palette has hidden options. To view these options, open the palette menu and select the Show command. To make the extra options disappear again, select the Hide command.

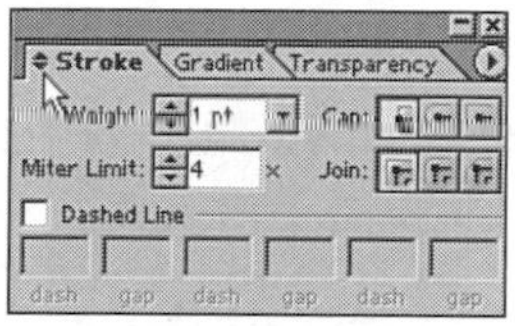

Figure 3.8

If an active palette tab contains two triangles, there are additional options for you to use. To view these options, open the Palette menu and choose the Show command.

Opening a New Document

The toolbox and the palettes aren't of much use until you get down to some actual computer illustration. Start by opening a new document window. Choose File → New from the menu, and the New Document dialog box appears, as shown in Figure 3.9.

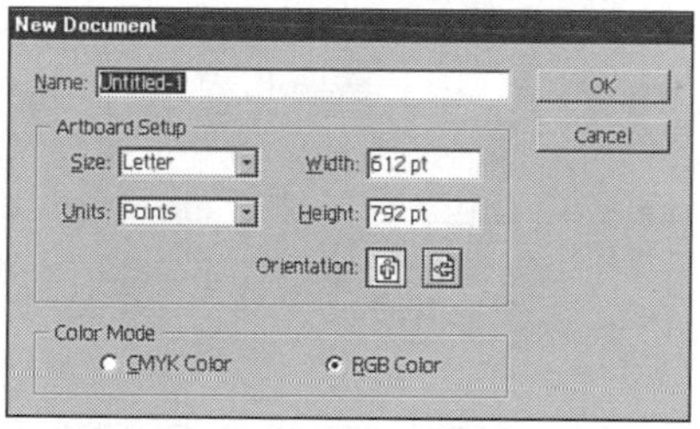

Figure 3.9

The New Document dialog box enables you to set up your drawing.

The New Document dialog box enables you to set up a few preliminary options for your drawing. None of the choices that you make here have to be permanent. You can modify these settings at any time.

In the Name field, give your drawing a title, if you know what the title is going to be.

Under Color Mode, you have the choice between RGB and CMYK. In most cases, pick RGB. You should only pick CMYK if you need to deliver color-separated art to your printer or publisher. I'll talk more about this in Chapter 8, "Coloring Fills and Strokes." But for now, knowing that you can easily switch to CMYK later, go with RGB.

Drawing Perspectives

Both RGB and CMYK can reproduce a wide portion of the visible spectrum using only a few simple elements. RGB color comes from mixing different levels of red, green, and blue light. CMYK color comes from mixing different quantities of cyan, magenta, yellow, and black ink.

Under Artboard Size, enter the width and the height of the paper you will use to print your work. As you can see in Figure 3.9, Illustrator gives the artboard size in points. The point (pt) is a common unit of measurement in the publishing world. You can type your measurements in inches or centimeters, followed by the abbreviation *in* or *cm*. Illustrator converts the inches or centimeters to points. To print on standard paper, you would type **8.5 in** in the width field and **11 in** in the height field. The corresponding measurements in points, by the way, are 612 and 792.

Click the OK button, and Illustrator opens the new document window according to your specifications.

As you can see in Figure 3.10, the document window contains two sets of borders. The outermost border represents the *artboard*, or the piece of paper to which you will print. The innermost border is the *imageable area*, or the space in which you can draw. Your printer determines the size of the imageable area. Because most printers have built-in page margins, the imageable area helps to keep you within the print zone. If a portion of your drawing bleeds into the *nonimageable area*, or the space between the artboard and the imageable area, your printer will probably crop off that portion of the drawing.

⟨ !#%@ ⟩ Word Balloon

In the document window, the **artboard** represents the paper to which you will print. The **imageable area** is the space in which you can draw. The **nonimageable area** represents your printer's built-in margins. The **scratch area** is the space for notes and sketches.

The sea of white surrounding the artboard is the *scratch area*. You can draw in the scratch area, but your printer ignores everything that you put there. Use the scratch area for notes, sketches, doodles, alternate designs, and so on.

Figure 3.10

The document window shows the artboard, or the work area.

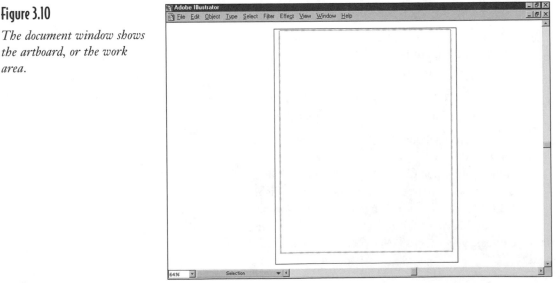

Taking a Test Drive

The time has come.

Move the mouse pointer to the toolbox and select the Rectangle tool. The Rectangle tool is the fourth tool from the top on the right. Now move the mouse pointer anywhere into the imageable area. Notice that the pointer changes into crosshairs.

Position the crosshairs, and then hold down the left mouse button and drag. (If you have a two-button mouse, always use the left mouse button unless I recommend otherwise.) A rectangular path tracks your mouse movements. You can adjust the shape and size of the rectangle as you go. When you're happy with the way it looks, release the mouse button. You have just drawn a rectangle!

Note that a blue selection outline traces the contour of the shape. The outline has a small dot in each corner. To deselect the rectangle, hold down Ctrl (Windows) or Command (Mac) and click anywhere in an empty space. You should now have a white rectangle with a thin black outline, as Figure 3.11 shows.

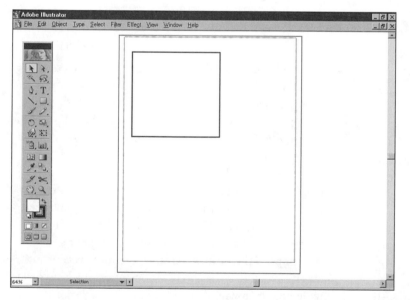

Figure 3.11

Use the Rectangle tool from the toolbox to draw a rectangular shape.

Because that was so successful, you should try another shape. This time, grab the Ellipse tool from the toolbox. The Ellipse tool hides under the Rectangle tool. To access it, click the Rectangle tool and hold down the mouse button. After about a second, the hidden toolset appears. The Ellipse tool is third from the left. Select it and release the mouse button. Then draw an ellipse shape just like you draw a rectangle. Deselect your ellipse by Ctrl-clicking or Command-clicking an empty area. (Ctrl-clicking and Command-clicking means holding down Ctrl or Command and clicking the left mouse button.) Your ellipse should be white, like the rectangle, with a thin black outline, as Figure 3.12 shows.

Figure 3.12

Use the Ellipse tool from the toolbox to draw an elliptical shape.

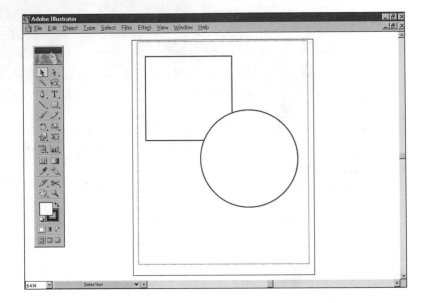

Art Alert

When you go for the Selection tool, make sure you get the black arrow, not the white arrow. The white arrow is the Direct Selection tool, and it has a different purpose.

Pointers

Holding down the Shift key while you draw with the Rectangle and Ellipse tools constrains the proportions of the shape. That is, the rectangle remains perfectly square, and the ellipse remains perfectly circular. The same trick works with many of the other drawing tools.

Now go back to the toolbox and grab the Selection tool. The Selection tool is the very first tool on the left—the black arrow. Click your ellipse with this tool. Then position the mouse pointer inside the ellipse, hold down the mouse button, and drag. The ellipse moves at your command. You can do the same thing with your rectangle. Move the shapes around the screen, one at a time, and deselect after each movement by clicking on empty space. (With the Selection tool, you don't need to hold down Ctrl or Command.) Notice that the ellipse always stays in front of the rectangle if you superimpose them. In Illustrator, the most recently drawn object gets the top position in the stacking order by default. You will play with the stacking order in Chapter 4, "Delivering Straight Lines."

Position your ellipse so that it partially covers the rectangle. Then, without deselecting the ellipse this time, take a gander at the toolbox. Underneath the tools, you should find two squares: a solid white square and a hollow black square. The solid square gives you the fill color of the current selection. The hollow square gives you the stroke color. The fill color is the inside color of the object, and the stroke color is the outside color.

Between the two squares on the right, there is a small curved-arrow icon, shown in Figure 3.13. Clicking this icon swaps the fill and stroke colors of the current selection. Go ahead and give it a try.

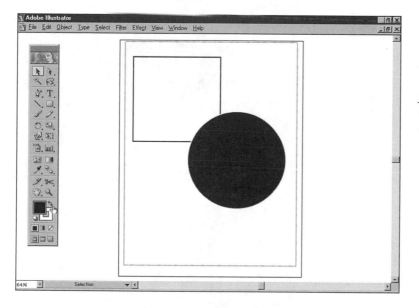

Figure 3.13

Click the curved arrow to swap the fill and stroke colors of the current selection. The fill color is the solid square on the toolbox. The stroke color is the hollow square.

It works. Your ellipse changes from white with a black outline to black with a white outline. You cannot see the outline, of course, because the imageable area is also white, but the outline is definitely there. To prove it, select the rectangle this time, and swap its colors. You can now see the white outline of the ellipse where the two shapes overlap, like in Figure 3.14.

Select the elipse again. Look at the toolbox, and make sure that the square for the stroke color is in front of the square for the fill color. (Remember, the fill color is the solid square, and the stroke color is the hollow square, so you want to have the hollow square in front of the solid square.) If the fill color is in front of the stroke color instead, click once on the hollow square. That should bring the stroke color to the foreground.

Look directly below the stroke color, and you will find a button with a red slash. This is the None button, shown in Figure 3.15. Click it, and the hollow square in the toolbox acquires the same red slash. This means that the current object has no stroke color. As a result, the outline vanishes.

Art Alert

Make sure you select the shape with the Selection tool before you try to swap the colors. If you don't, the colors will not swap.

Figure 3.14

Swapping the fill and stroke colors gives you black shapes with white outlines.

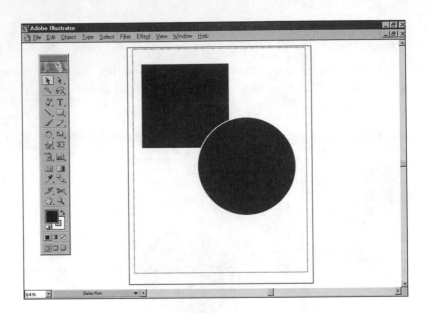

Figure 3.15

Click the None button to make the stroke or fill color disappear.

You can swap the None value just like you swapped the color values. Click the curved-arrow icon, and you get an ellipse with a black stroke and no fill. The inside of your ellipse is now transparent. The black rectangle shows through.

To see exactly which parts of your illustration are transparent, choose View → Show Transparency Grid. Transparent areas appear in a checkerboard pattern. To revert the document window to normal, select View → Hide Transparency Grid.

Adjusting the View

Illustrator lets you view your drawing at a number of magnification levels. You can find the current magnification at the bottom left of the document window. As you can see in Figure 3.16, my magnification is 100%, but yours depends on your monitor settings.

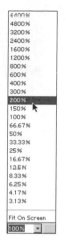

Figure 3.16

Change the magnification level of the document window with this drop-down list.

To change the level of magnification, click the drop-down list and select a new value. Choose the Fit On Screen option to make the artboard fit perfectly into the document window. As you increase the magnification, you get a closer look at your illustration. Decrease the magnification to zoom out.

Pointers

There is yet another way to adjust the magnification of your drawing. From the View menu, choose Zoom In, Zoom Out, Fit In Window, or Actual Size. The Actual Size command gives you 100% magnification.

Using the Zoom Tool

The Zoom tool is an easier, better way to magnify a particular area of your drawing (see Figure 3.17). The Zoom tool is the last tool on the right in the toolbox. Its icon is the magnifying glass. Grab the Zoom tool and click the area of the drawing that you want to magnify. The magnification level in the drop-down box changes as you zoom in closer and closer. To zoom out with the Zoom tool, hold down the Alt key (Windows) or Option key (Mac) while you click.

Notice that the edge of your ellipse maintains its sharpness as you zoom in (see Figure 3.18). That's the power of vector graphics. Try the same thing with a raster image, and it's block city.

Figure 3.17

The Zoom tool lets you enlarge a specific area of your drawing.

Figure 3.18

Thanks to vector graphics, the edge of the ellipse at 600% magnification still looks razor sharp.

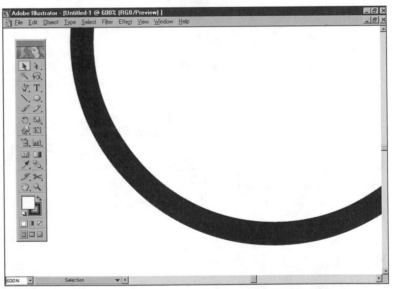

Using the Hand Tool

At high magnifications, you will not be able to see your entire image at a glance. Use the Hand tool to bring different areas of the artboard into view.

The Hand tool is directly to the left of the Zoom tool in the toolbox. To use the Hand tool, select it, and bring the hand-shaped mouse pointer anywhere into the document window. Hold down the mouse button, and the hand's fingers clasp. Then drag the mouse, and the artboard follows, as Figure 3.19 shows.

Figure 3.19

Use the Hand tool to change the position of the artboard in the document window.

Getting Help

Illustrator gives you a few nifty visual aids to help with your drawing: the rulers and the grid.

Using the Rulers

To turn on the rulers, choose View ➜ Show Rulers. The rulers appear along the top and down the left side of the document window. As you move the mouse, thin gray lines in the rulers give the position of the mouse pointer. This enables you to begin drawing at a precise location on the page, as Figure 3.20 shows.

> **Drawing Perspectives**
>
> One point equals 1/72nd of an inch.

Your rulers probably mark off measurement in points. If you want to change the units to something more useful like inches or centimeters, choose Edit ➜ Preferences ➜ Units & Undo. Under Units, find the General drop-down box. Choose a new unit of measurement from the list, and click OK. Your rulers instantly recalibrate themselves.

To make the rulers disappear, choose View ➜ Hide Rulers.

Figure 3.20

Rulers enable you to precisely position your illustration elements.

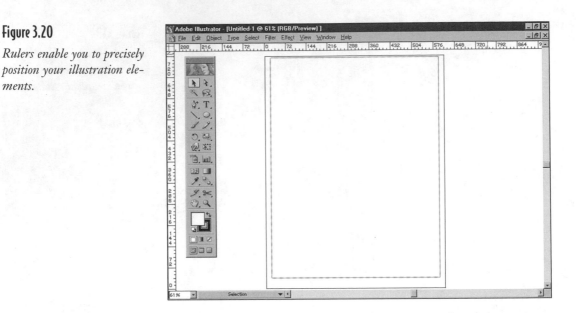

Using the Grid

Illustrator's grid drops a graph-paper texture across the entire document window (see Figure 3.21). The grid is especially useful for technical illustration. To turn on this feature, choose View → Show Grid. You can change the spacing and color of the grid lines under Edit → Preferences → Guides And Grid.

Figure 3.21

Illustrator's grid simulates graph paper.

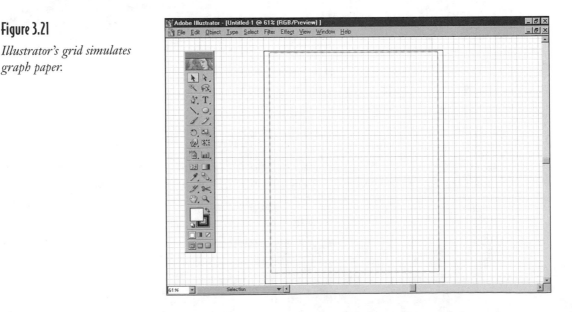

Illustrator can automatically grid-align the objects that you draw. Find the Snap To Grid option on the View menu. If there isn't a check mark next to this option, grid alignment isn't active. Highlight this option and click it if you want to turn it on.

Pointers

The grid only appears onscreen. It doesn't print out with your illustration.

Choose View → Hide Grid to make the grid disappear.

Undo Is Your Friend

Don't be ashamed to use Illustrator's Undo command, which you can find at the top of the Edit menu. Choosing Edit → Undo erases the most recent action. (If you're using a two-button mouse, right-clicking calls up a context menu that also gives you the Undo command.) This feature is extremely useful in correcting mistakes. Even though vector graphics are easy to edit, it's often easier just to undo a bad mouse stroke or an unintentional command.

Illustrator keeps track of your actions and gives you as many levels of Undo as your computer's memory can hold. This means that if you want to go back to your drawing the way it was 10 actions ago, just choose Edit → Undo 10 times in a row. It's like rolling back the clock to happier times, before everything went so wrong with your drawing. Illustrator's Undo command is a good friend to me, and it can be a good friend to you, too.

Saving Your Work

It's always a good idea to save your work. Go to the menu and choose File → Save. This calls up the Save dialog box.

Choose a location for your file. If you aren't used to working with your computer's operating system, you may want to save to the desktop. That way, you will not lose track of your file. You can also save to an external device such as a floppy drive or Zip drive by selecting it from the Save In drop-down list.

Select the Illustrator (AI) format from the Save As Type drop-down list. Then type a name for your file and add the extension *.ai* to the end of it. If your filename is *ostrich*, for example, you would type **ostrich.ai** in the File Name field. Click the Save button, and then click the OK button in the next dialog box.

For future saves, File → Save is the quickest option. It uses the filename and the location that you have already provided, overwriting the most recent version of the file. File → Save As lets you pick a different filename or a different location. Use this command if you want to keep the previous version of the file.

Art Alert _____

Watch out for spaces in your filename. They confuse some software applications. Use the underscore character (_) or the hyphen (-) instead of a space. For instance, type **My_Illustration.ai** or **My-Illustration.ai** instead of *My Illustration.ai*. Watch also the number of characters in the filename. Windows users have been able to cram 256 characters into a filename since Windows 95, and Mac users get the same capability with OS X. However, earlier Windows versions only support 8-character filenames plus 3-character extensions, and earlier Mac systems give you 31 characters total. If you really want to get picky about filename formats for the greatest compatibility, limit yourself to a maximum of 8 all-lowercase characters before the .ai extension, as in *myillo.ai*.

Drawing Perspectives

Easter eggs are undocumented, harmless, frequently humorous software features that developers slip past quality control. One of the first Easter eggs, if not the very first, was the secret room in *Adventure* for the venerable old Atari Video Computer System. Players who picked up the mysterious Gray Dot could enter this room, where they found the programmer's name in flashing color.

You Won't Find This in the Manual

To cap off this introduction of Illustrator, let me call your attention to a few undocumented features.

At the bottom of the document window, next to the magnification drop-down box, is the status bar. By default, it tells you the current tool. If you click the status bar, you can change it to display the date and time, the amount of free memory, and so on.

But if you press the Alt key (Windows) or the Option key (Mac), click the status bar, and hold down the mouse button, you receive some additional choices. Will these help you with your drawing? It's doubtful. But I'll bet they'll bring a smile to your face!

The Least You Need to Know

- ◆ You can customize the Illustrator interface to match your work preferences.
- ◆ The toolbox gives you drawing and editing tools.
- ◆ Close unneeded palettes to avoid clutter.
- ◆ The imageable area of the document window is the print zone.
- ◆ Use the Zoom tool to magnify and the Hand tool to reposition the artboard.
- ◆ The Undo command helps you to correct mistakes.
- ◆ Save your work with File → Save or File → Save As.

Part 2

Creating Line Art

After all that talk about policies and procedures, I'll bet you're ready for some action. This part provides. Here you put your virtual pen to metaphorical paper and begin to draw.

The following chapters explain how to create lines and shapes, the most basic elements of any illustration. You will learn the essential makeup of vector graphics, and you'll explore the differences between the Pen and the Pencil tools. By the end of this part, you will have composed a complete scene from a comic strip—character, background, and foreground. Don't believe me? Wait and see!

Chapter 4

Delivering Straight Lines

In This Chapter

- Drawing straight segments with the Pen
- Manipulating paths with the selection tools
- Joining, cutting, and erasing paths
- Drawing the arrow sign for the Astro Ape comic

When you work with vector graphics, you get irresistible straight lines, and I don't mean straight lines like "Who's on first?" or "Doctor, it hurts when I do this." I mean razor-sharp, picture-perfect, absolutely straight lines that hold up to the highest level of scrutiny.

It's easy, and you don't need a ruler. By the end of this chapter, you will be delivering *straight lines* as if you were George Burns.

Where It's Going

As promised in the introduction, you're going to create a comic strip in this book. Every chapter from here on out supplies some of the art, and the result will look something like a page from a comic book. I will talk you through the illustrations as you go. If you want to cut a few corners, the CD-ROM contains the comic strip art for each chapter.

The comic features Astro Ape, a character that I created especially for this book. Picture a monkey in a space suit, and you get the idea (see Figure 4.1). If monkeys aren't to your liking, you can find illustrations for Astro Ostrich and Astro Kangaroo on the CD-ROM.

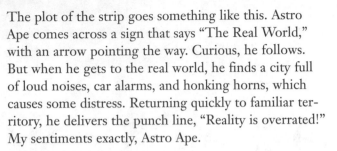

!#%@ **Word Balloon**

A **straight line** is the seemingly innocent utterance of the straight man that sets up the comedian for the punch line.

The plot of the strip goes something like this. Astro Ape comes across a sign that says "The Real World," with an arrow pointing the way. Curious, he follows. But when he gets to the real world, he finds a city full of loud noises, car alarms, and honking horns, which causes some distress. Returning quickly to familiar territory, he delivers the punch line, "Reality is overrated!" My sentiments exactly, Astro Ape.

Figure 4.1

You will draw this ape.

You will get to your first project—creating the arrow sign—a bit later in the chapter. Let's start at the beginning with the most fundamental element of illustration: the straight line.

Getting Down to Business

If you haven't already done so, launch Adobe Illustrator and open a new document window. (That's File ➜ New, remember?)

Drawing Perspectives

In Adobe Photoshop and Macromedia FreeHand, the tool is the Pen. In Deneba Canvas, the tool is the Curve. In CorelDRAW, the tool is the Bezier Pencil.

Now grab the Pen tool from the toolbox. The Pen is third from the top, on the left (see Figure 4.2). Move the mouse pointer into your workspace, and the pointer changes to the tip of a pen. Notice also a tiny X to the right of the pen pointer. I will go into this later.

To draw a straight line, pick a starting point, click the mouse button, and release. Move the pointer away for a moment, and take a look at what you have drawn.

Figure 4.2

Use the Pen tool to deliver an irresistible straight line every time.

What you see on the screen is a single *anchor point.* Recall from Chapter 2, "Of Pixels and Paths," that vector graphics create images with paths, or shape definitions. An anchor point tells the path which way to go. In this case, the anchor indicates the starting point for the line.

Move the mouse to the place where you want the line to end, and click the mouse button again. The Pen tool creates another anchor point, and a *segment* stretches between the points. A segment is a section of a path. It always falls between two anchor points, as you can see in Figure 4.3.

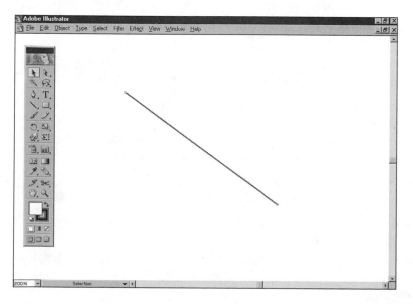

Figure 4.3

A segment always falls between two anchor points.

Position the Pen over the original anchor point. You will know you have it when the little X next to the pointer changes to an O. Click the original anchor point to close the line.

So, drawing a straight line with the Pen tool is really a three-step process:

1. Position the pointer, and click to create the starting anchor point.
2. Position the pointer, and click to create the ending anchor point.
3. Move the pointer back to the starting anchor point, and click again to close the line.

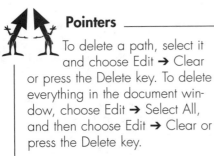

Word Balloon

An **anchor point** tells a path which way to go. A **segment** is a section of a path that falls between two anchor points.

Pointers

To delete a path, select it and choose Edit → Clear or press the Delete key. To delete everything in the document window, choose Edit → Select All, and then choose Edit → Clear or press the Delete key.

Position the mouse pointer over an empty area of the workspace, hold down Ctrl (Windows) or Command (Mac), and click to deselect your line. The anchor points become invisible. This is how your line really looks, without the bulging anchor points at either end. Click your line with the Selection tool (the black arrow), and you can move the path freely across the screen.

Take the Pen tool again and try a few more lines. Don't forget that third step, where you click the original anchor point. Make a diagonal line, and click it a few times with the Zoom tool (magnifying glass). Notice that the line retains its edge at absurd levels of magnification. Ah, vector graphics! How good you are to us!

Adding More Straight Segments

The simplest path consists of two anchor points and a single segment between them. But you can use the Pen tool to create more complex shapes, as Figure 4.4 shows.

Grab the Pen tool and plot the first two anchor points, just like before. Only this time, instead of clicking the original point to close the line, choose a different spot on the page, and click the mouse button. A new segment stretches between the second and third anchor points. Move the mouse and click again. Another new segment appears.

Add as many segments to the path as you want. To finish, you have two options, as Figure 4.5 shows.

Your first option is to close the path. A *closed path* doesn't have obvious start and end points, like a rectangle or a triangle. To close the path, move the mouse pointer to the original anchor point. Watch for the X to change into an O, and click. The path closes with one final segment.

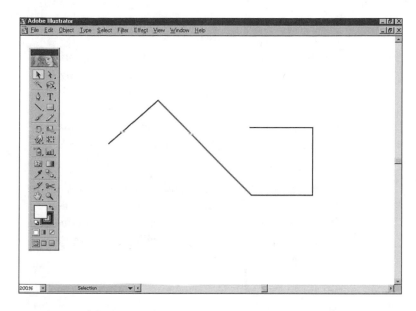

Figure 4.4

A path can contain multiple straight segments.

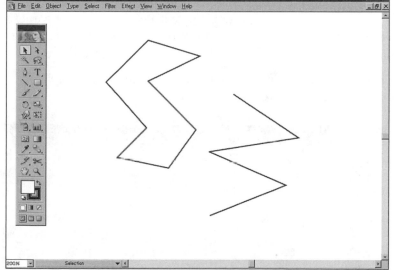

Figure 4.5

A closed path (left) doesn't have obvious start and end points, whereas an open path (right) does.

Your second option is to leave the path open. An *open path* has obvious start and end points, like a zigzag or the letter Z. To leave the path open, choose a blank area of the page, hold down Ctrl (Windows) or Command (Mac), and click. If you forget to deselect the path like this before you start drawing a new line, Illustrator gets confused and thinks that you want to add a new segment to the original line. Always deselect an open path before you resume drawing.

Continuing the Path

If, after careful reflection, you decide that an open path needs a few more segments, you can easily tack them on. First, click the path with the Selection tool. Then grab the Pen from the toolbox. When you position the Pen over one of the end anchor points, the X in the icon changes to a slash (/), which means that you can extend the path from that point. Click the mouse button, and add new anchors to your heart's content.

When continuing an open path, don't confuse the slash (/) in the Pen pointer icon with the minus sign (-). These symbols mean two different things. If you see a minus sign, clicking the anchor will actually remove it from the path.

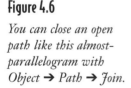

Word Balloon

A **closed path** doesn't have obvious start and end points, like a rectangle or a triangle. An **open path** has obvious start and end points, like a zigzag or the letter Z.

Closing the Path

An open path doesn't have to stay open forever. Consider my sloppily drawn parallelogram in Figure 4.6. Do you see how the segments don't quite match up in the left corner? I can remedy that by clicking the shape with the Selection tool and choosing Object ➔ Path ➔ Join from the menu. The awkward open path becomes a crisp, closed shape.

You can also close your path like before by moving your mouse pointer to the original anchor point. Watch for the X to change into an O, and click.

Figure 4.6

You can close an open path like this almost-parallelogram with Object ➔ Path ➔ Join.

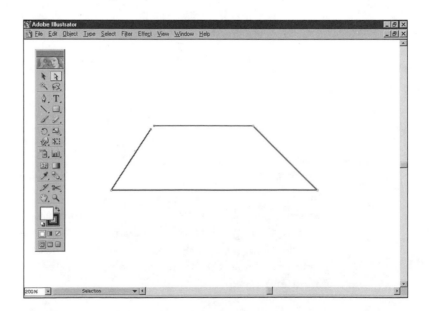

Keeping It on the Level

If you want to draw a perfectly horizontal, vertical, or diagonal segment, you can eyeball it, of course, and you can also turn on the grid, but why go to the trouble? Illustrator provides a perfectly reasonable alternative.

Make sure that the mouse pointer is in the neighborhood, and simply hold down the Shift key before you plot the second anchor point with the Pen. You get a perfectly horizontal segment if the mouse pointer roughly lines up with the horizontal position of the first anchor point. Likewise, you get a perfectly vertical segment if the mouse pointer roughly lines up with the vertical position of the first anchor point. Anything in between creates a diagonal segment at a 45-degree angle.

Modifying the Path

Whether your path is open or closed, you can modify it easily. To get the most editing power out of Illustrator, it is important to know the difference between the two arrow icons in the toolbox: the Selection tool and the Direct Selection tool.

You have used the Selection tool a number of times already. When you click a path with the Selection tool, a bounding box appears around the line or shape. Notice that the bounding box has eight small squares that look something like anchor points. There is a square in each corner and a square in the middle of each line. These squares are the handles of the bounding box. By dragging the handles, you can scale, or change the size of, your path.

Position the mouse pointer on a handle, and the pointer changes into a two-way arrow. The directions of the arrow tell you which ways you can scale the path. Hold down the mouse button, and drag in one of these directions. The path stretches dutifully. To finish, release the mouse button.

Incidentally, you can also rotate the path by positioning the mouse pointer slightly to the left or the right of a handle. Watch for the pointer to change into a curved two-way arrow. Then hold down the mouse button, and drag the mouse to rotate the path. This trick comes in handy throughout—I'll mention it many times before the end of this book.

Drawing Perspectives

In Adobe Illustrator, the tools are Selection and Direct Selection. In CorelDRAW, they are Pick and Shape. Other illustration programs give you a single selection or pointer tool. Whether that tool selects or direct-selects depends on how you use it.

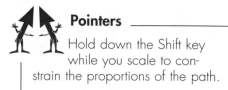 **Pointers**

Hold down the Shift key while you scale to constrain the proportions of the path.

You could say that the Selection tool enables you to modify the path as a whole. By comparison, the Direct Selection tool (the white arrow) enables you to adjust the individual anchor points and segments that make up the path. When you click a path with the Direct Selection tool, you don't get a bounding box. Instead, you see the anchor points of the path, as shown in Figure 4.7.

Figure 4.7

When you click a path with the Direct Selection tool, you gain access to the anchor points and segments that make up the path.

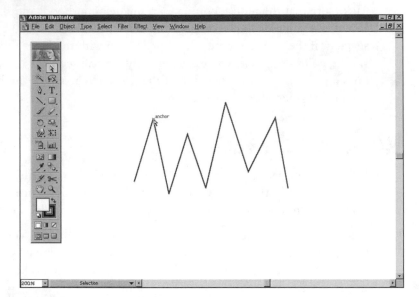

To move an anchor point, hover over it with the Direct Selection tool. Hold down the mouse button and drag. The path changes direction as you go. Release the mouse button to drop the anchor point in its new location. If you don't like the new location, pick up the anchor point and try another spot.

To move a segment of a path, position the white arrow anywhere along the segment (but not on an anchor point), hold down the mouse button, and drag.

With a little practice, you can change many-sided figures into simpler ones by dragging around the anchor points and segments. For instance, I changed an octagon, or an eight-sided shape, into a parallelogram, and then I changed the parallelogram into a triangle, as you can see in Figure 4.8. Just so you know, there's an even better way to transform shapes, which I discuss in Chapter 12, "Manipulating Paths."

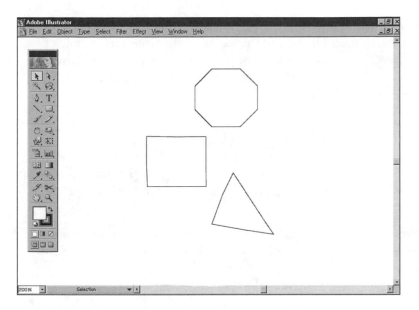

Figure 4.8

By manipulating the positions of anchor points and segments, you can put a shape through some fundamental changes.

Connecting Paths

Let's say you have two open paths, like the straight lines in Figure 4.9, and you want to connect them. To do so, you need to choose the end points of the paths. Sounds like a job for the Direct Selection tool.

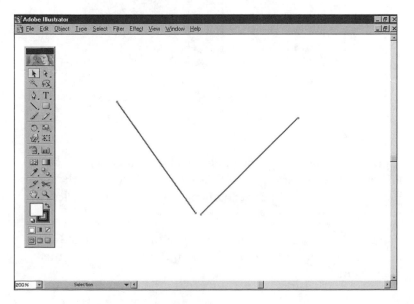

Figure 4.9

Use the Direct Selection tool and the Join command to connect two paths.

First, click the end point of the first path with the Direct Selection tool. Then hold down the Shift key and select the connection point of the second path. Make sure it's one of the end points, or the Join command will get upset with you. Choose Object ➔ Path ➔ Join, and a segment bridges the two paths.

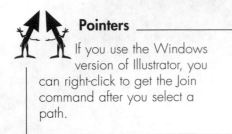

Pointers

If you use the Windows version of Illustrator, you can right-click to get the Join command after you select a path.

Cutting Paths

Illustrator gives you a couple of ways to cut a path. One way is to use the Scissors tool; another is to use the Knife tool.

The Scissors tool makes cuts in the segments of a path. You can use the Scissors to divide a path in two, or you can extract a portion from the middle of a path. Find the Scissors directly above the Zoom tool in the toolbox (see Figure 4.10).

Figure 4.10

Use the Scissors to cut a path in two or to snip a portion from the middle.

To divide a path in two, grab the Scissors from the toolbox and click anywhere along the path. A new anchor point appears at the cut. Use the Selection tool to separate the pieces. You can get rid of the part you snipped off by selecting it and choosing Edit ➔ Clear or pressing the Delete key.

To remove a portion from the middle of a path, click twice with the Scissors: once at the beginning of the cut, and once again at the end. Remove the cut portion with the Selection tool, as shown in Figure 4.11.

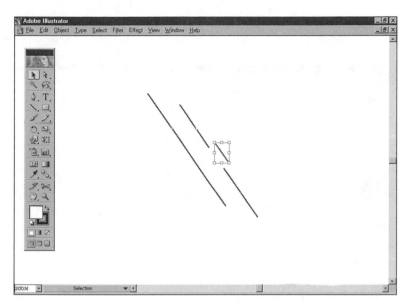

Figure 4.11

Make two snips with the Scissors, and extract a section from the middle of a path.

Remember hidden tools from Chapter 3, "Illustrating Illustrator"? The Knife hides under the Scissors in the toolbox. (Don't confuse the Knife tool with the Slice tool, which sits to the left of the Scissors.) To select the Knife, hold down the mouse pointer on the Scissors tool until the hidden toolset appears (see Figure 4.12).

Figure 4.12

Use the Knife to slice a closed path.

Use the Knife to divide a closed path, like the shape in Figure 4.13. Start with the mouse pointer outside the path. Then press and hold the mouse button and drag the Knife all the way through the shape. Don't release the mouse button until you come out the other side. This ensures that the tool makes a good clean cut. Afterward, separate the pieces with the Selection tool.

Figure 4.13

This shape went under the Knife.

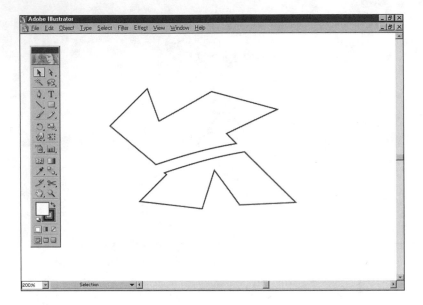

Art Alert

The Scissors works on open and closed paths, but the Knife works best on closed paths. If you try to use the Knife on an open path, you may get strange and undesirable results.

You can use the Knife to make multiple cuts at the same time. To do so, make the first cut, remembering to go all the way through the shape, but don't let go of the mouse button. Instead, run the Knife across the shape to make another cut. Repeat as often as you want, and release the mouse button to finish.

To cut with the Knife in a straight line, hold down Alt (Windows) or Option (Mac) before you start dragging.

Drawing Perspectives

The erasers in image editors work differently than their vector graphics counterparts. In programs such as Photoshop, you can rub the eraser back and forth to eliminate pixels. In Illustrator, you have to trace the portion of the path that you want to erase.

Erasing Paths

Another way to get rid of a portion of a path is to rub it out with the Erase tool. The Erase tool hides under the Pencil tool in the toolbox. To find the Pencil tool, look directly below the Rectangle tool (see Figure 4.14).

Before you erase, you have to click the path with the Selection tool. If you forget to do this, the Erase tool will not work. After you select the path, grab the Erase tool and move it onto the path. Then hold down the mouse button and trace the portion of the path that you want to erase. Don't rub the Erase tool back and forth across the path, like you would a real pencil line with a real eraser. Think of the Erase tool as Wite-Out instead. Apply it with a smooth stroke. When you release the mouse button, the portion that you traced disappears, as you can see—or not—in Figure 4.15.

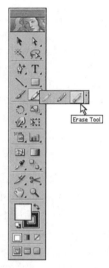

Figure 4.14

Use the Erase tool to rub out a portion of a path.

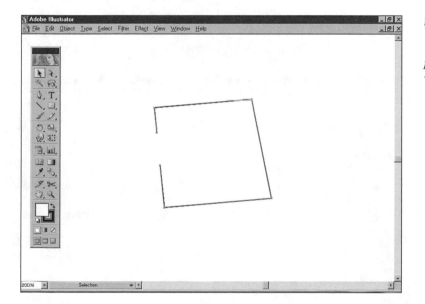

Figure 4.15

Trace the Erase tool over part of a path, and that part vanishes.

A Sign for the Times

What better way to practice using these tools than to create some art for Astro Ape? You can create the arrow sign that marks the way to the real world at the beginning of the strip.

First things first: Clear away your practice lines and shapes. Choose Edit ➔ Select All and press the Delete key or choose Edit ➔ Clear.

Art Alert

If you plan on drawing at a larger scale than you need for the final illustration, choose Edit ➔ Preferences ➔ General from the menu, and make sure that the Scale Strokes & Effects option doesn't have a check mark next to it. This way, the thickness of the outline will not change in proportion to the scale.

Now make sure that you can see what you're doing. Bump up the magnification to at least 100%. For smaller illustrations like this, I tend to work at 150% or 200%. Also, don't be afraid to draw the shape much larger than it will be in the final comic strip. Vector graphics lose absolutely no image quality when you shrink them down, and it's easier to work with large shapes than miniscule ones.

The arrow sign for Astro Ape is just a series of straight segments. Start out with the Pen tool, and plot the anchor points so that they create a closed shape like in Figure 4.16. If you make a mistake, remember: Edit ➔ Undo is your friend. Don't worry about doing anything too fancy at this stage. Just go for a uniform placement of anchor points. You will add some character to the illustration in the next step.

Figure 4.16

Start out by plotting a serviceable—if uninteresting— arrow design with the Pen tool.

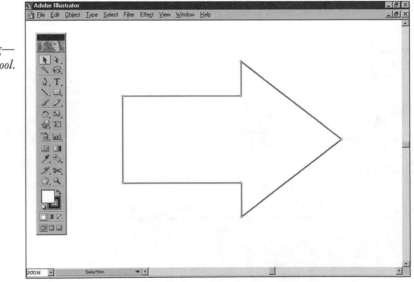

You should now have a serviceable, straightforward-looking arrow shape in the workspace. If you were doing a technical drawing, you could save the file now and go home for the evening. But the comic style in which you're working demands a little distortion. The sign should look believable but just over the top.

You might be wondering why I didn't tell you to draw a more comic-booky arrow shape to begin with. That's how an illustrator would have done it on pen and paper. But remember, computer illustration offers a different kind of approach. Because anchor points and segments are so easy to edit, you can bend and tweak the path as the mood strikes you. This feature enables you to test out many, many different designs for the arrow and choose the one that appeals to you the most. If you don't like the way a particular design is going, rectify it with Edit → Undo.

So, with the Direct Selection tool, shuffle the anchor points and segments until you get a pleasingly playful yet still recognizable arrow shape. It doesn't take much distortion to get the right effect. Figure 4.17 shows the design I liked the best of those I tried.

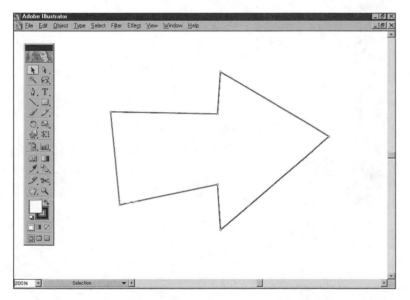

Figure 4.17

Use the Direct Selection tool to give the arrow some cartoony character.

Now, to make this arrow into a sign, you need a signpost. Pick a clean spot on the screen to draw it.

Again, if you're wondering why I didn't tell you to draw the signpost behind the arrow in the first place, I'll bet you can predict my response. Computer illustration has a different rhythm than pen and paper. You can easily move the signpost behind the arrow after you get it looking the way you like. I'll mention over and over again throughout this book that, in computer illustration, it's helpful to visualize a drawing in terms of its parts. More often than not, you will create each part individually and then assemble the pieces into a final design.

To make the signpost, you could take the Pen and make a tall, thin rectangle. For that matter, you could use the Rectangle tool to do the same thing. But to give the design a little depth, start out with an ellipse instead, courtesy of the Ellipse tool. Then, with the Pen, add two straight lines for the sides, as you see in Figure 4.18. Note that the lines don't touch the ellipse—at least not yet. Finally, with the Selection tool, click the ellipse and choose Edit → Copy and then Edit → Paste. This gives you an identical ellipse shape that you can position at the bottom of the signpost.

Pointers

To fine-tune the position of a shape, click the shape with the Selection tool and tap the arrow keys.

Figure 4.18

To begin the signpost, create two ellipses and two straight lines in close proximity.

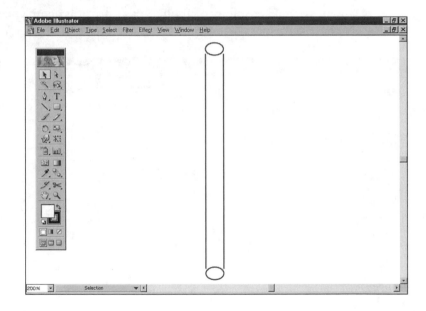

Snip off the bottom half of the first ellipse and the top half of the second ellipse with the Scissors tool, and delete the unused portions. Then position the half-ellipses just above and just below the vertical lines. Don't make the pieces touch just yet. You will probably want to zoom in to 600% or so to get the alignment just right, as shown in Figure 4.19.

When you finish positioning the pieces, grab the Direct Selection tool. Click the left anchor point at the bottom of the first half-ellipse. Hold down Shift, and click the anchor point at the top of the corresponding vertical line. Now choose Object → Path → Join, and the left side of the half-ellipse fuses to the line. Repeat this process for the other three pairs of anchor points. When you finish, you have a signpost design much like the one in Figure 4.20.

Figure 4.19

Zoom in and align the bottom of the ellipse with the top of the vertical line.

Figure 4.20

Use the Join command four times, and you get the finished design for the signpost.

Move the signpost to the arrow shape with the Selection tool, and adjust their relative sizes and positions accordingly. See Figure 4.21 for my interpretation.

Notice that the signpost appears to be in front of the sign. This is because of the *stacking order*. Illustrator stacks, or places in the foreground, the most recently drawn path. That means that the sign, which was the very first path you drew, is all the way at the bottom of the stack.

Figure 4.21

When you bring the two paths together, the signpost appears to be in front of the sign.

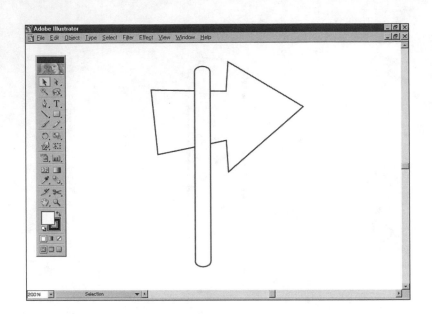

You can easily remedy this situation. Click the sign with the Selection tool and go to Object ➔ Arrange. Out slides a menu with these choices: Bring To Front, Bring Forward, Send Backward, and Send To Back. Each of these commands relates to the stacking order.

Word Balloon

The **stacking order** determines which paths appear in front of which other paths in the document window. By default, the most recently drawn path sits at the top of the stack.

The Bring To Front command moves the selected path all the way to the top of the stack. Bring Forward moves the path one step up in the stacking order. Likewise, Send Backward moves the path one step down, and Send To Back moves the path all the way to the bottom.

In this drawing, there are only two paths to stack, so Bring To Front and Bring Forward produce identical results. Choose the one that suits your fancy. The sign repositions itself in front of the signpost, as in Figure 4.22.

We have the beginnings of something here! True, neither of the objects appears in color, and the sign doesn't say "The Real World," but I address these and other details in Chapters 9, "Applying Brushes" and 11, "Inserting Type."

For the time being, choose File ➔ Save to store your work in a convenient location on your hard drive. I'm using the filename *aa_sign.ai*. The *aa_* portion refers to Astro Ape, which is the name I've chosen for this project. Get into the habit of labeling your files this way. As a computer illustrator, you store many, many files for many, many different projects. Using project-specific filenames makes hunting down the right ones that much easier. It also makes a good, professional impression on the people who write the checks.

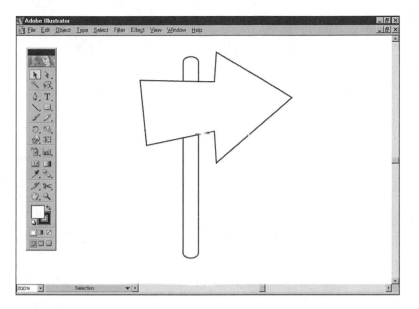

Figure 4.22

*Bring the arrow to the fore-ground under Object →
Arrange.*

Don't look now, but you just completed the first piece of art for the comic strip! You owe
yourself a little reward. Truly I say to you, a computer illustrator you shall be.

The Least You Need to Know

◆ Every path has at least two anchor points and one segment.

◆ Use the Pen tool to plot anchor points.

◆ Use the Selection tool to manipulate a path as a whole.

◆ Use the Direct Selection tool to rearrange the anchor points and segments that
make up a path.

◆ Use tools such as the Scissors, Knife, and Erase to change a path.

◆ In computer illustration, it is helpful to visualize a drawing in terms of its parts.

Creating Curves

In This Chapter

- ◆ Drawing curved segments with the Pen
- ◆ Mixing curved and straight segments
- ◆ Drawing the cartoon landscape for the Astro Ape comic

So far I've shown you how to draw straight lines. This technique is surprisingly versatile. As you saw in Chapter 4, "Delivering Straight Lines," you can create many kinds of shapes from different combinations of straight segments. But the time will come when you want to add some roundness to your computer line technique. For the purposes of this book, that time is now.

The best way to draw graceful arcs and smooth, flowing curves is to use your old friend, the Pen tool. Unfortunately, out of all the procedures in this book, drawing curves with the Pen is the least intuitive and the least like traditional illustration.

The technique isn't hard, but it does take some getting used to. If you're still practicing curves with the Pen long after you've mastered everything else in this book, don't take it as a sign that you should abandon computer illustration in favor of counted cross-stitching. Not an artist alive completely understands this procedure. I wouldn't say that computer illustrators hate using the Pen to draw curves, they simply dislike it intensely.

Playing It Smooth

Before I taint your attitude completely, have a look at the dreaded beast. Open up a fresh document window, and grab the Pen from the toolbox.

When you drew straight lines with the Pen, I asked you to click once and release the mouse button to plot an anchor point. There wasn't any dragging of the mouse. This is because dragging is the difference between *corner points* and *smooth points* when it comes to the Pen.

A corner point is an anchor point whose segments come out at angles, like in a rectangle or triangle. You used corner points in Chapter 4. But a smooth point is an anchor point whose segments come out as curves. If you drag the Pen instead of clicking and releasing, you create a smooth point.

> **!#%@ Word Balloon**
>
> A **corner point** is an anchor point whose segments come out at angles. A **smooth point** is an anchor point whose segments come out as curves.

Give it a try. Hold down the mouse button and drag in any direction. The Pen appears to draw a straight segment, but this isn't the case. The entire figure is actually a single smooth point with two *direction lines*—one on each side, as shown in Figure 5.1. The direction lines determine the slope and the depth of the curved segment that comes out. The angle of the direction lines gives you the slope of the curve, and the length of the direction lines gives you the depth of the curve. The longer the direction lines, the deeper, more pronounced the curve will be.

Figure 5.1

The direction lines of a smooth point determine the slope and depth of the curved segment to come.

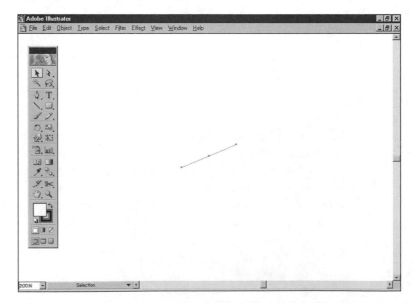

Make the direction lines good and long, and release the mouse button. Notice that the curve does not yet appear. Why not? Remember from Chapter 2, "Of Pixels and Paths," that you need two anchor points for each straight segment. The same holds true for curved segments. So far you have plotted exactly one anchor point. You need exactly one more to create the curve.

Move the mouse pointer elsewhere on the page, and click the mouse button. (Keep the button held down, but don't drag the mouse just yet.) Now that's more like it! A precise, fluid curve fills in between the two anchor points, as you can see in Figure 5.2.

Drag the mouse to create a pair of direction lines on the anchor point that you just plotted. Notice how the shape and size of the curve change as you adjust the length and angle of the direction lines. When you have the direction lines the way that you want them, release the mouse button. Then, to see what the curve looks like without the anchor points and direction lines in the way, move the mouse pointer to an empty area of the page, hold down Ctrl (Windows) or Command (Mac), and click (see Figure 5.3).

Drawing Perspectives

Adobe Illustrator and Deneba Canvas use the terms *corner points* and *smooth points*. In Macromedia FreeHand, anchor points are called *corner points* and *curve points*. In CorelDRAW, anchor points are called *cusp nodes* and *smooth nodes*.

 Pointers

A direction line always has a round bulge at the end of it, whereas a straight segment falls between two square anchor points. That's how you can tell a direction line from a straight segment. Incidentally, the name for the round bulge is the *direction handle*.

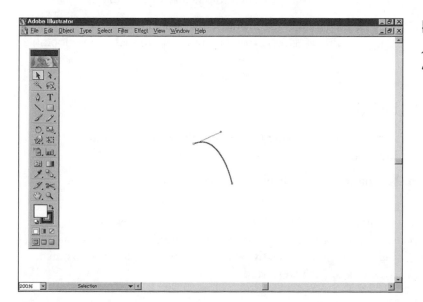

Figure 5.2

Add a second anchor point, and the curve appears.

Figure 5.3

Adjust the second anchor point's direction lines and deselect the path to see the curve in its final form.

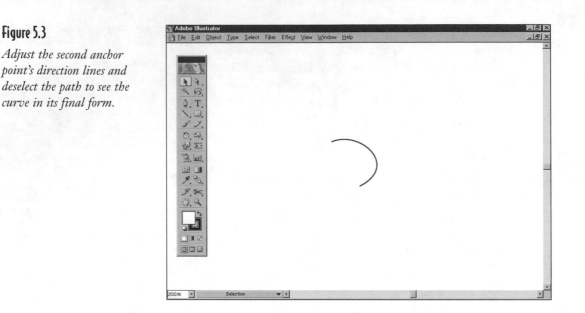

Drawing Perspectives

In Adobe Illustrator, you use *direction lines* and *direction handles*. In Macromedia FreeHand, you use *point handles* and *point knobs*. Deneba Canvas uses *tangent lines* and *handles,* and CorelDRAW uses *control points.*

There! That wasn't so bad. It goes without saying that you can magnify the heck out of the work area with the Zoom tool, and your curve retains its fluidity, thanks to the power of vector graphics. If you had drawn this curve in an image editor instead, it wouldn't take much magnification before the essentially rectangular shape of the pixels degraded the quality of the curve.

Take this opportunity to draw some more curved segments. Don't worry about trying to make them look like anything at this point. Just get a feel for the process.

Controlling the Curve

After you're familiar with the ritual of drawing curves with the Pen, it's helpful to look at some of the nuances of the tool.

"Nuances?" you might be tempted to say. "Is he crazy? This is the clumsiest thing I've ever worked with."

I have uttered those words many, many times. But in spite of appearances, the Pen is probably the most precise tool of them all. It can draw nearly anything that you can imagine. The trick is being able to tell the Pen exactly what you want it to do, and this takes practice. Here are some pointers to get you started.

Going with the Flow

The direction in which you drag the mouse when you create the initial anchor point determines the direction of the curve. If you drag the mouse to the right, for instance, the curve flows to the right. If you drag the mouse to the left, the curve flows to the left. If you drag the mouse up, the curve flows upward, and if you drag the mouse down, the curve flows downward. You get the idea.

You won't necessarily catch a dragging-direction mistake until you plot the second anchor point. You can use the Direct Selection tool to adjust the direction of the first anchor point after the fact, or you can invoke Edit ➔ Undo two times: once to get rid of the most recent anchor point, and once to remove the original anchor point.

Minding Your C's and S's

The direction in which you drag the mouse when you create the second anchor point also affects the direction of the curve. When you plotted the first point, the way you dragged the mouse determined the direction of the curve. When you plot the second anchor point, you can either maintain the original direction or bend the curve in the opposite direction midway. This gives you either a C-shaped curve or an S-shaped curve. A *C-shaped* curve maintains its original direction from start to finish. An *S-shaped* curve changes directions in the middle.

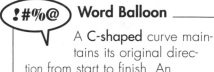 **Word Balloon**

A **C-shaped** curve maintains its original direction from start to finish. An **S-shaped** curve changes direction in the middle.

Dragging in the *opposite* direction for the second anchor point gives you a C-shaped curve. Dragging in the *same* direction gives you an S-shaped curve.

For example, assume that you dragged to the left when you plotted the initial anchor point. This creates a curve that flows to the left. Now, if you drag to the right when you create the second anchor point, the curve continues its graceful leftward arc and ends up looking similar to the letter C. But if you drag to the left instead, the curve starts out flowing in a leftward direction, but then it bends to the right before it comes to the second anchor point, much like the letter S changes direction in the middle. See for yourself in Figure 5.4.

Figure 5.4

A C-shaped curve maintains its original direction from start to finish, like the letter C. An S-shaped curve changes direction in the middle, like the letter S.

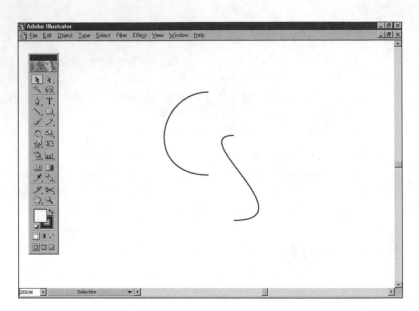

Changing Direction

Use the Selection tool to scale and move the path, and use the Direct Selection tool to adjust the anchor points and segments that make up the path, just like you did in Chapter 2.

The Direct Selection tool also enables you to edit the direction lines of a smooth anchor point. Click a smooth point with the Direct Selection tool, and the direction lines appear. Drag the round handles at either end to change the length and angle of the direction lines. To change a C-shaped curve into an S-shaped curve, for instance, you could click the starting anchor point with the Direct Selection tool and twist the direction lines around.

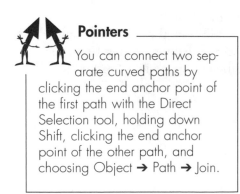

Pointers

You can connect two separate curved paths by clicking the end anchor point of the first path with the Direct Selection tool, holding down Shift, clicking the end anchor point of the other path, and choosing Object ➜ Path ➜ Join.

Adding More Curved Segments

A path can have multiple curved segments. If you don't Ctrl-click (Windows) or Command-click (Mac) after you draw a curve, the next anchor point that you plot will become part of the current path. Drag the direction lines of this anchor point in the same way as the others. If you drag in the direction opposite the most recent point, you get a C-shaped segment. If you drag in the same direction as the most recent point, you get an S-shaped segment. Figure 5.5 shows these multiple curved segments.

Figure 5.5

You can attach multiple curved segments to the same path.

To close the path, move the mouse pointer back to the original anchor point, just like you did for paths made of straight segments. Note that the Pen icon shows a tiny O to tell you that you have the right anchor point. When you see the O, click and drag the direction lines. If you drag in the same direction as you did when you first plotted the point, the original segment maintains its shape. If you drag in the opposite direction, the original segment changes from an S-curve to a C-curve or a C-curve to an S-curve.

Here is a simple example to show you what I mean. Start off with a smooth anchor point that you drag to the right. Plot another smooth point a few inches underneath, and drag this one to the left. This gives you a C-shaped curve. Now go back to the original anchor point to close the path *but do not release the mouse button yet*. Here's where the process gets interesting, because the second anchor point of the second segment and the first anchor point of the first segment are one and the same. Drag the direction lines to the right, and you get a species of ellipse, with two happily conjoined C-shaped curves. Drag the direction lines to the left, and you get a figure eight instead, as you can see in Figure 5.6. The C-curve that comes out of the original anchor point twists into an S-curve, because dragging the

Art Alert

When you start working with multiple curved segments, it gets harder to make the Pen do what you want it to do. The same rules for creating C-shaped and S-shaped curves apply, although anticipating the end result becomes trickier. The best policy here is to experiment. See what happens to the path when you drag the mouse in different directions after plotting a new point.

original anchor point to the left changes its rightward direction. You could have made the same figure eight by dragging to the left each time. This way, when you drag to the left during the close, you don't end up changing the original anchor point's direction.

Figure 5.6

Depending on the way you drag the mouse when you close this curved path, you can create a round shape or an Arabic numeral.

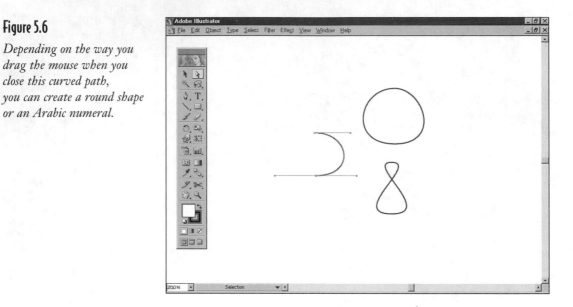

You don't have to close a curved path if you don't want to. Ctrl-click or Command-click on an empty area of the page to leave the path open.

Combining Straights and Curves

You can create paths of all curved segments. You can create paths of all straight segments. And you can create paths that combine straight and curved segments. It all depends on how you drag the mouse.

Say that you want to draw a straight segment immediately after a curved segment. Start by drawing the curved segment, which means dragging the mouse to make a smooth anchor point. Then, when you plot the second point, click the mouse button and release. Don't drag a new pair of direction lines, or you will end up with another smooth point.

Clicking once and releasing creates a corner anchor point, like the kind you used in Chapter 2. A curve flows from the first anchor point and ends at the second. Now, to continue in a straight line, plot the third anchor as a corner point—in other words, click and release.

Now say that you want to add a curved segment. No problem. When you plot the fourth anchor point, make it a smooth one by dragging a pair of direction lines. A curved segment flows between the third and fourth points, as shown in Figure 5.7. Add as many segments as you want, dragging for smooth points, and clicking and releasing for corner points.

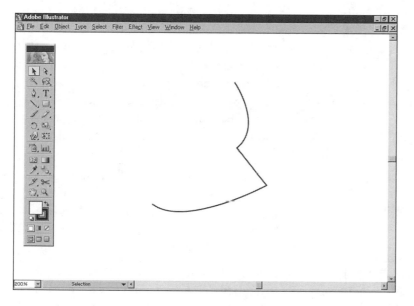

Figure 5.7

Mixing curved and straight segments is easy. It all depends on how you handle the mouse.

Here's another trick that you can use to do the same thing. Assume that you start out by drawing a curved segment, and you drag direction lines for the first anchor point as well as the second. You now have a beautifully flowing curve between two smooth points. How can you get a straight segment to come out of the second smooth point?

Move the Pen back to the second anchor point, and notice the caret character (^) in the lower right. The caret tells you that, if you click again, you will convert the anchor point from corner to smooth or smooth to corner. Going from smooth to corner is exactly what you want, so click away. Now move the mouse and plot the third anchor as a corner point, and a straight segment fills in. If you want to convert this corner point to a smooth point, position the mouse pointer and look for the caret. When you see it, hold down the mouse button and drag a direction line. Plot a new anchor, and a curved segment flows from the converted corner point. Nice!

Pointers

If you rummage through the hidden toolset under the Pen, you will find a dedicated Convert Anchor Point tool. Use this tool to convert any anchor point from corner to smooth or smooth to corner. I explore some of the creative possibilities of anchor-point conversion in Chapter 12, "Manipulating Paths."

There's No Place Like Home

In this section you use the Pen tool to create the cartoon environment for Astro Ape.

Recall that the comic strip begins and ends in a fantasy setting, with an unpleasant detour to the Real World in between. You're going to process a photographic backdrop for the Real World panels toward the end of this book, but you can anticipate that the source photo will have lots of jagged corners and rough, rectangular shapes. It will look even more inhospitable by the time you're finished with it. You need something different for the background of the fantasy panels—something rolling and pleasant and friendly. How convenient that the Pen tool, with its graceful curves, offers an excellent contrast to the hard angles of the Real World photo.

Art Alert

In Illustrator, all paths— even open paths—have a fill color and a stroke color by default. You haven't noticed the fill color so far because it matches the white background of the page. You may notice the color in this exercise, however, if part of what you've drawn seems to mysteriously disappear. If you don't turn off the fill color, the "invisible" white fill may partially obscure the line work beneath it.

Pointers

You can easily make sure that the start points and end points of the curves stay at about the same level. With the Pen tool, create a horizontal line that stretches the length of the page. Then plot the start points and the end points of the curves so that they fall just above or just below this line. Delete the guide rule when you finish.

Open a new document window, or clean up the current window, and set the magnification to at least 100%. For this drawing, it will be helpful to see the left and right sides of the imageable area at a glance, so watch that you don't zoom in too much at first.

It will also be helpful to turn off the fill color. Remember how to do that? Look in the toolbox for the solid white square and the hollow black square. The solid square is the fill color, or the inside color, and the hollow square is the stroke color, or the outside color. Click once on the solid square to bring it to the foreground. Then click the None button, which is the icon with the red slash through it. The solid square should now also have a red slash. Leave the stroke color as black. You don't want to turn that one off, or you will not be able to see the Pen strokes.

All right. For the cartoon landscape, you need a pair of C-shaped curves that flow upward. Get the Pen tool and plot a smooth anchor point by dragging up. Release the mouse button, move across the page, and plot another point, dragging down this time. Ctrl-click or Command-click, and you have your first curve. Draw another one just like it. If your curves look a bit like rolling hills, you're on the right track. If they don't, take the Direct Selection tool and edit them into shape. When you finish, you should have something resembling Figure 5.8.

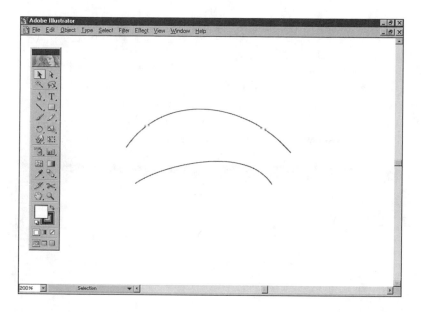

Figure 5.8

Use the Pen tool to draw two C-shaped curves.

With the Selection tool, position the curves so that one curve overlaps the other curve slightly, as in Figure 5.9. If you squint, you should be able to imagine a cartoony, comic-booky landscape.

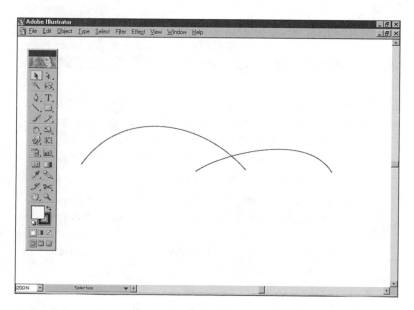

Figure 5.9

With some deft arrangement, the curves become the beginning of hills in a cartoon landscape.

Now remember that you're creating these hills for the background of a comic strip panel. You know that the panels will be rectangular, so you should square off the sides and the bottom of the hills. This way, you can fit the hills nicely into the panel when you get around to creating it.

Pick up the Pen tool again, and position the mouse pointer under the outside end point of the curve on the right. Draw a straight segment down a short way, continue with another straight segment to the left, and finish with a third straight segment going up. Use the Direct Selection tool to adjust this path so that the vertical segments line up with the edges of the curves, as Figure 5.10 shows. Zoom in if you need to.

Figure 5.10

Create a path with three straight segments, and line up the verticals with the edges of the curves.

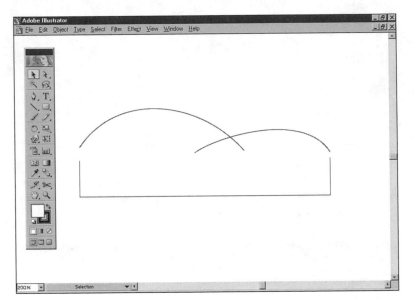

When the fit is just right, click the end point of the right curve with the Direct Selection tool. Hold down Shift, and click the end point of the corresponding vertical segment.

Art Alert

If you erase too much of the overlapping segment, the entire path could disappear! The trick is to get as much of the line as possible without also erasing part of the intersection. If you go too far, use Edit → Undo.

Choose Object → Path → Join to attach the two paths. Repeat this procedure on the left side, and you get something resembling Figure 5.11.

Almost finished! All you have to do now is remove the overlapping portion of one of the hills. This is a precise maneuver, so zooming in well past 100% is smart. Make it so the overlapping lines dominate the workspace.

Click the path with the Selection tool. Then find the Erase tool. It's hiding under the Pencil, remember? Drag the Erase tool across one of the overlapping segments—it doesn't matter which segment. I'm choosing the segment that belongs to the hill on the right, so that the hill on the left appears to be in front. If you want the hill on the right to be in front, then make it so.

Zoom back out, and your screen should look similar to Figure 5.12.

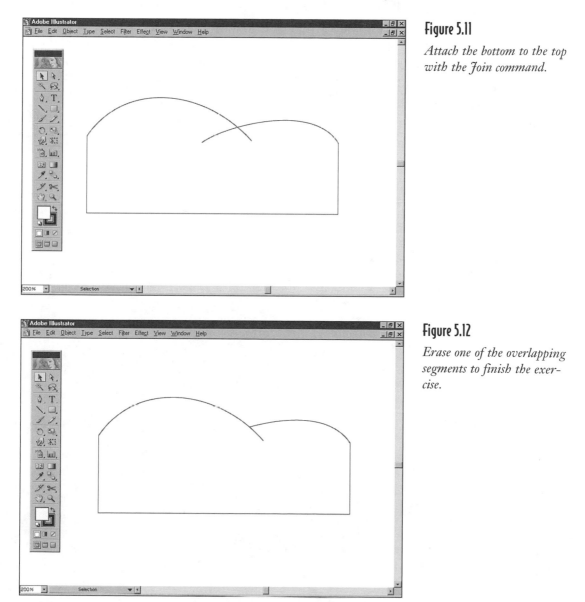

Figure 5.11

Attach the bottom to the top with the Join command.

Figure 5.12

Erase one of the overlapping segments to finish the exercise.

You have some rolling hills for the cartoon landscape. Congratulations on another job well done! Save your work under the filename *aa_hills.ai* or some such. You will revisit this drawing when it comes time to add color.

The Least You Need to Know

◆ Dragging the Pen creates a smooth anchor point.

◆ Direction lines determine the slope and the depth of a curved segment.

◆ Depending on how you drag the mouse, you can create a C-shaped or an S-shaped curve.

◆ You can use the Direct Selection tool to edit the direction lines of a smooth point.

◆ You can combine curved segments and straight segments in the same path.

Chapter 6

Going Freeform

In This Chapter

Let's face it. If the Pen were the only drawing tool, computer illustration would only appeal to mathematicians, engineers, and people who use the term *hypotenuse* in casual conversation. The Pen is precise—maybe a little *too* precise. Sometimes illustrators must sacrifice precision for expedience.

Fortunately for the non-scientists among us, Illustrator offers an alternative to the plot-the-anchor-point, determine-the-slope-and-depth procedure that you have been good enough to endure for the sake of your art. This alternative enables you to draw in a more intuitive way: by dragging the mouse. The path goes where the mouse goes. Illustrator is smart enough to calculate the positions and directions of the anchor points for you as you draw.

Call this technique *freeform drawing*. The tool for the job is the Pencil, and I show you how to use it in this chapter.

Pushing the Pencil

Open a new document window, and pull out the Pencil tool. The Pencil is the fifth tool from the top, on the right, as shown in Figure 6.1.

Figure 6.1

Illustrator's Pencil tool helps you draw freeform paths.

The Pencil is very easy to use. Position the mouse pointer where you want to start drawing, hold down the mouse button, and drag. A thin, dotted line traces your movements.

Release the mouse button, and a path appears in the shape of the dotted line. Your path should contain a series of smooth anchor points and segments, as shown in Figure 6.2. These smooth points and segments work exactly like the ones you plotted with the Pen in Chapter 5, "Creating Curves."

Figure 6.2

In freeform drawing, you just drag the mouse. Illustrator calculates the positions and directions of the anchor points as you go.

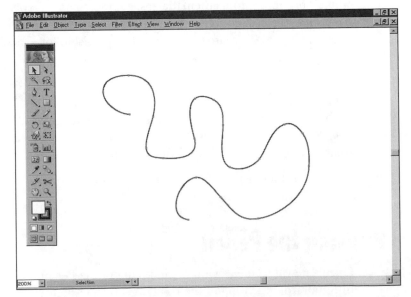

To see the Pencil's resemblance to the Pen, hold down Ctrl (Windows) or Command (Mac) and click on an empty area of the page. Now grab the Direct Selection tool from the toolbox and click anywhere along the path that you just drew. You should get at least one direction line—you will probably get more. Feel free to adjust the direction lines as well as the anchor points and segments. Note that you can reshape the Pencil line with ease. The experience of doing so should be much like you remember it from Chapters 4 and 5.

> ### Drawing Perspectives
>
> The freeform drawing tool in Macromedia FreeHand is, appropriately enough, the Freehand tool. In CorelDRAW it is also called the Freehand tool.

So what's the difference between a Pencil path and a Pen path? Nothing, as far as Illustrator is concerned. Both contain the same basic elements. Anything that you can draw with the Pencil, you can also draw with the Pen. The difference between the two isn't theoretical but practical. With the Pen, you explicitly define the anchor points that make up the path. With the Pencil, Illustrator defines them for you as you draw. This makes using the Pencil more intuitive and much faster.

The only catch is that the Pencil is not as precise a tool as the Pen. The Pencil creates a more natural-looking, noisier, less efficient path, while the Pen creates a quieter, sharper, mathematically pristine one.

 Pointers

Even the Pencil may be too precise when you're just starting out, before you develop a good technique for drawing with the mouse. If your Pencil lines look too shaky for your taste, try adjusting the Pencil preferences. Double-click the Pencil icon in the toolbox to call up the Pencil Tool Preferences window. Adjust the Fidelity slider to make your Pencil lines more forgiving—higher fidelity causes Illustrator to ignore slight variations in mouse movement. Adjust the Smoothness slider to make your Pencil lines smoother in general. Click OK to set your preferences. Be warned, though, that these adjustments make detailed Pencil work more challenging.

Which is the better drawing tool? It depends on what you want to illustrate. If you want to draw a perfect right angle, you need the corner-point power of the Pen. The Pencil can give you a very close approximation of a right angle, but it will never give you a perfect right angle, as you can see if you look closely at Figure 6.3.

Of course, much that you would care to illustrate doesn't require the exacting precision of the Pen. If you're drawing somebody's elbow, for instance, you don't need a perfect right angle. In fact, you don't want a perfect right angle—it would make your subject look like a robot.

Figure 6.3

Freeform paths are easy to draw, but they just aren't as precise as Pen paths. The Pen's version, on the left, is dead-on accurate. The Pencil's version, on the right, doesn't quite achieve the same glory.

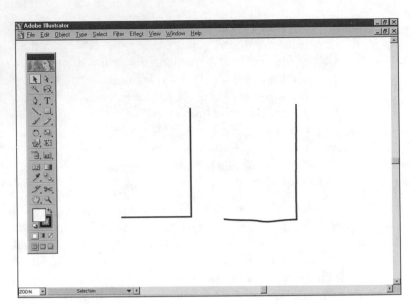

If precision is essential to the task at hand, the Pen is the tool for you. But if precision isn't necessary or even desirable, make your choice the Pencil.

Adding On

It's easy to add to an existing path with the Pencil. Simply click the path with the Selection tool and grab the Pencil from the toolbox. Note that when you move the Pencil into the work area, the mouse pointer shows an X in the lower right corner, just like the Pen. This signifies that the Pencil is ready to draw a new path. If you start drawing with the Pencil now, the new path will not attach to the one that you have selected.

Move the mouse pointer to the end point of the path that you want to extend. The X disappears from the Pencil icon. Now when you draw with the Pencil, the new path attaches to the old one.

This works, by the way, with all kinds of paths, not just ones that you draw with the Pencil.

Redrawing the Path

You can also use the Pencil to redraw any portion of an existing path. This trick is faster and more intuitive than the Direct Selection tool.

Click an existing path with the Selection tool. Get the Pencil, and move the mouse pointer onto the path. The little X next to the Pencil icon disappears. Now, to redraw the path from that location, hold down the mouse button and drag. Draw the rest of the path as you would like it to be. When you release the mouse button, the first portion of the path remains as it was, but the second portion reshapes itself according to its new definition.

Art Alert

Sometimes Illustrator gets confused about which part of the path you want to keep and which part of the path you want to redraw. As a rule of thumb, if you draw the new portion from left to right, Illustrator keeps everything to the left of the insertion point. If you draw the new portion from right to left, Illustrator keeps everything to the right of the insertion point. If you try this and Illustrator still doesn't cooperate, you may need to re-create the path from scratch.

Closing the Path

To close a freeform path, hold down the Alt key (Windows) or Option key (Mac) while you draw. The Pencil icon acquires a tiny O in the lower-right corner, which, as you remember from the Pen, is the close-path signal. Release the mouse button, and the path snaps closed.

You don't have to be in the vicinity of the starting anchor point to close the path. Illustrator shoots a closing segment from the current mouse position to the original anchor point, no matter where you are on the page.

Make sure that you hold down Alt or Option *after* you start drawing, though. If you press the key before you start drawing, the Pencil turns into the Smooth tool, as you will soon see, and you will not get any line at all.

And the Crooked Made Straight

The Pencil may not be as precise as the Pen, but it is certainly more sensitive. If your hand twitches slightly, or if your elbow hits something, or if your mouse runs off the mouse pad, the Pencil registers it.

You already know of several good ways to fix mistakes. You can bring out the Direct Selection tool and manually adjust the anchor points, direction lines, and segments of the path. You can redraw the botched portion with the Pencil tool. And let's not forget my favorite, Edit ➔ Undo.

Drawing Perspectives

What is the Smooth tool's icon supposed to represent? That is a very good question. It seems to be a round-body pencil, the kind that rolls off your desk.

Here's another method that works especially well for ironing the kinks out of an otherwise good freeform path: the Smooth tool, shown in Figure 6.4. The Smooth tool hides under the Pencil tool in the toolbox. It is the middle icon in the Pencil toolset.

Figure 6.4

Use the Smooth tool to iron out the kinks in a freeform path. The Smooth tool hides under the Pencil in the toolbox.

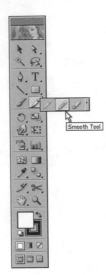

The Smooth tool works on any path, not just freeform paths. But because you rarely need the Smooth tool on Pen paths because of their innate mathematical perfection, Illustrator wisely associates this tool with the Pencil. In fact, if you select the Pencil tool and then hold down Alt (Windows) or Option (Mac), the Pencil automatically changes into the Smooth tool. This feature enables you to draw a freeform path and then smooth it out without going back to the toolbox. This shortcut only works when you aren't using the Pencil. If you press Alt or Option while you're in the middle of drawing something, Illustrator thinks that you want to close the path.

Pointers

If the Smooth tool doesn't smooth enough for your tastes, you can increase its effectiveness by opening the Smooth Tool Preferences window. Double-click the Smooth tool to access the preferences. Crank up the Fidelity, and the Smooth tool eliminates lumps and bulges. Increase the Smoothness value, and the tool irons out all but the sharpest corners. Be careful, though, that you don't smooth out too much detail under such high settings.

To smooth out a path, first click the path with the Selection tool, and then take the Smooth tool from the toolbox. The Smooth tool works much like the Erase tool, in that you don't rub the Smooth tool back and forth across the path. Instead, hold down the mouse button and trace the Smooth tool across the portion of the path that you want to smooth out. Release the button to see the effect.

This is what I like best about the Smooth tool: The more often you apply it to a path, the smoother the path becomes. You may need a few swipes of the Smooth tool to iron out particularly gnarled paths, as you can see in Figure 6.5.

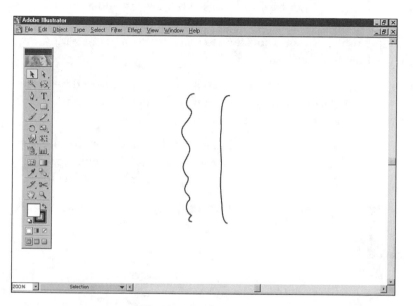

Figure 6.5

After a few swipes with the Smooth tool, a shaky path feels much better about itself.

The Same Rules (and Tools) Apply

You already know that Pencil paths and Pen paths are the same thing as far as Illustrator is concerned. You can use the Selection and Direct Selection tools on both paths. You can attach freeform paths to Pen paths with ease. You can even redraw Pen paths with the Pencil.

It should come as no surprise that the other tools and techniques that you've explored so far work equally well on Pencil paths.

Use the Scissors to snip off sections of a Pencil path. Use the Knife to cut closed Pencil shapes in two. Fuse two separate Pencil paths together by selecting their end points and choosing Object → Path → Join. Rub out portions of a Pencil path with the Erase tool.

Drawing Perspectives

You can even use Illustrator's editing tools on paths that you create in some other vector graphics program. Illustrator can read, or import, vector graphics files from many different pieces of software.

Remember that the Pencil and the Pen are different tools for doing the same thing: creating paths. Once you create a path, you can manipulate it with all the commands at your disposal.

Show Me the Monkey

The Astro Ape character is a collection of freeform paths, a few circles, and a single straight line. You know how to make straight lines with the Pen tool. You know how to make circles with the Ellipse tool. And you know how to make freeform paths with the Pencil tool. You now know how to draw Astro Ape!

I mentioned before that, in computer illustration, it makes sense to visualize a drawing in terms of its parts. You draw each part separately and assemble the pieces afterward. This is exactly the approach you will take for drawing the monkey.

I'm going to cheat a little and show you the finished character design before you get started (see Figure 6.6). This will give you an idea about how the individual pieces will come together in the end. Astro Ape consists of 20 separate paths in all.

Figure 6.6

Here it is at last: the design for Astro Ape. This illustration uses 20 separate paths, most of which are freeform.

Open a new document window, adjust the magnification, and grab the Pencil tool. Now crack your knuckles, rub your palms, and take a firm grip on the mouse. Ready? Good!

Start with the head. The head is like a deflated playground ball, as you can see in Figure 6.7. As you draw it with the Pencil, don't forget to hold down the Alt key (Windows) or the Option key (Mac) so that the path closes when you release the mouse button.

Ctrl-click or Command-click to deselect the head shape, and add some ears in the vicinity. Each ear is just a single, simple, open Pencil path. Don't hold down Alt or Option to close the ears as you draw them.

The face contains the most paths—seven total (see Figure 6.8). The face itself is another deflated playground ball, this one lopsided. Use the Pencil and hold down Alt (Windows) or Option (Mac) to close the path. The nose is an arc that is slightly pinched at the top. The smiling mouth, by comparison, is wider and not as deep.

Art Alert

Staring intently at a computer screen for a long period of time can give you a headache, to say nothing of staring at goofy monkey pictures. When you feel like you need to take a break, take it. Save your work and come back to it later.

Figure 6.7

Here are the monkey's head and ears. The head is a closed path.

Grab the Ellipse tool to draw an eye and an eyeball. The eyeball is a perfect circle, so hold down Shift to constrain the proportions of the path as you create it. The eye isn't quite a circle. It's slightly wider than it is tall. When you finish, get the Selection tool and click the eyeball. Hold down Shift and click the eye. This selects both paths. Choose Edit → Copy and then Edit → Paste to create the matching set, shown in Figure 6.8.

!#%@ Word Balloon

Monkeys are generally smaller primates that have tails. **Apes** are generally larger primates that have no tails. Astro Ape, with his tail, may not be a very good ape, but he is an excellent astronaut.

Figure 6.8

Seven paths make up Astro Ape's face. Use the Ellipse tool to create the eyes and eyeballs.

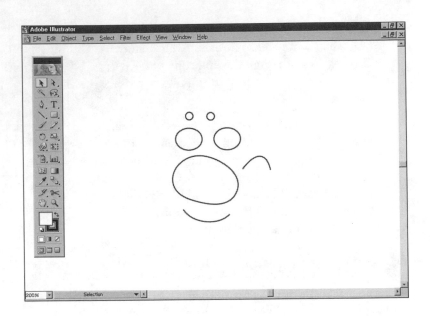

Grab the Pencil again for the body (see Figure 6.9). The body is a closed path that looks something like a bean crossed with a peanut. The tail is also a closed path. The upper extremity of the tail is flat, and the lower extremity is round, like the head of an earthworm. The path with the notch in the top is the breastplate of Astro Ape's space suit. What else? Every space suit needs a breastplate. Notice that it vaguely resembles the shape of the body, with a very slight dip in the left side.

Figure 6.9

Astro Ape's body pieces are all closed freeform paths.

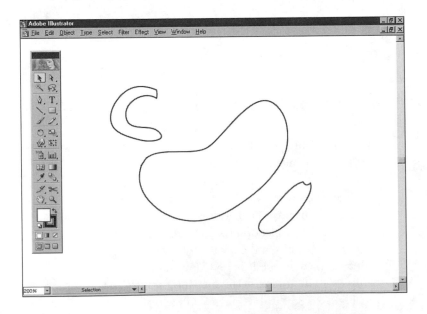

On to the arms and the legs, shown in Figure 6.10. Each arm is an open path. Start at the top left, add the shape of the hand at the bottom, and finish at the top right. Each leg is a closed path. Watch out for the knees—they bulge a bit.

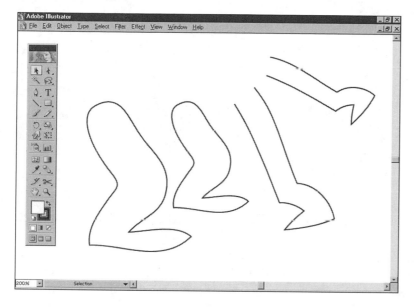

Figure 6.10

The arms and legs are freeform paths, too. Close the leg paths, but leave the arms open.

You will finish with the space helmet. The helmet proper is an ellipse, the antenna is a straight line, and the bulb at the end of the antenna is a perfect circle. I decided to give these pieces of technology a more geometric look, contrasting them subtly with the looser and more organic body design, so I used the Ellipse tool and the ever-precise Pen to create these paths.

Draw the antenna and the bulb first. Get the Pen, plot a pair of corner anchor points, and you have the antenna. Then, with the Ellipse tool, hold down the Shift key and create the bulb (see Figure 6.11).

The helmet is also an ellipse, but it has two unique features. First, it doesn't have a fill color, so that you can see the face underneath when you arrange the pieces. Before you draw the helmet, click the fill-color square on the toolbox, and then click the None button. Second, the right side of the helmet tilts downward. You achieve this effect by rotating the ellipse after you draw it. I discussed rotation briefly in Chapter 4. You may have also stumbled across this trick while experimenting with the Selection tool. Just in case you haven't, here's what you do.

Pointers

Feel free also to experiment with Illustrator's Rotate tool, which can tilt objects with a greater degree of control than the bounding-box method. I explore the Rotate tool more fully in Chapter 14, "Applying Transformations."

Figure 6.11

The antenna for the space helmet is a simple Pen stroke. Use the Ellipse tool to create the bulb at the top.

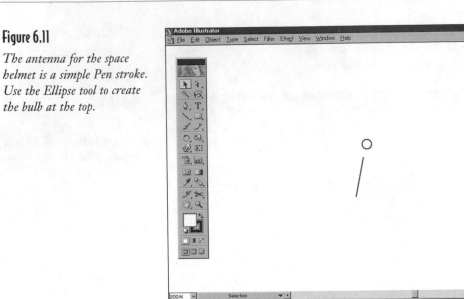

Draw the ellipse with the Ellipse tool, and grab the Selection tool from the toolbox. This should create a bounding box around the shape. If it doesn't, just click the ellipse. Now move the mouse pointer to the handle in the lower right corner of the bounding box. The pointer should change to a diagonal two-way arrow. Don't press the mouse button just yet. Instead, slowly move the mouse to the left, along the bottom of the bounding box. The pointer should change to a curved, two-way arrow. Ah-ha! That's the rotation indicator. Hold down the mouse button and drag the mouse down and to the left. The bounding box and the ellipse inside it begin to rotate clockwise. Release the button when the helmet has the right amount of tilt (see Figure 6.12).

Figure 6.12

Create the helmet itself with the Ellipse tool, and then rotate the path slightly in a clockwise direction.

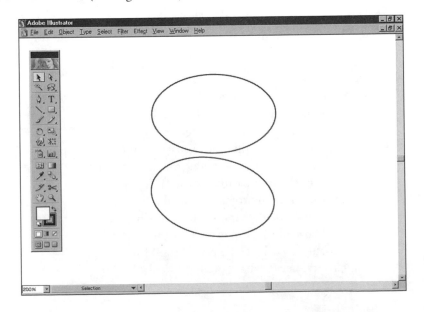

You have 20 paths. There is only one monkey. The task now is to assemble the pieces. With the Selection tool, drag each path into place. Refer to Figure 6.6. Remember, you can scale the individual parts if something looks too small or too large in context.

You will also need to adjust the stacking order of the paths. As you may recall from Chapter 4, the stacking order determines which paths sit in front of which other paths on the page. By default, the most recently drawn item is at the top of the stack. Because you drew Astro Ape's head before you drew his body, the head is further down in the stack, which means that the body will cover part of the head when you bring the paths together. You want the head to sit on top of the body, not the other way around.

To fix this, all you have to do is select the body and send it backward a few steps in the stacking order. Choose Object → Arrange → Send Backward several times, until the head pops out from behind the body. Avoid the hassle of opening the menu over and over by holding down Ctrl (Windows) or Command (Mac) and tapping the left bracket key ([). This shortcut does the same thing as the Send Backward command.

You will run into a similar situation with the arms and legs. The larger limbs should sit in front of the body, and the smaller ones should sit behind it. As you have it now, all the limbs will appear in front of the body. Use the Object → Arrange commands to get every path in its proper place.

In case you have trouble figuring out which paths belong in front of which other paths, here is the stacking order of the finished illustration from top to bottom: antenna bulb, antenna, helmet, nose, mouth, right eyeball, left eyeball, right eye, left eye, face, right ear, head, left ear, right arm, breastplate, right leg, body, tail, left arm, left leg.

To help you assemble the paths, you can take advantage of a technique called grouping. Grouping allows you to combine separate paths into a single package, if you will. When you click a group with the Selection tool, you can move it around the document window as if it were a single path.

After you assemble an eye, for instance, hold down Shift and click both eye paths with the Selection tool. Then choose Object → Group from the menu. (For those with a right mouse button, you can also right-click and pick Group from the

Art Alert

You may have trouble selecting a path if another path covers it completely. If this happens, Windows users can select the visible path, right-click, and choose Select → Next Object Below or Select → Last Object Below from the context menu.

Pointers

When you create the helmet for the rear view, don't forget to turn off the fill color so that the inside is transparent.

context menu.) Now, when you select either path in the group, you select both paths automatically. You can drag the eye around the screen without readjusting the relative position of the component paths.

Do the same thing to all the paths of the head, including the two eye groups. A group can contain individual paths as well as other groups. By grouping the head, you can position it on the body faster and with less hassle. I'll talk more about groups in Chapter 13, "Organizing Objects." When you finish, save your work as *aa_side.ai*.

Don't stop now! You're on a roll! Open up a new document window, and give this rear view of Astro Ape a try (see Figure 6.13).

I will not take you through this one step by step. I don't need to! You're getting too good. But I will give you some hints to start you off.

Figure 6.13

You will also use a rear view of Astro Ape in the comic strip. There are 13 paths in this illustration.

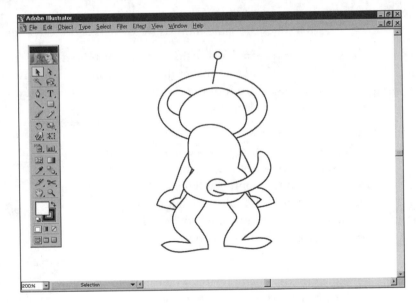

There are 13 paths in all. I group them together for you in Figure 6.14. Nine of these are Pencil paths. The helmet, the antenna, the antenna bulb, and the hole for Astro Ape's tail are not. The final stacking order, from top to bottom, is tail, tail hole, body, right leg, left leg, right arm, left arm, antenna bulb, antenna, helmet, head, right ear, left ear.

Draw each piece individually, as before, and then arrange them to form the final design. I have full confidence in your ability to do this. If you get stuck, the art for this chapter is on the CD-ROM.

And that, as they say, is that! Save your work as *aa_rear.ai* and shower yourself with praise for another brilliant success.

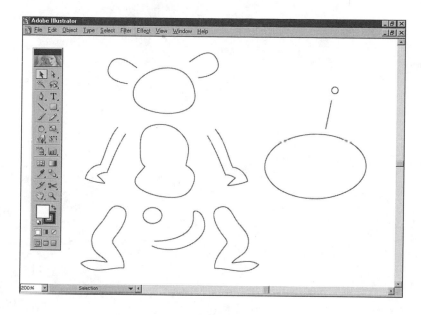

Figure 6.14
Here are the paths that make up the rear view.

The Least You Need to Know

◆ You can create freeform paths with the Pencil tool.

◆ The Pencil tool is faster and more intuitive than the Pen.

◆ The Pen is more precise than the Pencil.

◆ Use the Smooth tool to rub out small mistakes in Pencil lines.

Generating Shapes

In This Chapter

♦ Drawing ellipses and circles

♦ Drawing rectangles and squares

♦ Drawing polygons, stars, and other shapes

♦ Drawing the sky for the Astro Ape comic

So far, you have created paths by hand, with deft manipulation of the Pen and Pencil. Some geometric shapes come easy this way. Consider the rectangle. It isn't hard to plot four anchor points with the Pen to get a solid, satisfactory rectangular shape.

But what about drawing circles and ellipses? Creating one of these with the Pen is a form of torture in some countries. And even though Pen-drawn rectangles are easy, the process could be faster.

That's why illustration programs give you special tools for creating simple geometric forms. Some computer illustrators call these forms *primitives* (or simple geometric shapes). But I'll call them by their completely appropriate and less connotative nickname: shapes. This chapter explores Illustrator's shape-drawing tools.

Drawing Ellipses

You have been drawing ellipses since Chapter 3, "Illustrating Illustrator." But for those of you just joining in, a review may be in order.

To draw an ellipse, take the Ellipse tool from the toolbox. The Ellipse tool hides under the Rectangle. Move the mouse pointer into the document window, and the pointer changes into crosshairs. Now position the crosshairs where you want to start drawing, hold down the mouse button, and drag. You can adjust the shape and size of the ellipse as you go. To finish, release the mouse button.

This is the way you have been drawing ellipses so far. It's probably the most intuitive way. But it isn't the only way.

Suppose that you need to create an ellipse with a specific width and height—say, six inches wide and four inches tall. You could be dragging the Ellipse tool around for hours before you get the shape exactly right. Or you could simply specify the width and height from the get-go.

How? It's easy. Take the Ellipse tool from the toolbox, and bring the mouse pointer into the document window as before. But instead of holding down the mouse button and dragging, click once and release. This calls up the Ellipse dialog box, shown in Figure 7.1.

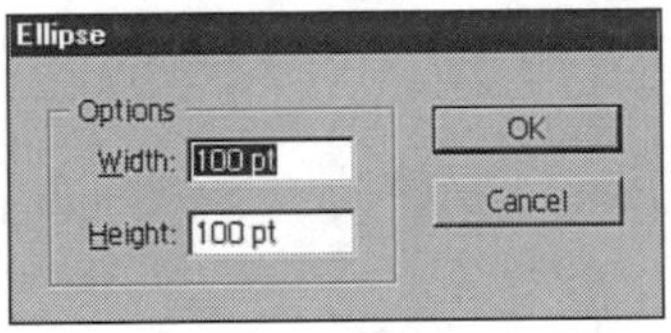

Figure 7.1

Use the Ellipse dialog box to create an ellipse of a particular width and height.

Now all you have to do is type values in the fields for width and height. By default, Illustrator calculates measurements in points, a typographical unit that publishers and printers find useful. There are 72 points in an inch, so an ellipse with a width of 72 points and a height of 72 points is an ellipse that is one inch by one inch.

> **Drawing Perspectives**
>
> In the world of computer graphics, it is standard practice to give measurements as width followed by height. When somebody asks for an ellipse of four by five, you can interpret that as four units wide by five units high.

Fortunately, you don't have to convert measurements to points if you don't feel like it. Illustrator can do it for you. To create an ellipse that is six inches by four inches, type **6 in** for the width and **4 in** for the height. The software calculates the equivalent measurement in points.

If you prefer the metric system, you can type values for centimeters and millimeters in the width and height fields. Use the abbreviations *cm* and *mm*, respectively.

When you click the OK button, Illustrator creates an ellipse to your exact specifications.

You may notice that, when you select the ellipse, what looks like an anchor point appears in the center of the shape, as shown in Figure 7.2. Appropriately enough, this is the center point of the shape. Rectangles also have this characteristic point, as you will soon see.

The center point isn't an anchor point, per se. It doesn't behave like the other anchor points in the drawing. It works more as a convenience to you, the artist. Use it to help you align objects and paths to the center of the shape.

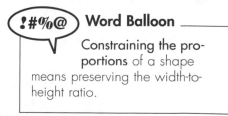

Pointers _____

If you don't like the look of a center point, you can make it invisible. Click the shape with the Pointer tool, and then call up the Attributes palette under Window → Attributes. Click the button with the hollow square to hide the center point. To make the center point visible again, click the button with the dotted square.

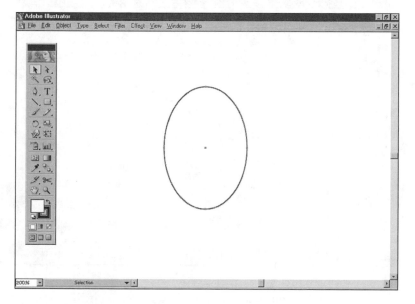

Figure 7.2

The center point helps you to align other objects and paths with the center of an ellipse or rectangle.

Drawing Circles

It stands to reason that if you specify the same value for the width and height in the Ellipse dialog box, your ellipse will come out as a perfect circle.

If you need a circle of a specific size, this method beats the old way—holding down the Shift key and dragging the Ellipse tool. Holding down Shift *constrains the proportions* of the ellipse. Constraining

Word Balloon _____

Constraining the proportions of a shape means preserving the width-to-height ratio.

the proportions means nothing more than preserving the width-to-height ratio of the shape. When you use the Rectangle and Ellipse tools, constraining the proportions also keeps the width equal to the height.

Creating Cheap Curves

If drawing curves with the Pen makes your head spin, try this sneaky workaround.

First, create an ellipse or circle that looks something like the curve you want to draw. Then get the Scissors tool from the toolbox and snip off a portion. Adjust the size of the curve with the Selection tool, and modify the direction handles and the placement of the anchor points with the Direct Selection tool. Clear away the unused portion of the shape, and no one will be the wiser (see Figure 7.3).

Figure 7.3

I used the Pen to create one of these curves, and I snipped a circle in half with the Scissors to create the other curve. Which is which? I'll never tell! Never! (Hint: The one on the left is the Pen curve.)

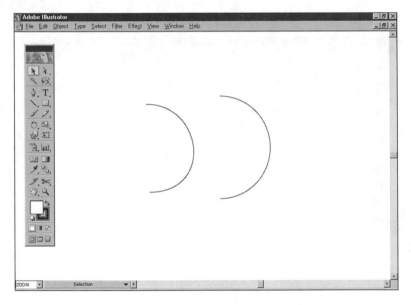

This trick requires some practice, but it is quicker than using the Pen in a pinch.

Drawing Rectangles

You have also used the Rectangle tool before. It works just like the Ellipse tool. Choose the Rectangle tool from the toolbox, drag the mouse, and release to create a rectangular path.

You can also click once with the Rectangle tool to call up the Rectangle dialog box, shown in Figure 7.4. Enter the exact measurements in the width and height fields to draw a rectangle of a specific size.

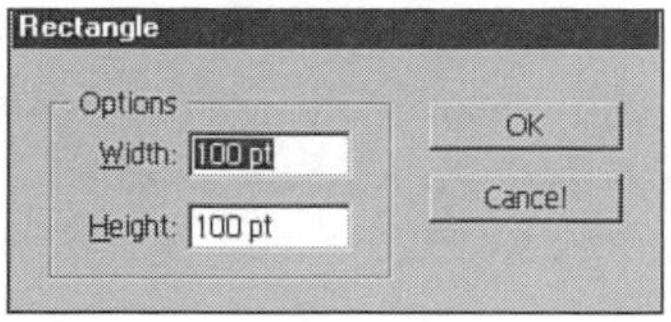

Figure 7.4

Use the Rectangle dialog box to create a rectangle of a particular width and height.

Drawing Squares

To create a perfect square instead of a rectangle, do one of two things:

◆ Hold down the Shift key as you drag the Rectangle tool (constraining proportions again).

◆ Enter the same values for width and height in the Rectangle dialog box.

You can change the square into a rectangle if the need arises. Click the square with the Selection tool, and drag one of the handles on the bounding box.

Drawing Rounded Rectangles

Hiding under the Rectangle in the toolbox is the Rounded Rectangle tool, as Figure 7.5 shows. This tool works very much like the Rectangle tool, only it creates rectangles with rounded corners. Give it a try.

> **Drawing Perspectives**
>
> Web builders often use rounded rectangle shapes for button designs.

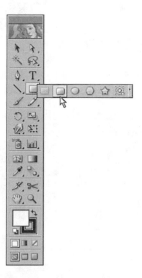

Figure 7.5

Use the Rounded Rectangle tool to create rectangular paths with rounded corners.

If you click the Rounded Rectangle tool once instead of holding down the mouse and dragging, the Rounded Rectangle dialog box appears. You can enter precise values for the width and height of the shape in addition to the radius of the corners. As you can see in Figure 7.6, the higher the corner radius, the rounder the edges of the rectangle.

Figure 7.6

The higher the corner radius, the rounder the edges of the shape. The top rectangle has a corner radius of 12 points, and the bottom rectangle has a corner radius of 36 points.

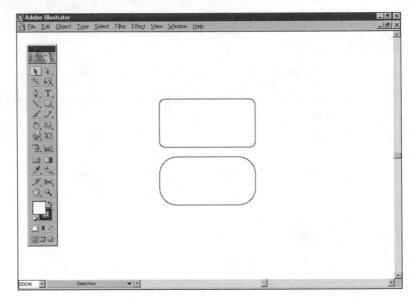

To create a rounded square, hold down Shift as you drag, or enter identical values for the Width and Height fields in the Rounded Rectangle dialog box.

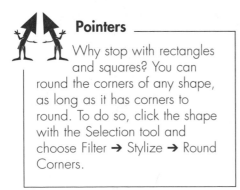

Pointers

Why stop with rectangles and squares? You can round the corners of any shape, as long as it has corners to round. To do so, click the shape with the Selection tool and choose Filter ➔ Stylize ➔ Round Corners.

Cutting Corners

Just like the Ellipse tool gives you cheap curves, the Rectangle tool gives you cheap right angles.

Create a rectangle, click it with the Selection tool, and snip off one of the corners with the Scissors tool. Discard the excess, and you have an instant right angle—yours to scale with the Selection tool and manipulate with the Direct Selection tool as Figure 7.7 demonstrates.

Chapter 7: Generating Shapes **107**

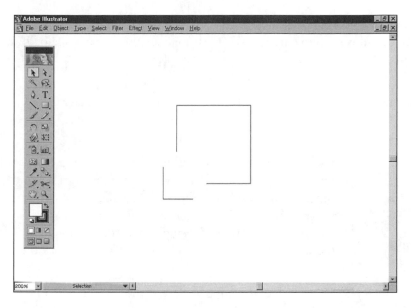

Snip a corner from any rectangle or square, and you have a perfect right angle at no extra cost.

Drawing Other Shapes

The Rectangle's hidden toolset offers some interesting alternatives to plain old circles, squares, and ellipses. These are the Polygon tool and the Star tool as Figure 7.8 shows. For those who missed geometry class, a *polygon* is a many-sided figure. In strictest terms, a polygon has more than four sides. But you can use the Polygon tool to create three-sided and four-sided figures, too.

!#%@ **Word Balloon**

A **polygon** is a shape with more than four sides. Illustrator enables you to cheat a bit and use the Polygon tool to create figures with as few as three sides.

Figure 7.8

Hidden under the Rectangle are tools for drawing polygons and stars.

Both tools work as you might expect. Drag them with the mouse to create the specified shape, or click them once and release to enter precise measurements by way of a dialog box.

You will notice that the Polygon dialog box enables you to give the number of sides in the shape, and the Star dialog box enables you to enter the number of points. To create an equilateral triangle, for instance, specify a three-sided polygon. To create a hexagram, specify a six-point star. The higher the number of sides or points, the rounder the shape.

Pointers

The Polygon tool is great for equilateral triangles, which have three 60-degree angles. But if you want to create a right triangle, which is a triangle with one 90-degree angle, use the Rectangle tool instead. Draw a rectangle and click it with the Selection tool. Then get the Pen, and click one of the anchor points. The anchor point disappears, and the figure becomes a right triangle.

Unlike the Rectangle and Ellipse tools, dragging the mouse doesn't change the proportions of polygons and stars, and holding down the Shift key doesn't constrain the proportions of these shapes. In fact, these shapes always have constrained proportions. You cannot alter the width relative to the height until after you draw the shape.

So what does dragging achieve with these shapes? I'm glad you asked. Dragging the mouse up and down changes the size of the shapes, and dragging the mouse to the left or right causes the shapes to rotate. Holding down the Shift key prevents the shape from rotating at all.

To alter the width or height of a polygon or star, first draw the shape with the appropriate tool. Then click the shape with the Selection tool, and drag the handles of the bounding box.

Table 7.1 helps you remember how each shape tool works.

Table 7.1 Using the Shape Tools in Illustrator

Tool	Dragging Up/Down	Dragging Left/Right	Holding Down Shift
Ellipse	Changes size	Changes proportions	Constrains proportions
Polygon	Changes size	Rotates	Prohibits rotation
Rectangle	Changes size	Changes proportions	Constrains proportions
Rounded Rectangle	Changes size	Changes proportions	Constrains proportions
Star	Changes size	Rotates	Prohibits rotation

Stars and Garters

You drew the ground on which Astro Ape walks in Chapter 5, "Creating Curves." In this chapter, you will draw the starry heavens into which his bold eyes gaze, and you will use the shape tools to do it.

Scientists estimate that at least 100 billion billon stars exist in the universe, but you only need six for Astro Ape, along with two ellipses, one circle, and one rectangle.

You know the drill. Open a new document window and bump up the magnification. Choose a conservative level for now, say 150% or 200%. You can zoom in later for detail work.

Start with the rectangle. This will be the back-drop, or the "canopy of the sky," if you want to get poetic about it. Remember that you squared off the bottom of the landscape in Chapter 5. By creating the sky from a rectangle instead of some other shape, you will be able to fit the rolling hills into place with ease. Also, the combined rectangular ground/sky illustration will slide perfectly into a rectangular panel for the final comic strip.

So taking the Rectangle tool, draw a path to match the one you see in Figure 7.9.

Drawing Perspectives

Stars are hot, dense balls of hydrogen and helium gas. The largest and hottest stars create heavier elements in their cores and release these elements when they explode. Scientists believe that most of the material in our bodies originally came from stars.

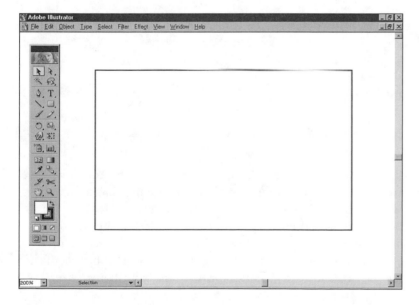

Figure 7.9

The background of the sky in Astro Ape is a simple geometric shape, courtesy of the Rectangle tool.

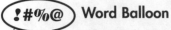

Word Balloon

In the media game, **repurposing content** for a project means reusing existing material instead of developing something new. Although this practice is creatively suspect, it is often quicker, easier, and cheaper than the alternative. Many media consumers prefer inexpensive things to original ones.

Now look under the Ellipse for the Star tool, and add a sextet of twinkling celestial bodies in different sizes and angles of rotation. Don't use the same shape six times! I like a good computer-illustration shortcut as much as the next person, but these shape tools are so easy and quick that there's no good excuse for *repurposing content*, as they say.

With the Selection tool, position your six original, unique, nonrepurposed stars at the top of the rectangle, as shown in Figure 7.10. Notice that there is some space between the star on the left and the five-star cluster on the right. That space will shortly be occupied by the crown jewel of your sky—a ringed planet of the Saturn variety.

Figure 7.10

Add six stars of different sizes and angles of rotation.

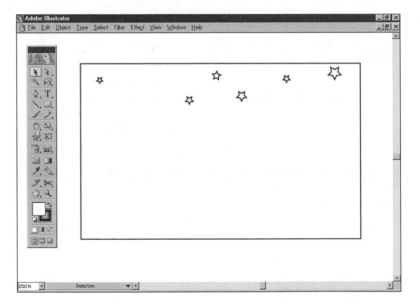

As you may know, small bits of rock and dust make up the rings of Saturn. You don't have a Dust tool or a Rock tool in the Illustrator toolset, but you can use the Ellipse tool as a workaround. Start out with a single ellipse—make it short and wide, because it's going to be part of the rings. When you get the shape you want, choose Edit → Copy and then Edit → Paste from the menu to create an identical twin. Now select the pasted ellipse with the Selection tool, hold down the Shift key, and drag the bottom right handle of the bounding box. This gives you two ellipses of identical proportions but different sizes.

Line up the center points of the ellipses. Then select the smaller ellipse and tap the up-arrow key until its top edge matches that of the larger ellipse, as Figure 7.11 shows.

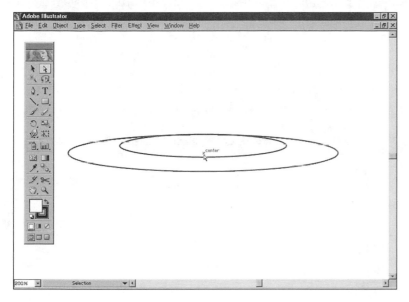

Figure 7.11

Using the center points as a guide, position two ellipses to form the rings of the planet.

Now hold down the Shift key and draw a circle to represent the planet. Line up the center point of the circle with the center point of either ellipse, and tap the up-arrow or down-arrow key to fine-tune the planet's vertical position in relation to its rings. When you finish, your screen should look something like Figure 7.12.

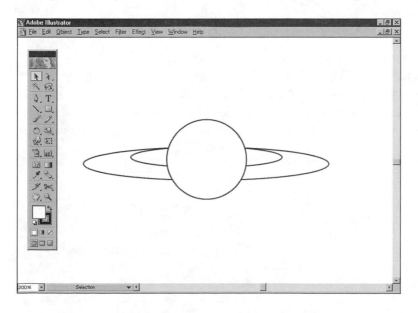

Figure 7.12

The center point of the disc of the planet has the same horizontal position as the center points of the ellipses.

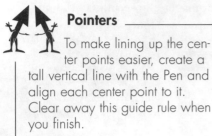

Pointers

To make lining up the center points easier, create a tall vertical line with the Pen and align each center point to it. Clear away this guide rule when you finish.

Select the circle, and choose Object → Arrange → Send Backward two times in a row. This positions the circle behind the ellipses in the stacking order. Now grab the Scissors from the toolbox and get ready for some snipping. Cut each ring where it intersects the circle. Zoom in to 400% or even 600% if necessary. You will make four cuts in total. Remove the inner parts of the ellipses with the Selection tool and delete them. Figure 7.13 shows the finished result.

Figure 7.13

Snip off the tops of the ellipses with the Scissors.

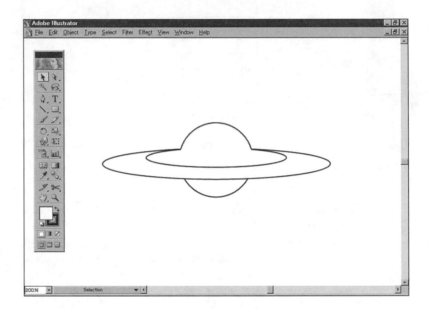

Now for a new trick: Select the circle and choose Edit → Cut. This gets the circle out of the way for the time being. You will bring it back soon with Edit → Paste In Back. The Paste In Back command returns the circle to the exact position from which it was cut (at the bottom of the stacking order, no less), which saves you the trouble of repositioning it and rearranging it. Handy! (The Paste In Front command works similarly, only the object goes to the top of the stacking order.)

Art Alert

You may be tempted to use the Cut command to erase unwanted paths. Cutting a path does remove it from your illustration, but the path doesn't disappear entirely. It goes to the Clipboard, where it replaces anything you may have copied there. To avoid potential hassles, always use the Clear command when you want to delete a path, and only use the Cut command when you intend to paste the path later.

After you cut the circle, get out the Direct Selection tool. Go to the larger ellipse first, and click the anchor point on the left side of the gap. Hold down Shift, click the corresponding anchor point on the smaller ellipse, and choose Object → Path → Join. Repeat this procedure on the right side of the gap, and the two ellipses fuse into a single shape, as shown in Figure 7.14.

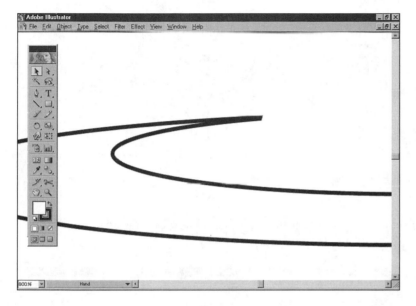

Figure 7.14

Select the anchor points on the left side of the gap, and choose Object → Path → Join. Repeat on the right side.

Return the planet to its rightful position with Edit → Paste In Back. Zoom in, and check that the tips of the rings don't poke into the circle. If they do, simply make the circle smaller.

Zoom back out to a comfortable distance, and click the planet with the Selection tool. Hold down Shift and click the rings. This selects both paths. Move the mouse pointer to the lower right corner of the bounding box, and slowly inch the pointer to the left. When the pointer icon changes to a curved arrow, you can rotate the selected paths. Hold down the mouse button, and drag the mouse upward to rotate the paths in a counterclockwise direction. Release the button when the planet sits at a nice tilt, like in Figure 7.15.

Drawing Perspectives

The giant planet Saturn has nearly 100 times the mass of Earth, but its density is so low that it would float in water.

Figure 7.15

Rotate the planet counter-clockwise to give it a tilt.

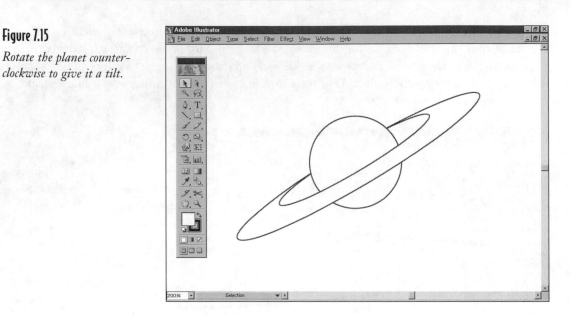

With both paths still selected, move the planet into position on the sky. Scale it down as needed. Check Figure 7.16 for my design.

Figure 7.16

Scale down the planet and move it into position.

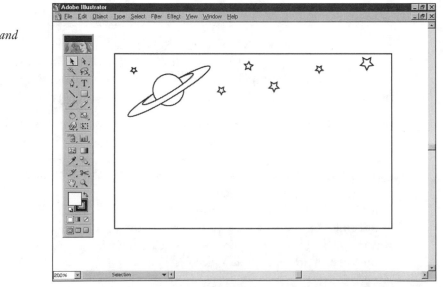

Finished! Save this piece as *aa_sky*. You're making some serious progress on this comic strip. To show you just how serious, I invite you to compose a complete scene. You have created all the art you need. In fact, you have created more than enough.

Using File ➜ Open from the menu, load the following Astro Ape artwork from previous chapters: *aa_sign.ai*, *aa_hills.ai*, and *aa_side.ai*. That's the arrow sign, the landscape, and the side view of the character, in case you used different filenames. After you open these files, choose Window ➜ Tile from the menu. This lets you view the three previous illustrations plus the current sky picture at the same time.

Click the top of the sign's document window. Choose Edit ➜ Select All and then Object ➜ Group. Remember groups from Chapter 6, "Going Freeform"? Groups allow you to collect paths. Select a group, you automatically select all the paths that it contains, allowing you to move and manipulate the group as if it were a single path.

After you group the sign, choose Edit ➜ Cut from the menu. Then click the top of the sky's document window, and choose Edit ➜ Paste. The sign group appears.

Repeat this procedure for the hills and the character design. Don't forget to group each set of paths. This will make working with them easier.

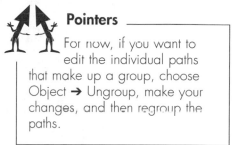

Pointers ⎯⎯⎯⎯⎯⎯⎯⎯

For now, if you want to edit the individual paths that make up a group, choose Object ➜ Ungroup, make your changes, and then regroup the paths.

When you finish, all four illustrations should be in the same document window. Close the other, empty document windows by clicking the X icons in the upper right. Illustrator asks whether you want to save the changes to the file. Click the No button each time.

Choose Window ➜ Tile again to maximize the document window that remains. All you have to do now is assemble the pieces. Use the Object ➜ Arrange commands as necessary to adjust the stacking order of the separate illustrations. Scale them with the Selection tool to make them the right size in relation to each other. Bring them together piece by piece, and a scene appears! See my rendition in Figure 7.17.

Art Alert ⎯⎯⎯⎯⎯⎯⎯⎯⎯⎯⎯⎯⎯⎯⎯⎯⎯⎯⎯⎯⎯⎯⎯⎯⎯⎯⎯⎯⎯⎯⎯

When you position the sign, you may notice that the landscape seems to show through the signpost. Likewise, the stars and planets might show through the hills. This happens because I told you to turn off the fill color when you drew these paths, making them transparent. Few situations are easier to remedy. Position the sign with the Selection tool, choose Object ➜ Ungroup, and click a blank area of the page to deselect everything. Then click the signpost, and click the Default Fill And Stroke icon on the toolbox. (The Default Fill And Stroke icon is directly under the fill-color square. It looks like a miniature version of the color squares.) This inserts the default white fill into the signpost. Do the same thing with the hills, and you're back on track.

Figure 7.17

Bring in art from previous chapters to create a complete Astro Ape scene.

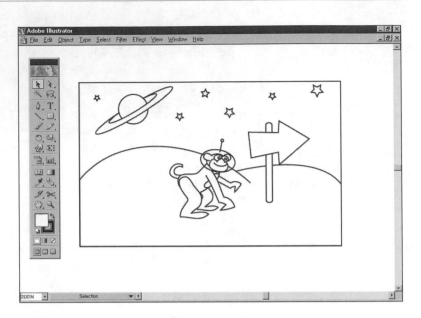

Print out this piece for your refrigerator door using File ➔ Print, and then save it as *aa_mockup.ai*. It's typical in the graphics world to call sample pieces *mockups*. The term may seem derogatory, but it isn't intended to be. When you create computer art for a living, you almost always need to let your client see what you have in mind before you deliver a finished piece. Often you allow the client to choose between two or three alternatives. Creating mockups saves you from putting too much time into concepts that the client will eventually pass over. When you get the green light on a particular look or design, you can use its mockup as the starting point for the complete, fully rendered illustration.

A mockup has psychological benefits, too. Your initial idea begins to take shape there. The pieces start to come together. You can see what works and what doesn't. You have something to post on your refrigerator door. I like to think of the mockup as the first of many rewards to come.

The Least You Need to Know

◆ Shape-drawing tools are quicker than the Pen or Pencil for drawing geometric figures.

◆ Hold down Shift to create circles and squares from ellipses and rectangles.

◆ Ellipses and rectangles have center points.

◆ Create cheap curves and right angles by cutting them from ellipses and rectangles.

◆ Hold down Shift to prohibit the rotation of polygons and stars.

◆ Create quick equilateral triangles by specifying a three-sided polygon.

Part 3

Adding Color, Style, and Type

It's time to dress up those line drawings. To choose from more colors than your eye can accurately distinguish. To make strokes stand out with paint-brush styles. To create attention-grabbing gradients. To fill paths with patterns instead of color. To insert text of all shapes and sizes. The next four chapters give you everything you need to bring your artistic vision to life as only you can do it.

Coloring Fills and Strokes

In This Chapter

◆ Exploring RGB and CMYK color models

◆ Applying color to fills and strokes

◆ Changing stroke weight, cap style, and join style

◆ Coloring the character designs for Astro Ape

Illustrator gives you precise control over the colors in your art. In fact, you might think that Illustrator gives you too much control, especially if this is your first experience with big-league graphics software. "RGB? CMYK? In gamut? Out of gamut?" you might be tempted to ask. "I just want to make the fire engine red!"

Now consider that coloring vector graphics isn't as straightforward as it seems like it should be, and you can see why people get cranky.

I promise you, it isn't as bad as it seems. Battle through the theory and the terminology in the early throes of this chapter, and your art will reap the rewards of several million colors.

Deciphering Color Modes

You're familiar with the term, at least, if not the concept. You see it every time you open a new document window. The New Document dialog box asks you to specify the *color mode* of your art: RGB or CMYK.

When this topic first came up in Chapter 3, "Illustrating Illustrator," I told you to go with RGB unless you were preparing your work for a commercial print shop. I don't believe I offered any kind of explanation as to why. This section provides some answers.

!#%@ **Word Balloon**

A **color model** is a method for reproducing color. Setting the **color mode** of a document prepares your work for one of these models.

Look at the cover of this book, and you see the color orange. Look at a picture of the cover on your computer screen, and you see the color orange again. But the orange of the printed book cover is a different kind of orange than that of the computer image, even if the shades are absolutely identical. Why? Because different media use different *color models*, or different methods for reproducing color. The book cover is orange for a different reason than the computer image.

The computer image is orange because of the RGB color model. RGB reproduces color by mixing different levels of red, green, and blue light. Shine all three at full intensity, and you get white. Turn them all off, and you get black. Use various combinations of red, green, and blue at different intensities for everything in between. To create a shade of sea green, for instance, you might mix 0% red light, 100% green light, and 50% blue light. That is, you would turn the red light all the way off, you would turn the green light all the way on, and you would add blue light at half intensity.

The book cover is orange because of the CMYK color model. CMYK reproduces color by mixing different tints of cyan, magenta, yellow, and black ink. (Cyan is a species of greenish blue, and magenta is a kind of reddish purple.) Combine all four undiluted inks on a piece of white paper, and you get a very rich black. If you don't put any ink on the paper at all, you get white. Create in-between shades by mixing different tints and combinations of inks. A shade of sea green similar to the one that you mixed for RGB translates to CMYK as a 90% tint of cyan ink and a 75% tint of yellow ink, with no magenta or black. A tint, by the way, is just a lighter shade of the ink color in question. That 90% tint of cyan is closer to pure, undiluted, 100% cyan than, say, a much paler 20% tint.

Illustrator and other graphics programs can prepare your art for RGB as well as CMYK. Setting the color mode of the document gets your work ready for one of these models. If you choose CMYK mode, Illustrator simulates CMYK colors on the computer screen, and it can create *color separations* for your commercial printer. A color separation has four

Drawing Perspectives

The K in CMYK stands for *key color*. The key color is black. It's the color that commercial printers use to register the other colors.

separate color plates, one for each of the four CMYK inks. The cyan plate contains only the cyan portions of the image. The magenta plate contains only the magenta portions, and so on. Stack the four plates, and you get a full-color image. In your travels, you may have heard the term *four-color* in reference to color printing. Now you know exactly which four colors.

Four-color process printing is the standard method for getting color on paper in books and magazines. This is why CMYK mode is essential for preparing art for the press. As you follow along with this book, though, Illustrator's RGB mode makes more sense. If you plan to distribute your computer illustrations on the web or by e-mail, you will want to use the RGB color mode, because your audience will enjoy your work on RGB monitor screens. Even if you plan to print out your art, most color desktop printers don't use the CMYK model. They do just fine interpreting RGB color information.

To change the color mode of your document, choose File ➔ Document Color Mode from the menu, and pick RGB or CMYK from the list that slides out.

‽#%@ Word Balloon

A **color separation** has four separate color plates—one for each of the four CMYK inks.

Exploring Coloring Guidelines

Whether you work in RGB or CMYK, vector graphics behave the same when it comes to coloring them.

Every path in vector graphics has two color values: one for the stroke and one for the fill. The stroke color applies to the outline or the contour of the path, and the fill color applies to the interior of the path, as you can see in Figure 8.1.

Figure 8.1

Every path has a stroke color and a fill color. The stroke (black) traces the contour of the path, and the fill (gray) colors the interior space.

You can turn off the stroke color or the fill color for any given path. Remember when you drew Astro Ape's helmet? I asked you to turn off the fill color, which made the interior of the helmet transparent. But turning off one color or the other doesn't delete the stroke or the fill for good. Turn the color back on again, and the stroke or fill reappears.

It is easy to anticipate where the fill color goes in closed paths such as ellipses and triangles. The fill color appears inside the closed area that the stroke creates. The fills of open paths behave strangely sometimes. As Figure 8.2 shows, some open paths have well-behaved fills, whereas others have more unruly fills. To eliminate unexpected results, it is often a good idea to turn off the fill color entirely when you draw open paths.

The stroke and the fill can have the same color value, or the values can be different. If the values are the same, the stroke and the fill blend together. You cannot easily tell where one ends and the other begins. If the values are different, the path acquires a visible outline.

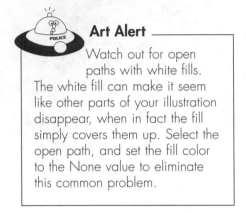

Art Alert

Watch out for open paths with white fills. The white fill can make it seem like other parts of your illustration disappear, when in fact the fill simply covers them up. Select the open path, and set the fill color to the None value to eliminate this common problem.

For example, assume that you want to draw a solid red circle. You could set the fill color and the stroke color to the same shade of red, or you could just turn off the stroke color. Either way, you get a red circle with no visible outline. Now assume that you want to draw a red circle with a black border. You don't have to add the border as a separate path. Set the fill color to red and the stroke color to black, grab the Ellipse tool, hold down Shift, and draw. The black stroke color automatically traces the contour of the path.

But enough theory! It's time to put these strokes, fills, and document color modes into practice. Launch Illustrator, open a new document window, set the color mode for RGB, and get ready for greatness.

Figure 8.2

Open paths have fills (gray), too. The shape of the path determines where the fill goes.

Using the Color Palette

There are many ways to add color to your art in Illustrator. One of the easiest is to use the Color palette.

Choose Window → Color, and the Color palette appears, as shown in Figure 8.3. The Color palette has a solid fill-color square and a hollow stroke-color square, just like the toolbox. The palette also gives you sliders for color mixing. If you don't see these features in your Color palette, click the triangle icon at the top of the palette and choose Show Options from the menu that slides out.

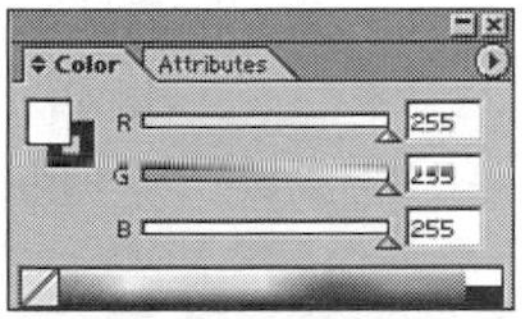

Figure 8.3

The Color palette gives you a fill color square, a stroke-color square, and sliders for mixing.

Now, to take the Color palette for a test drive, you should have a path to color. Pick the tool of your choice from the toolbox and draw something. I'm going with a square. I wonder if this says anything about my personality.

There it sits in my document window. A square. Default black stroke. Default white fill. Cold. Lifeless. Colorless.

Not for long.

Click your path with the Selection tool. Then venture into the Color palette and click the solid fill-color square. This brings the fill color to the foreground. If you glance at the toolbox, you will notice that its fill-color square has also moved to the foreground.

The color sliders tell you that the current fill color, white, comes from red value 255, green value 255, and blue value 255. In the RGB color model, 255 is the highest possible value, equivalent to 100% intensity; 0 is the lowest possible value. If you dragged all three sliders to 0, the fill for the square would turn black.

You don't want to make a black fill, though. You want to make a red fill. To do it, leave the red slider at 255 and drag the green slider and the blue slider to 0. You can physically drag the sliders with the mouse, or you can type values directly into the fields. The slider method automatically changes your fill as you move; however, if you type in the value, you must press Enter or Return to register your change.

Pointers

If you come from an Adobe Photoshop background, you might be interested to know that double-clicking the color squares on the toolbox calls up the Color Picker. The Illustrator Color Picker works exactly like the one in Adobe Photoshop. Use it as an alternative to the Color palette for selecting colors.

Drawing Perspectives

In the RGB color model, setting all three component colors to the same value creates black, white, or a shade of gray.

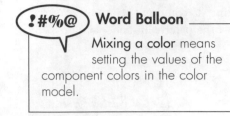
The fill-color square in the Color palette changes to red, as does the fill-color square in the toolbox. And, more important, the fill of the path becomes a brilliant red. This is the most brilliant red you can make, by the way. You cannot go higher than 255 on the red slider, and you cannot go lower than 0 on the green and blue sliders. This is pure, perfect red, with no green or blue light *mixed* in.

Drag the red slider to the left, and notice that the fill-color squares on the Color palette and the toolbox get darker. As you approach 0 on the slider, the red becomes so dark that it looks black. When you get to 0, the red *is* black. Go back to about 151 on the slider and release the mouse button. The path changes to the color you mixed.

Bring in some blue by dragging the blue slider to the right. This gives the red a purplish hue. At about 100 or so, the red fill becomes very purplish indeed. As the blue surpasses the value of the red, the blue component begins to dominate the color. Now add some green, and the color changes again.

Manually mixing colors like this can be intellectually stimulating, but unless you're an expert at the RGB color model, it becomes an exercise in trial and error. Most people can figure out that purple comes from mixing red and blue. But it isn't intuitively apparent that pure yellow, for instance, comes from 255 red and 255 green.

Fortunately, you don't have to mix colors by hand. At the bottom of the Color palette, you will find the RGB Spectrum (see Figure 8.4). The RGB Spectrum gives you access to all the possible colors that the RGB color model defines. There are 16,777,216 distinct shades in total—more than the human eye can differentiate. That's quite a crayon box.

Figure 8.4

The RGB Spectrum lets you choose from nearly 17 million possible colors.

To use the RGB Spectrum, move the mouse pointer into it. The pointer changes to an eyedropper icon. Now hold down the mouse button and drag. The sliders automatically readjust themselves to mix whatever color the eyedropper selects. When you see a shade that looks close to the one that you want, release the mouse button. The path in your drawing acquires this color as the fill. Make manual adjustments to the sliders as needed to mix the perfect shade.

At the extreme left of the RGB Spectrum is a red slash, like the None button on the tool-box. To turn off the fill color, click this area. At the extreme right, you see rectangles for pure white and pure black. Click these areas to create white and black fills.

Running the Gamut

Don't deselect your path just yet. This is just getting interesting.

Type 204 in the red slider field, drag the green slider all the way to 255, and drag the blue slider to 51. Your path fills with one of my favorite shades of chartreuse.

When you mix this color, a caution icon appears under the color squares in the palette, as Figure 8.5 shows. Contrary to appearances, this icon is not activated when Illustrator detects a tasteless color selection. The caution icon appears when a color goes *out of gamut*.

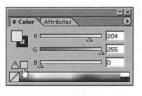

Figure 8.5

If you mix an RGB color that CMYK cannot repro-duce, Illustrator warns you that this color is out of gamut. Click the little swatch next to the warning triangle to substitute the closest in-gamut color.

An RGB color is out of gamut when the CMYK color model cannot reproduce it. In other words, you cannot use this color in an illustration that will end up at the printing press.

The small square color swatch to the right of the caution icon gives the closest in-gamut equivalent to my beloved hue. Click the swatch to substitute the in-gamut color for the out-of-gamut one. When you do, the caution icon goes away, and the slider configuration changes slightly to red 203, green 231, and blue 47. This shade of chartreuse isn't quite as intense as the original, but it is in gamut, which means that a printing press can reproduce it correctly.

If you don't plan on sending your work to the printer's, you can ignore the caution icon. Computer monitors don't have a problem with out-of-gamut colors.

!#%@ Word Balloon

An RGB color is **out of gamut** when the CMYK color model cannot reproduce it.

Keeping Colors Web-Safe

When you switch from the out-of-gamut chartreuse to the in-gamut version, a cube icon appears in the Color palette. This cube icon is also a warning. It indicates that the in-gamut chartreuse is not a *web-safe color*.

Of all the millions of colors that the RGB color model defines, only 216 of these are web-safe. That is, only 216 RGB colors reproduce correctly across all Mac and Windows systems on the web today. Click the swatch next to the cube icon to correct the color for the web. (Which, incidentally, knocks the color back out of gamut! Some days you just can't win.)

Why are there so few web-safe colors? Because there are still a good many older computers browsing the web. Maybe you own one of them! Older Macintosh and Windows computers can display a maximum of 256 colors at a time. Of this 256, 216 colors look the same on Windows and Mac platforms. The web-safe color palette contains exactly these 216 common colors.

 **Word Balloon**

A **web-safe color** is one of the 216 most common RGB colors. Nearly every Windows and Mac computer can display these colors, so you can use them with confidence in web graphics.

If you plan on distributing your work electronically, either by way of a website or by e-mail, restrict your color choices to the web-safe palette as much as possible. You never know who will end up seeing your work, using a who-knows-what type of antiquated machine. Work with too many nonweb-safe colors, and your art may look strange on older computers.

 Pointers

You can set the Color palette to display only web-safe colors. Open the Color palette menu and choose Web-Safe RGB. When you do so, the values in the Color palette switch from decimal to hexadecimal numbers. Web designers use hexadecimal numbers in HTML code to indicate color choices. The hexadecimal system is base 16, not base 10, and it uses the letters A through F to represent the six digits above 9. The number 11, for instance, equals the digit B in hexadecimal nomenclature.

Still, 216 colors is quite a crayon box. Compared to nearly 17 million, though, the web-safe palette seems somehow unfair. Most newer computers can display *high color*, for 65,536 simultaneous shades, and many give you *true color*, for the entire RGB spectrum. If you know for a fact that your audience uses newer equipment, don't worry so much about color correcting for the web.

Different Strokes

So far, you have been coloring fills to great success. You can add color to strokes just as easily.

Click the hollow stroke-color square on the Color palette. This brings the stroke-color square to the foreground, of course. Mix a color for the stroke manually, or choose one from the RGB Spectrum. The stroke color of the selected path promptly changes.

You might not always be able to tell that the stroke color has changed. By default, Illustrator gives you a light, 1-point stroke. This stroke has a thickness of only 1/72nd of an inch, and you can lose it easily, especially if you have an overpowering fill color.

If you want a more prominent outline for your path, you can get one. Choose Window → Stroke from the menu, and the Stroke palette appears. Open the palette menu by clicking the triangle icon, and choose Show Options. Your stroke palette should now look similar to the one in Figure 8.6, with the extra options showing. If your palette belongs to a different group than the one in the figure, don't sweat it. Remember, it doesn't matter where the palette sits on the screen, just as long as it's on the screen.

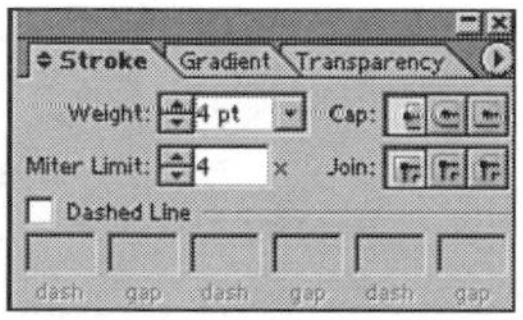

Figure 8.6

Use the Stroke palette to change the weight and style of a stroke.

To increase the thickness, or *weight*, of the stroke, pick a new value from the Weight drop-down list. A 70-point stroke is just about an inch thick—this is probably too thick for most paths; 4-, 5-, and 10-point strokes give good, clear outlines without looking too conspicuous, as Figure 8.7 shows.

The Stroke palette also enables you to choose a cap style and a join style for the path.

A *cap* appears at either end of an open path. If you define a cap for a closed path, you will not see the results until you open up the path with the Erase tool or the Scissors.

There are three kinds of caps: *butt* caps, *round* caps, and *projecting* caps. As you can see in Figure 8.8, the round cap has a rounded tip, but the difference between the butt cap and the projecting cap may not be as apparent. Look carefully at the figure, and you will see that, with a butt cap, the stroke stops exactly on the starting and ending anchor points. With a projecting cap, the stroke extends slightly beyond the starting and ending anchor points.

!#%@ Word Balloon

A **cap** appears at either end of an open path. A **join** appears at the connection point of two segments.

Figure 8.7

These circles have stroke weights of 4, 5, 10, 20, and 40 points, clockwise.

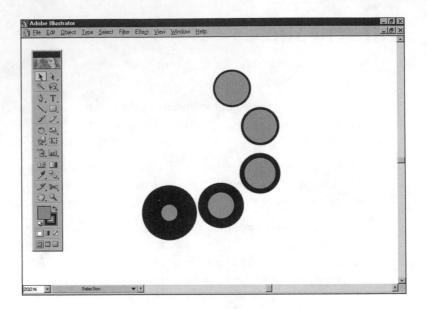

Figure 8.8

Here are the three kinds of caps for a path, from top to bottom: butt, round, and projecting.

A *join* appears at the connection point of two segments. Again, there are three types: *miter* joins, *round* joins, and *bevel* joins. See Figure 8.9 for an example of each type.

Figure 8.9

Here are the three kinds of joins for a path, from top to bottom: miter, round, and bevel.

Miter joins come with an optional limit property. The miter limit determines the threshold at which a miter join automatically becomes a bevel join. You can see the results of the miter limit most dramatically in paths with steep angles, as in Figure 8.10. The figure shows a 10-point stroke with a miter limit 4 (top left), a 10-point stroke with a miter limit 10 (top right), a 4-point stroke with a miter limit 4 (bottom left), and a 4-point stroke with a miter limit 11 (bottom right).

Figure 8.10

The miter limit can change the appearance of a path.

The default miter limit is 4. Mathematically speaking, this means that a miter turns into a bevel when the length of the join exceeds four times the weight of the stroke. A miter join

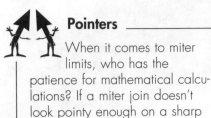

Pointers

When it comes to miter limits, who has the patience for mathematical calculations? If a miter join doesn't look pointy enough on a sharp angle, click the path with the Selection tool and bump up the miter limit one notch at a time until the bevel disappears.

on a 10-point stroke, then, can extend 40 points past the connecting anchor and still be a miter join. If the join goes beyond the 40-point threshold, Illustrator bevels off what would be a tapering, pointy tip.

To conclude, I should mention that each path has only one weight, cap style, and join style, just like each path has only one stroke color. You cannot get a 4-point stroke with butt caps and a 10-point stroke with round caps on the same path, in other words. You have to draw two separate paths and then position them next to each other to create the effect of a single path.

Using the Coloring Tools

Illustrator provides two coloring tools: the Eyedropper and the Paint Bucket. Both can save you time and effort.

Find the Eyedropper in the toolbox two steps above the Hand tool. The Paint Bucket hides underneath the Eyedropper, as you can see in Figure 8.11.

Figure 8.11

Use the Eyedropper and the Paint Bucket to apply color to your art.

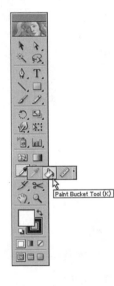

When you click the Eyedropper on a path, you capture the *appearance attributes* of that path. These appearance attributes include the fill color, the stroke color, the stroke weight and style, and other effects; I cover these attributes later in this book.

For instance, if you click the Eyedropper tool on a rectangle with a red fill and a 10-point blue stroke, the fill-color square on the Color palette turns red, the stroke-color square turns blue, and the Weight drop-down menu in the Stroke palette shows 10 points.

To use this information, switch from the Eyedropper to the Paint Bucket. Click the Paint Bucket on any path in your illustration, and that path acquires the appearance attributes you soaked up with the Eyedropper.

This combination of tools saves you from defining the same set of appearance attributes over and over again. If you want several paths in your illustration to have the same attributes, define these attributes once, in one path. Then capture the attributes with the Eyedropper, and apply them to all the other paths with the Paint Bucket.

You can also use these tools with the Selection tool. Select a path in your illustration, and then pull out the Eyedropper. Click any other path with this tool, and the selected path acquires the clicked path's appearance attributes. Pull out the Paint Bucket instead, and the clicked path acquires the selected path's attributes.

> **!#%@** **Word Balloon**
>
> The **appearance attributes** of a path include the fill color, the stroke color, the stroke weight and style, and the effects.

Palette of the Ape

After all that theoretical talk, coloring Astro Ape should be a welcome diversion.

Choose File ➔ Open from the menu, and load up the side-view character design from Chapter 6, "Going Freeform." If you followed my example, you saved this file as *aa_side.ai*.

This view of Astro Ape uses seven web-safe RGB colors, as Table 8.1 shows.

> **Drawing Perspectives**
>
> Apes and monkeys can see in color. Like humans, they appear to have trichromatic vision, or sensitivity to red, green, and blue light.

Table 8.1   Colors for Astro Ape

Color	Red Value	Green Value	Blue Value
Black	0	0	0
Brown	153	102	51
Cyan	0	255	255

continues

Table 8.1   Colors for Astro Ape   (continued)

Color	Red Value	Green Value	Blue Value
Dark green	102	153	102
Light green	153	204	153
Peach	255	204	153
White	255	255	255

To begin, mix black on the Color palette as the fill color and the stroke color. You can keep the stroke weight at the default value of 1 point. In fact, you can keep 1-point strokes for all the paths in this illustration.

After you mix the color for black, get out the Paint Bucket and click each of the eyeballs. Astro Ape's eyes should become solid black circles.

Art Alert ——————

Computer graphics people talk about black and white as colors for convenience's sake. In strictest terms of color theory, though, pure white is a tint, and pure black is a shade. Neither are colors.

Drawing Perspectives

Color blindness in humans (and apes) isn't blindness, per se, but a difficulty in perceiving one or more of the three RGB component colors. About 10 percent of human males have some kind of color deficiency. The most common form is red-green color blindness, which comes from a lack of red color receptors in the eye.

Do brown next, but this time, only mix it as the fill color. Keep the stroke color as black so that the character retains its cartoony black outline. Use the Paint Bucket again on the tail and the head. See how easy this is?

Mix cyan as the fill, and apply it to the bulb at the top of the antenna.

The dark green fill goes with Astro Ape's left limbs, and the light green fill goes with the right limbs and the body.

Finally, the peach fill goes with the face, the nose, the mouth, and the ears. Leave the breastplate and the eyes white, and keep the helmet fill turned off for now. I have something special planned for that one later.

So much for the side view. Your screen should look something like Figure 8.12—only in color, of course.

Save your work as *aa_side_color.ai* using the File ➔ Save As command instead of File ➔ Save. It is always a good idea to save each new version of an illustration as a separate file. That way, no matter what unexpected and terrible things happen as you experiment, explore, and modify, you can go back to an earlier version of your work and start fresh.

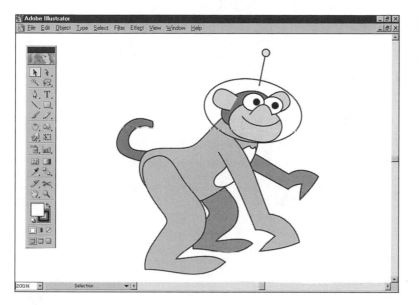

Figure 8.12

They say the clothes make the man, but the color makes the monkey.

Care to try another?

Close the current document window and open *aa_rear.ai*, the rear-view character design. This illustration uses the same colors as the side view, with the exception of dark green and white. The head, the tail, and the tail hole have brown fills. The arms, legs, and body have light green fills. The antenna bulb is cyan, and the ears are peach. All the strokes are 1-point black.

When you finish, you should see something like Figure 8.13. Choose File ➔ Save As again, and *aa_rear_color.ai* is one for the books.

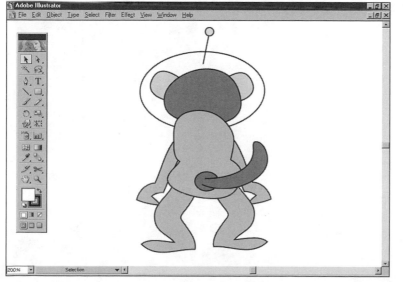

Figure 8.13

When your rear view looks this good, you don't mind it if they don't see your face.

The Least You Need to Know

- ◆ The RGB color mode works best for personal use and electronic distribution.
- ◆ The CMYK color mode works best for commercial printing and publishing.
- ◆ Use the Color palette to mix fill and stroke colors.
- ◆ An RGB color is out of gamut if it doesn't have a CMYK equivalent.
- ◆ A web-safe RGB color displays the same on just about everyone's computer.
- ◆ You can change the weight of a stroke with the Stroke palette.
- ◆ Apply fill and stroke colors to paths with the Eyedropper and Paint Bucket tools.

Applying Brushes

In This Chapter

◆ Using the Paintbrush tool

◆ Applying brush styles to paths

◆ Punching up the arrow-sign design for Astro Ape

A regular old stroke may be loyal and reliable, but it isn't terribly interesting visually.

Don't get me wrong. Regular strokes are perfect for some drawings. Take the Astro Ape character designs. The linework shouldn't call too much attention to itself in these, or it will detract from the overall effect. But if you wanted to draw calligraphy with the computer, where the shape and richness of the line is essential to the overall effect, the standard Pen and Pencil tools may not be up to the task.

What you need is a tool that gives you interesting-looking strokes—the Paintbrush. In this chapter, I'll show you how to use the Paintbrush, and I'll show you how to apply brush styles to paths that you have already drawn.

Yet Another Drawing Tool?

The Paintbrush is another drawing tool. It sits in the toolbox to the left of the Pencil, as Figure 9.1 shows.

Figure 9.1

Use the Paintbrush to draw paths with visually interesting, brushed strokes.

"Another drawing tool?" I can hear you say. "I just finally mastered C-curves and S-curves last night! I can't handle yet another tool with its own set of bizarre mouse movements."

You should know by now that I would never cause you undue distress. The Paintbrush may be new, but it works just like the Pencil. It's a freeform drawing tool. Hold down the mouse button and drag, and the Paintbrush line follows. Illustrator calculates the positions and directions of the anchor points as you go.

Paintbrush lines are paths, just like Pen lines and Pencil lines. You can move and scale a Paintbrush line with the Selection tool. You can adjust the anchor points of a Paintbrush line with the Direct Selection tool. You can use the Scissors, the Knife, the Erase tool, and the Smooth tool on a Paintbrush line, and you can connect it to other paths with the Join command.

Because Paintbrush lines are paths, they have a fill color and a stroke color. Remember, all paths have fills and strokes. The fill of a Paintbrush line is no fancier than the fill of a Pencil line or a Pen line. The fills of these paths look and work exactly the same.

> **!#%@ Word Balloon**
>
> A **brushed path** is a path that has the additional appearance attribute of a brush style, which makes the stroke more visually interesting.

The stroke of a Paintbrush line, however, is different. It has a weight, just like other strokes, and it can have caps and joins, but it also has a brush style. The brush style is what makes Paintbrush lines more visually interesting than regular Pencil lines and Pen lines. For convenience's sake, when I talk about a Paintbrush line, I'm going to call it a *brushed path*. You will understand that I mean a path with a stroke as well as a fill, with the stroke having the additional appearance attribute of a brush style.

The great thing about the Paintbrush tool is that you can choose from many different brush styles. The Brushes palette gives you access to these styles (see Figure 9.2). So before you begin drawing with the Paintbrush, call up the Brushes palette under Window → Brushes.

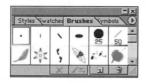

Figure 9.2

Choose from many different brush styles with the Brushes palette.

To draw a brushed path, first click one of the brush icons in the palette. Then grab the Paintbrush from the toolbox and draw. Your path will look something like the one in Figure 9.3, depending of course, on the brush style you chose.

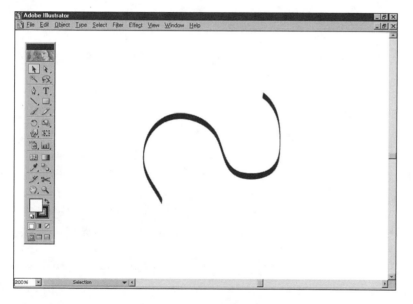

Figure 9.3

The stroke of a brushed path looks more visually interesting than that of a non-brushed path.

The Paintbrush follows the same procedures as the Pencil tool. To close a brushed path, hold down Alt (Windows) or Option (Mac) while you draw. When you release the mouse button, the path closes automatically, just like with the Pencil. If you hold down Alt or Option before you start drawing, the Paintbrush changes into the Smooth tool, just like the Pencil.

Draw as many paths with the Paintbrush as you like. You don't need to go back to the Brushes palette until you want to change the brush style. Use as many different brushes in your drawing as you need, with one proviso: Each individual path can have only one brush style, just like it can have only one stroke weight and only one stroke color.

Art Alert _____

You may notice that, after you draw with the Paintbrush, all the other drawing tools automatically use the same brush style. This happens because the New Art Maintains Appearance option is on. To turn this option off, open the Appearance palette under Window ➔ Appearance. Then click the first button on the left at the bottom of the palette. Now, new art has the basic appearance, which means that special attributes like brushes don't apply unless you specifically add them.

Brushing Up on Brushes

As you experiment with different brushes, you may notice that some of them behave differently than others. Some brushes seem to follow the drawn path faithfully, while others spill outside the boundaries of the path. Is this just your imagination, or are you on to something?

You are definitely on to something. Illustrator provides not two, not three, but four different kinds of brushes. These are calligraphic brushes, scatter brushes, art brushes, and pattern brushes.

A *calligraphic brush* follows the shape of the path very closely. This type of brush is the easiest to control, and many calligraphic brushes work well for detailed linework.

!#%@ **Word Balloon** _____

A **calligraphic brush** follows the shape of the path closely. A **scatter brush** takes a separate illustration and places copies of it outside the boundaries of the path. An **art brush** places a separate illustration along the entire shape of the path. A **pattern brush** tiles, or repeats, a series of separate illustrations across the shape of the path.

A *scatter brush* takes a separate illustration and places copies of it outside the boundaries of the path, like the leaf or the pin in the Brushes palette. A stroke from this kind of brush may only vaguely resemble the path that you draw, so a scatter brush isn't the best choice for detailing.

An *art brush* places a separate illustration along the entire shape of the path, like the arrow in the Brushes palette. An art brush's illustration always appears only once along the path. It doesn't *tile*, or repeat.

A *pattern brush* tiles a series of separate illustrations across the shape of the path, like the frieze border in the Brushes palette.

See Figure 9.4 for an example of each type of brush.

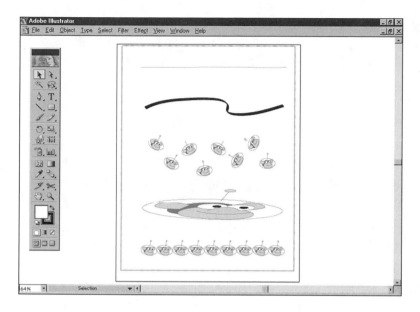

Figure 9.4

Different brushes work differently, from top to bottom: unbrushed path, calligraphic brush, scatter brush, art brush, pattern brush.

How can you tell a brush's type before you draw with it? There are a few ways, but the easiest is just to double-click the brush's icon in the palette. This calls up the options for that particular brush, which, by the way, you are free to modify. The top of the window tells you the brush type. Click the Cancel button to close the options window.

The Brushes palette can hide certain kinds of brushes from you. If you only want to use calligraphic brushes, for instance, you may want to follow this procedure.

Open the brush palette menu by clicking the triangle icon in the upper right corner. At the bottom of the menu, you should see the names of different kinds of brushes preceded by check marks. A check indicates that the palette shows brushes of that particular kind. Highlight a brush type and click to remove the check mark. All the brushes of that type disappear from the palette window. This operation doesn't delete the brushes. It simply hides them from view. To display them again, open the palette menu and click the option to show that type of brush.

Pointers _____

Another way to check the type of the brush is to draw with it and then look under the Edit menu. The Undo command tells you the type of brush that you will be undoing.

Using Brush Libraries

Illustrator comes with a number of brush libraries. Each library contains a bunch of new brushes for you to try.

To open a brush library, choose Window ➔ Brush Libraries, and pick a library from the list that slides out. The library opens in its own floating palette, which works just like the Brushes palette. Click the icon of the brush style that you want to use, grab the Paintbrush tool, and go.

You can also get brush libraries from third-party vendors and other computer illustrators. Many of these are available as free downloads from the creator's website.

To install a third-party brush library, download the library file into the Brush Libraries folder, which is inside the Adobe Illustrator program folder on your hard drive. The next time you launch Illustrator, you will find your new library under Window ➔ Brush Libraries.

The CD-ROM for this book contains some sample third-party brush libraries for your creative pleasure, as well as an Astro Ape brush library that I put together especially for you.

Adding Brushes to Paths

In Chapter 8, "Coloring Fills and Strokes," I talked about appearance attributes such as stroke color, fill color, and stroke weight. A brush style is another kind of appearance attribute. This means that any path, not just a Paintbrush path, can have a brush style, just like any path can have a stroke color.

Assume that you draw a path with the Pencil, and you decide afterward that the standard Pencil stroke looks too uninteresting. You realize that you should have used the Paintbrush.

Art Alert

Remember that brush styles apply to strokes, not fills. You cannot apply a brush style to a fill.

Not a problem. Just click the path with the Selection tool, go to the Brushes palette, and click the icon of the brush that you want to apply. The Pencil path instantly acquires the brush style that you selected, becoming in essence a Paintbrush path.

You can use this trick on any path in your illustration: Pen paths, ellipses, rectangles, polygons, and so on.

Removing Brushes from Paths

It is just as easy to change or remove a brush style from any path, even a Paintbrush path. To do so, click the path with the Selection tool and go to the Brushes palette.

If you want to change the brush style, click a different icon in the palette. If you want to remove the brush style completely, click the first button on the left at the bottom of the palette. Removing the brush style makes a path look as though you drew it with the Pencil or the Pen.

The Remove button doesn't alter any of the other appearance attributes on the path. In other words, the path retains its original stroke and fill colors, stroke weight, and the like. The only appearance attribute that goes is the brush style.

If you decide that you like the old style better, choose Edit ➔ Undo.

Pointers

The weight of a brushed path equals roughly the weight of the stroke times the weight of the brush style. Removing the brush style may make the stroke look thinner than you want.

A Mild Case of Sign-Stroke

For your Astro Ape experience in this chapter, you will punch up the arrow sign with some brush-style action.

The arrow sign is a good candidate for the fancy treatment. The sign is really the pivotal illustration in the cartoon. It sets up the premise of the strip as well as the joke. It should grab the reader's attention from the outset. At the same time, it shouldn't be so overpowering that it reduces the importance of the main character. This calls for some subtle brushwork—just enough to make the sign stand out.

Drawing Perspectives

If you give a chimpanzee a paintbrush, the chimp may use it to extract tasty termites from a mound or pull honey from a beehive. Chimps in the wild have been known to employ sticks or twigs in this fashion.

So, go to File ➔ Open and call up *aa_sign.ai*. The sign illustration appears as you left it.

First things first. You ought to color this piece of art. If the Color palette isn't already on your screen, use Window ➔ Color.

It goes without saying that the color of the sign can also help this illustration to stand out. Also keep in mind that the sign will eventually contain some words. Because dark letters against a light background are easier to read than light letters against a dark background, you should fill the arrow shape with a bright, vivid color.

A color, perhaps, like my beloved chartreuse.

The RGB values for this color are red 204, green 255, and blue 51. Select the arrow shape, click the fill-color square on the Color palette, and enter the values for chartreuse in the fields. Keep the stroke color as black.

I suppose that the signpost is metallic, so you should make the fill for this shape a light gray. Select the signpost and enter the following values in the Color-palette fields: red 204, green 204, and blue 204. As you can see, this gray is both web-safe and in gamut.

When you finish applying the fills, your illustration should resemble Figure 9.5.

Figure 9.5

Give the arrow shape a chartreuse fill and the sign-post shape a light gray fill.

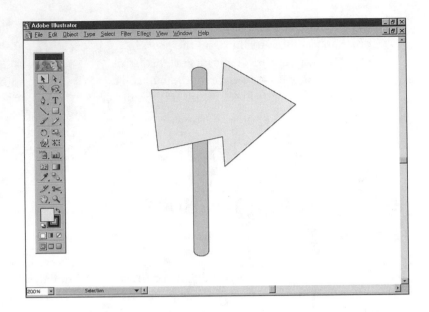

Now for the brushwork. Select the arrow shape again, go to the Brushes palette, and apply the second brush from the left at the top of the list. This is the 10-point oval calligraphic brush. Continue by selecting the signpost and applying the same brush style to it. Both paths in the sign illustration should now have brushes. Check your work against mine in Figure 9.6.

Figure 9.6

Apply the 10-point oval cal-ligraphic brush to both shapes.

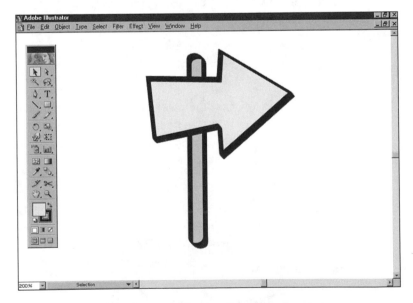

Notice how the brush style helps the illustration to pop off the page? This is exactly the effect that you want.

Pointers

If none of the brushes are satisfactory, you can create your own. To create a calligraphic brush, click the new brush icon at the bottom of the Brushes palette, and choose the Calligraphic option from the dialog box that appears. The dialog box gives you controls for defining the angle, roundness, and diameter of the point. Click OK, and your brush appears with the others in the Brushes palette.

My only concern is that the illustration now has too much emphasis, especially the signpost, which isn't nearly as important as the arrow shape to the premise. You need a way to tone down the effects of the brush.

Look no further than the Stroke palette. If you don't see it, choose Window → Stroke.

Click the arrow path. The Stroke palette tells you that the weight of this path is 1 point. We also know that there is a 10-point brush attached to this stroke, so the actual weight is in the neighborhood of 10 points, or 10 times 1. If you reduce the weight of this path to, say, ½ point, that would make the actual weight somewhere around 5 points, or 10 times ½. Five points just might do the trick.

Give it a try at least. Choose ½ point from the Weight drop-down list. The brushed path changes to match Figure 9.7.

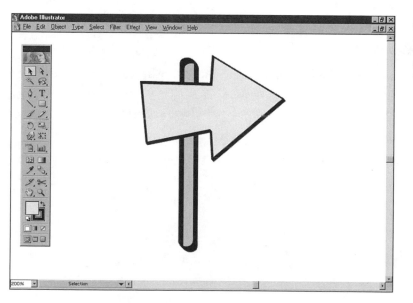

Figure 9.7

Reduce the weight of the arrow shape's stroke to ½ point.

This looks promising, although the heavier signpost stroke now really interferes. You can fix that. Select the signpost and reduce the weight to ½ point, just like you did for the arrow shape. Check the results in Figure 9.8.

Figure 9.8

Reduce the weight of the signpost's stroke to ¹/₄ point.

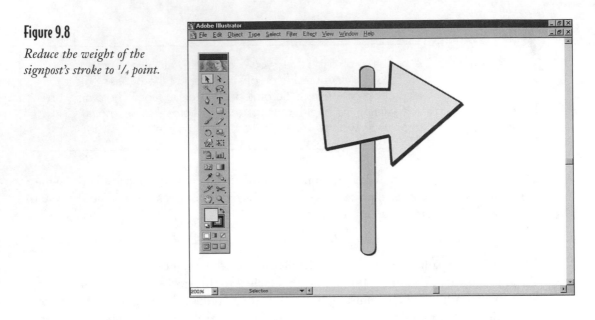

Success! Compare this illustration with the original in Figure 9.5, and I think you will agree that you have a better design.

Save this illustration with the File ➔ Save As command, and supply a filename like *aa_sign_color.ai*. You're getting very good at this!

The Least You Need to Know

- ◆ The Paintbrush works like the Pencil, only it applies a brush style to the stroke of its path.
- ◆ There are four kinds of brushes: calligraphic, scatter, art, and pattern.
- ◆ You can find additional sets of brush styles under Window ➔ Brush Libraries.
- ◆ The brush style is an appearance attribute that you can apply to any path.
- ◆ You can remove the brush style from any path, including Paintbrush paths.

Chapter 10

Using Patterns and Gradients

In This Chapter

- Applying patterns to fills and strokes
- Applying gradients as fills
- Creating and using color swatches
- Punching up the background design for Astro Ape

In Chapter 9, "Applying Brushes," you saw how brush styles can add some zing to ordinary strokes. It only stands to reason that you should be able to do something similar with ordinary fills.

Let me be absolutely honest with you here. Illustrator doesn't give you a way to do this.

It gives you two ways. This chapter explores the creative possibilities of patterns and gradients.

Using Patterns

A *pattern* is a separate piece of artwork that tiles, or repeats, throughout a path. You may recall from the preceding chapter that a pattern brush takes a separate piece of artwork and tiles it along the stroke. The idea here is very similar, with one important difference. A pattern brush restricts you to the stroke of a path, but a pattern can apply to the fill as well as the stroke. Figure 10.1 shows an example of a patterned fill.

Figure 10.1

This circle has a pattern instead of a flat color as its fill.

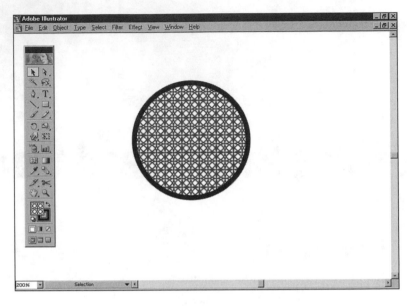

Illustrator comes with a handful of ready-made patterns for you to use. To access them, choose Window ➔ Show Swatches. This calls up the Swatches palette, shown in Figure 10.2.

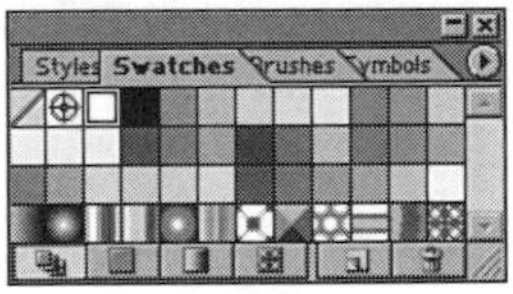

Figure 10.2

The Swatches palette gives you quick access to patterns as well as colors and gradients.

The Swatches palette gives you more than just pattern swatches. There are also color swatches and gradient swatches. I will talk more about these kinds of swatches later in this chapter. For now, let me draw your attention to the pattern swatches. Click the fourth button from the left at the bottom of the Swatches palette to show only the patterns.

A *swatch*, by the way, is just a small square that represents a particular appearance. As you see them now, the swatches represent the different patterns that you can use.

Filling a path with a pattern instead of a solid color is easy. To demonstrate, grab one of the shape tools and draw a path. When you finish, click the fill-color square in the toolbox to bring the fill to the foreground. Make sure that you keep the path selected. If you deselect it by mistake or force of habit, click it with the Selection tool.

At this point, if you were going to apply a solid color to the fill of your path, you would go to the Color palette and mix up the shade of your choice. Because you want to apply a pattern to the fill instead, go to the Swatches palette. Click the swatch of the pattern that you want to apply, and the pattern does its thing, repeating itself throughout the entire area of the fill.

In case you have any doubts about what just happened, have a look at the fill-color square in the toolbox. Notice that it shows the pattern instead of a solid color. The pattern is an appearance attribute of the path, just like a color.

To change a pattern fill to a solid color, click the patterned path with the Selection tool. Then go to the Color palette and pick a color from the RGB Spectrum.

Drawing Perspectives
In Illustrator, patterns tile from left to right.

Applying Patterns as Strokes

You applied a pattern to a fill, which is where patterns work the best. But you could have just as easily applied the pattern to a stroke instead. See Figure 10.3 for an example of a patterned stroke.

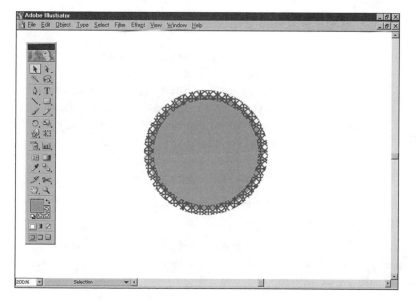

Figure 10.3

Patterns might work best with fills, but you can apply them to strokes, too. The weight of the stroke determines how much of the pattern you see.

To apply the pattern to the stroke of a path, select the path, click the stroke-color square in the toolbox, and click the pattern of your choice from the Swatches palette.

The weight of the stroke determines how much of the pattern you see. Most patterns are larger than a typical stroke weight, so you will probably need to increase the weight of the stroke to get the proper effect.

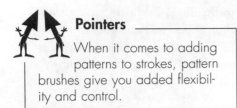

Pointers

When it comes to adding patterns to strokes, pattern brushes give you added flexibility and control.

The pattern value works the same as the color values in the toolbox for purposes of swapping. Assume that you have a path with a green fill and a patterned stroke. If you select this path and click the curved-arrow icon next to the toolbox's color squares, the pattern switches over to the fill, and the green value switches over to the stroke.

Moving a Patterned Path

You may have noticed that when you move a path that has a patterned stroke or fill, the appearance of the pattern changes. A patterned fill may start perfectly in the upper left corner of a rectangle, for instance. If you move the rectangle, the pattern may not start in the upper-left corner anymore.

By selecting the path and choosing Object ➔ Expand, you can prevent the pattern from changing position as you move the path around. In the Expand dialog box that appears, make sure that the check box for Fill or Stroke has a check mark, depending on which one contains the pattern. If you see check marks in both boxes, remove the check for the one that doesn't have the pattern. If the fill has the pattern, in other words, remove the check mark for the stroke.

Drawing Perspectives

Expanding creates two paths: one for the fill of the original path, and another for the stroke. The path for the stroke is actually a compound path. I will talk more about compound paths in Chapter 17, "Working with Transparency."

Click OK to expand the patterned stroke or fill. Expanding a pattern changes it from an appearance attribute, like a fill color, into a separate, independent path. When you click the original path with the Selection tool, the pattern no longer appears in the color squares of the toolbox. Why? Because the pattern is no longer an appearance attribute of the path. The expanded pattern is now a path of its own.

It's harder to modify the appearance of a path after you expand the pattern, so make sure that the path looks exactly the way you want it.

If you use the same pattern in different paths, you can expand the pattern of one path without altering the pattern of any other path. The other patterns remain as appearance attributes until you specifically expand them.

Creating Your Own Patterns

The patterns that come with Illustrator may be all right for playtime, but they aren't very useful for most actual illustrations. Thankfully, you can create your own patterns in a few simple steps.

I mentioned before that a pattern is a separate piece of artwork that repeats throughout a path. So to create a pattern, it makes sense to start with the separate piece of art.

Find a convenient spot in the document window where you can work without disturbing any other art that you might have in place. Then, using the drawing tools of your choice, create the design for the pattern. You only need to draw a single repetition. Illustrator automatically tiles the art when you apply it as a pattern.

As an example, create a simple star pattern. Take the Star tool, and make an arrangement of three star-shaped paths. Apply fill and stroke colors as you desire. See Figure 10.4 for my design.

Art Alert

Be careful not to use existing patterns in your pattern design. If you try to do this, Illustrator gets upset with you and sends you an error message.

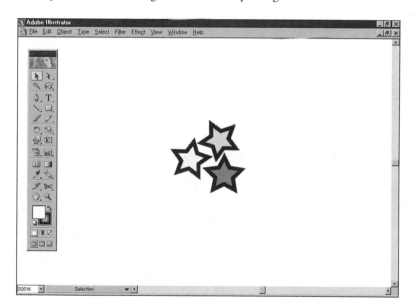

Figure 10.4

To create a pattern, first create the separate piece of artwork that you want to use as a pattern. Then select all the paths in the art and choose Edit → Define Pattern.

When you finish, take the Selection tool from the toolbox. Hold down the Shift key, and click each of the stars to select all three.

Now choose Edit → Define Pattern. The New Swatch dialog box appears. (For creating pattern swatches, Illustrator grays out most of the options on this dialog box, so don't be alarmed if the dialog box looks dead.) Type a name for the pattern in the Swatch Name field and click OK.

Look on the Swatches palette, and you will find a swatch for your new pattern ready to go. To test it out, draw a path and apply your pattern as the fill, as shown in Figure 10.5.

Figure 10.5

After you define a pattern, you can apply it to your art.

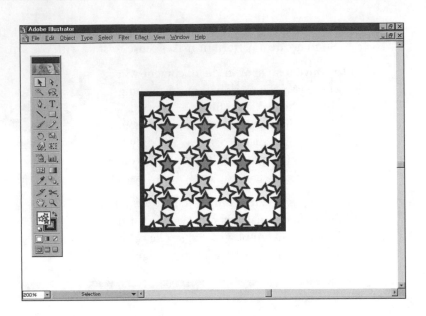

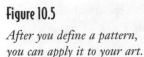

Pointers

Normally, the spaces between the paths in the pattern are transparent. If you want these spaces to be opaque, place a colored square behind all the paths in the pattern.

The pattern design remains in the document window after you create the new swatch, but you can safely delete the paths.

Editing Pattern Designs

Sometimes an otherwise useful pattern might not have the right color scheme for your current illustration, or the layout of the paths might not be quite right. In cases like these, it makes sense to edit the pattern design.

To do so, first deselect everything in your drawing. Then click the pattern on the Swatches palette, and hold down the mouse button. Drag the swatch into the document window. When you release the mouse button, the pattern design appears.

Illustrator automatically groups the paths of the pattern design. I will deal with groups more thoroughly in a later chapter. All you need to know for now is that, to edit the art, you can ungroup the paths. Click the group with the Selection tool and choose Object ➔ Ungroup from the menu. Click on an empty area of the page to deselect all the paths of the group.

Now, feel free to modify the pattern design as you choose. Treat it just like any other art in your illustration.

When you finish, hold down the Shift key and click all the paths in the pattern with the Selection tool. Release the Shift key, and hold down Alt (Windows) or Option (Mac). While holding down this key, drag the pattern design onto the Swatches palette.

Drawing Perspectives

The *pattern tile* is another term for the *pattern design*.

If you release the mouse button on an empty area of the palette, the edited pattern gets its own swatch. Art that uses the original version of the pattern remains as it was. If you release the mouse button on a swatch, the edited pattern replaces the current swatch. Art that uses the pattern of the old swatch automatically updates to the new swatch.

As before, the pattern design remains in the document window after you create the new swatch. As before, you can safely delete the paths.

By the way, if you want to get rid of the swatch, simply drag it to the Trashcan icon at the bottom of the Swatches palette, or click the swatch and then click the Trashcan icon.

Using Gradients

A *gradient* is a gradual blend of two or more colors. Unlike patterns, gradients can only apply to the fill of a path. Figure 10.6 shows an example of a gradient fill.

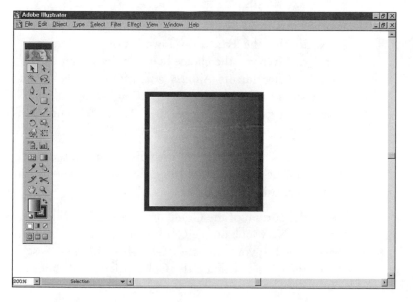

Figure 10.6

A gradient fill gradually blends two or more colors.

The Swatches palette gives you a few gradients to get you started. To view them, click the third button from the left at the bottom of the Swatches palette.

Apply a gradient swatch to a path just like you apply a pattern swatch. First, draw or select the path. Then click the gradient swatch of your choice on the Swatches palette. The fill-color square in the toolbox automatically comes to the foreground, and the gradient applies to the fill of your path.

To replace a gradient fill with a solid color, click the path in question with the Selection tool, and make sure that the fill-color square is in the foreground in the toolbox. Then go to the Color palette and select a solid color from the RGB Spectrum.

Making Gradients

You will outgrow Illustrator's built-in gradient swatches in a hurry, which is just as well. Creating your own gradients is not only easy but fun.

To get started, call up the Gradient palette under Window → Show Gradient. If your Gradient palette looks shorter than the one in Figure 10.7, open the palette menu by clicking the triangle icon and choose Show Options.

Figure 10.7

The Gradient palette makes defining your own gradient fills a thoroughly enjoyable experience.

Drawing Perspectives
The starting color of a linear gradient appears at the left side of the path, and the starting color of a radial gradient appears in the middle of the path.

Notice that the Type drop-down list on the Gradient palette gives you the choice between linear gradients and radial gradients. A *linear gradient* blends the colors in a straight line, and a *radial gradient* blends the colors in concentric circles. See Figure 10.8 for an example of each type.

Pick a type from the drop-down list to match the kind of gradient that you want to create. Now comes the fun part: choosing the colors.

Click the first crayon-shaped slider at the bottom of the Gradient palette. This slider represents the starting color of the gradient. Now look on the Color palette, and you should find that the values of the color have loaded. If you don't see RGB values, simply adjust the Color palette's color model. Click the triangle icon on the Color palette and choose RGB from the menu that slides out.

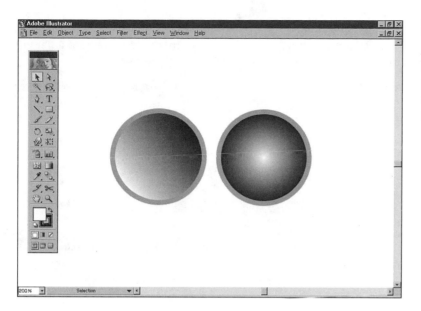

Figure 10.8

A linear gradient (left) blends the colors in a straight line, and a radial gradient (right) blends the colors in concentric circles.

Mix a color, or choose one from the RGB Spectrum. The color of the first gradient slider changes as you work.

After you get the right starting color for the gradient, click the second crayon-shaped slider, which represents the ending color. Go to the Color palette again, and mix or choose the tone of your choice. Don't forget to adjust the color model if you don't see RGB values on the Color palette.

Go back to the Gradient palette, and drag the diamond-shaped gradient slider. This slider determines the point at which the changeover from one color to the other occurs. If you drag the slider toward the left, the changeover happens sooner, and the ending color dominates the gradient. Drag the slider to the right, and you delay the changeover. The starting color dominates the gradient.

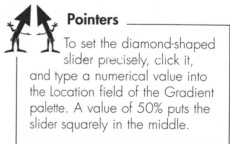

Pointers

To set the diamond-shaped slider precisely, click it, and type a numerical value into the Location field of the Gradient palette. A value of 50% puts the slider squarely in the middle.

You can adjust the positions of the crayon-shaped sliders, too. Move them closer to the diamond-shaped slider to create a steeper color shift. Back them away from the diamond-shaped slider for a more gradual color shift. Switch their positions in relation to the diamond-shaped slider to reverse the gradient.

Now create a swatch for the gradient. This is a simple matter of clicking the new-swatch icon at the bottom of the Swatches palette. If you want, you can give the gradient a name by double-clicking the swatch.

Your gradient is ready to use. Give it a try! Draw a path and click the swatch to apply your gradient.

Making Gradients with Multiple Colors

A gradient can have more than two colors.

To demonstrate, click your gradient swatch on the Swatches palette. Look at the Gradient palette, and you will find the gradient that you defined.

Now click anywhere between the two crayon-shaped sliders. Don't click in the band of color itself, but just below it, on the surface of the palette. When you do, a new crayon-shaped slider appears for the color, as does a new diamond-shaped slider for the change-over position.

Click the new crayon-shaped slider, and go to the Color palette to mix the new color. Then go back to the Gradient palette to adjust the positions of the various sliders. They all work exactly as you remember.

Repeat this process for as many colors as you want to add. When you finish, you will want to update the gradient swatch. Hold down Alt (Windows) or Option (Mac), and drag the fill-color square in the toolbox to the old gradient swatch on the Swatches palette. When you release the mouse button, the new swatch replaces the old one, and all the art that uses the old gradient automatically updates.

Art Alert

At a minimum, a gradient must have two colors. Illustrator will not let you remove the starting or ending color of a gradient if there isn't a third color to pick up the slack.

If you decide that you want to remove a color from a gradient, drag its crayon-shaped slider down, off the Gradient palette. Release the mouse button when the slider disappears.

Using the Gradient Tool

Use the Gradient tool to adjust the position and direction of a path's gradient fill.

You can find the Gradient tool two steps above the Scissors in the toolbox, as Figure 10.9 shows. Be careful that you don't select the Gradient Mesh tool by mistake. The Gradient Mesh tool enables you to create more sophisticated gradients than I discuss in this book.

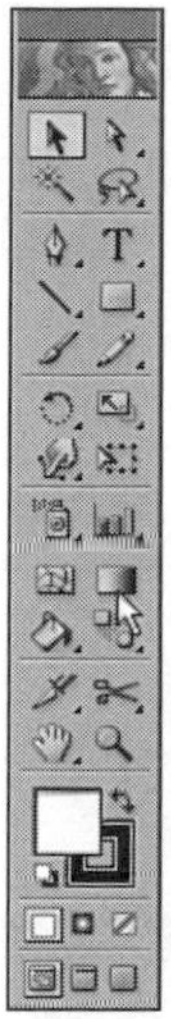

Figure 10.9

Use the Gradient tool to adjust the position and direction of a gradient fill.

You need a gradient before the Gradient tool does anything, so draw a path and apply a gradient fill to it. Select the path if need be, and grab the Gradient tool from the toolbox. The mouse pointer changes into crosshairs when you move it into the document window.

Drawing Perspectives

A mesh object is a path that breaks the rule of having only one fill color. The mesh itself is a network of crossing lines that fall across the fill of a path like a grid. Each intersection point of the mesh lines can have a different color value. Use Illustrator's Gradient Mesh tool to create and edit mesh objects. You can also change an ordinary gradient into a mesh object with the Object → Expand command. Be sure to select the Gradient Mesh option in the Expand dialog box.

Position the crosshairs where you want the gradient to begin, and hold down the mouse button. Drag the mouse to where you want the gradient to end, and release. The gradient fill adjusts itself as you specified.

You can make the gradient smaller than the fill area of the path. Simply choose a start point and an end point inside the fill area. The gradient restricts itself to the zone you define, and the start and end colors of the gradient fill out the remainder of the space.

Likewise, you can make the gradient larger than the fill area of the path. Choose start and end points outside the boundaries of the fill area. The selected path shows the portion of the gradient that falls across it.

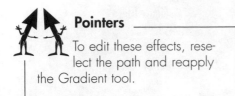

Pointers

To edit these effects, reselect the path and reapply the Gradient tool.

You can even spread a gradient across several different paths, as shown in Figure 10.10. To do so, hold down the Shift key and click all the paths in the spread with the Selection tool. Now click the gradient swatch of your choice. Notice that the gradient applies to each path individually.

Figure 10.10

With the Gradient tool, you can spread a single gradient across several different paths.

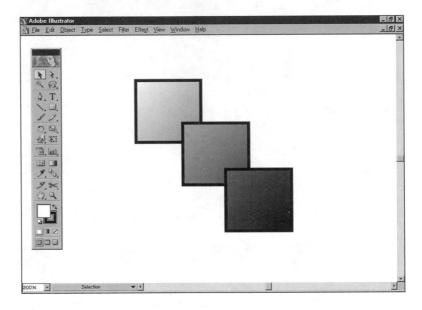

You can fix that in a hurry. Go back to the toolbox for the Gradient tool, and define the start point and end point of the gradient. When you release the mouse button, the gradient spreads itself across the fills of the selected objects as if they were a single path.

Creating and Using Color Swatches

Swatches provide a convenient way to work with patterns and gradients. You may find it just as convenient to create and use color swatches as pattern and gradient swatches.

As you might expect, a color swatch represents a flat color instead of a fancy pattern or gradient. To see Illustrator's built-in color swatches, click the second button from the left on the bottom of the Swatches palette.

Color swatches work just like the other kinds of swatches. You can apply a color swatch to the fill of a path by selecting the path, clicking the fill-color square in the toolbox, and clicking the swatch. You can apply the color swatch to the stroke by following the same procedure—only click the stroke-color square in the toolbox instead.

To create a color swatch of your own, mix a fill or stroke color on the Color palette. Then click the New-Page icon at the bottom of the Swatches palette. If you want to name the color, double-click the swatch.

It is a good idea to create color swatches for colors that you use often in your illustrations. This prevents you from having to remix colors every time you need them. Sure, you could pick up the color that you want with the Eyedropper tool, but clicking a color swatch is faster and more intuitive.

> ### Drawing Perspectives
>
> The Registration color swatch becomes important for CMYK illustrations, as does the color type in the Swatch Options dialog box. For RGB illustrations, you can ignore the Registration color swatch, and you don't have to set the color type.

Time for an Upgrade

Are you thinking what I'm thinking?

I'm thinking that a gradient would work nicely with the sky for the Astro Ape comic. This would give the background just the right touch of depth. Besides, gradients look cool. You have to work one in there somehow.

While you're at it, you should also officially combine the background elements into a single illustration. Right now, you have two separate files for the background: *aa_hills.ai* and *aa_sky.ai*. By the end of this exercise, you will have one file: *aa_background.ai*.

The first task is to get the hills and the sky in the same illustration, so open *aa_hills.ai*. Choose Edit → Select All and then Edit → Cut, and click the X icon at the top of the document window to close the file. Illustrator asks whether you want to save the changes. Click No.

Now open *aa_sky.ai* and Edit → Paste the hills onto the artboard. Grab the Selection tool, and move the hills into place on the sky. You squared off the bottom of the hills for a reason, and this is it: Line up the bottom of the hills with the bottom of the sky for a perfect fit. Drag the handles of the bounding box to scale the hills to just the right size. When you finish, your screen should look something like Figure 10.11.

Figure 10.11

Paste the hills into the sky illustration and drag the bounding-box handles to scale the hills to the perfect size.

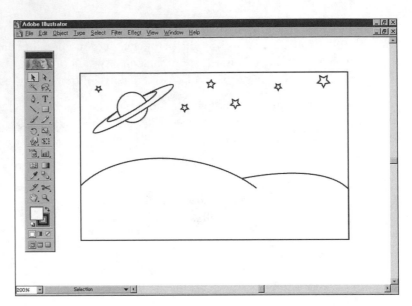

You may have noticed that the fill color for the hills is the None value, which is as you left it back in Chapter 5, "Creating Curves." Take this opportunity to give the path the default white fill by clicking the Default Fill And Stroke icon, which is directly under the fill-color square in the toolbox. Hold off on coloring the hills anything but white for now, because you will do something special with them later.

Now add some color to the stars and the planet. I recommend a light, pale color for the fill, so that the stars and planet stand out against the sky, with a somewhat darker color for the stroke. I also suggest that you use the same color scheme for all the celestial bodies, including the planet and the rings. With 17 million colors at your disposal, the temptation is great to make the stars different colors. But remember, these are background elements in a comic strip, and your audience's attention is a finite quantity. The more of it you draw to the background, the less of it remains for the main character and the story.

> **Drawing Perspectives**
>
> The color of a star says something about its temperature. Red stars are the coolest, and blue stars are the hottest. Our sun, a yellow star, is on the cool side, as far as stars go.

For the stars and planet, go with web-safe RGB red 255, green 255, and blue 204 as the fill, which gives you a pale yellow. Click the fill-color square in the toolbox or on the Color palette to bring the fill color to the foreground. Then mix the color in the Color palette, click the new-page icon at the bottom of the Swatches palette, and double-click the new color swatch to give this color a name, such as *Stars (fill)*. A descriptive, project-specific color name like this is better than a generic one like *pale yellow*. Your eyes can see that the color is pale yellow just by looking, but you might not remember that this particular shade of pale yellow is the fill color for the stars.

For the stroke, do orange to the tune of web-safe RGB red 255, green 204, and blue 102. Click the stroke-color square, mix the color, and create a new color swatch called *Stars (stroke)*.

The stroke-color square should be orange now, and the fill-color square should be pale yellow. If not, click the fill-color square and select the fill swatch, or click the stroke-color square and select the stroke swatch.

When the toolbox shows the proper color scheme, get out the Paint Bucket tool, which hides under the Eyedropper. Click the star and planet paths with the Paint Bucket to apply the stroke and fill colors.

You're ready for the gradient now. I'm thinking of a linear gradient that goes from a light purplish color at the bottom of the illustration, just below the hills, to a dark shade of blue at the top. This should give the sky a glowing, alien-atmosphere effect.

Go to the Gradient palette, and choose Linear from the Type drop-down list. Click the first crayon-shaped slider, go to the Color palette, and mix web-safe RGB red 255, green 191, and blue 234. Now click the second crayon-shaped slider on the Gradient palette, return to the Color palette, and mix web-safe RGB red 27, green 19, and blue 133. You don't have to adjust any of the sliders for this gradient.

Click the new-page icon at the bottom of the Swatches palette, and double-click the new gradient swatch to give it a name. I'm calling it *Sky*.

Now to apply it: Select the rectangular path that you're using as the background of the sky, and click the new gradient swatch. You should get something like Figure 10.12.

Pointers

Remember, when you mix the colors for the gradient, you may have to switch the color model on the Color palette to RGB. Click the triangle icon on the Color palette and choose RGB from the menu that slides out.

Clearly, you're getting somewhere. But you wanted the gradient to begin at the bottom of the illustration and end at the top. As it is now, it begins at the left and ends at the right. The star on the left gets lost in the light purple color.

This looks like a job for the Gradient tool. Click its icon in the toolbox and choose a starting point just under the hills. Hold down the mouse button and drag to the top of the illustration. When you release, the gradient reconfigures itself nicely, as Figure 10.13 shows.

Figure 10.12

Mix the gradient colors, create a new gradient swatch, and apply it to the rectangular path in the background.

Figure 10.13

Adjust the direction of the gradient with the Gradient tool.

Save this file as *aa_background.ai* and call it done for the day. Not only did you make the grade, you also made the gradient.

The Least You Need to Know

- ◆ A pattern is a separate illustration that tiles across a path.
- ◆ You can apply patterns to fills as well as strokes.
- ◆ Expand a pattern to keep it properly aligned on the stroke or fill as you move the path.
- ◆ A gradient is a gradual blend of two or more colors across a path.
- ◆ You can apply gradients to fills but not strokes.
- ◆ Use the Gradient tool to adjust the position and direction of a gradient on a path.
- ◆ Create color swatches for colors that you use frequently in your illustration.

Inserting Type

In This Chapter

♦ Adding type to your illustration

♦ Setting type properties

♦ Creating area, path, and vertical type

♦ Applying color to type

♦ Creating pieces of text for the Astro Ape comic

You might think it odd that a book about computer illustration devotes an entire chapter to type. You have to admit, you've been doing pretty well so far without it.

In fact, computer illustration usually involves text in one form or another. Technical illustrations and diagrams have captions. Advertisements have tag lines. And don't forget that comic strips have word balloons.

Any kind of serious computer illustration software needs to give you plenty of control over the printed word. You will find that Illustrator does not come up short in this regard. Illustrator isn't a word processor, of course. If I handed in this manuscript as an .ai file, my editor would pull me aside for a long talk. Nevertheless, the software offers many useful features for working with type (some word-processor-like, some not), as this chapter demonstrates.

Comparing Methods for Adding Type

You can add type to your work in two ways. You can insert it directly into your illustration, or you can put it inside a *type area*, which is a predefined container for text. Both methods have their advantages.

In either case, use the Type tool. You will find the Type tool above the Rectangle tool in the toolbox, as Figure 11.1 shows.

Figure 11.1

Use the Type tool to insert text.

Taking the Direct Approach

Choose the Type tool, and the mouse pointer becomes an I-beam when you move it into the document window. Click the mouse button, and a flashing cursor appears. You may now insert text directly into your illustration with the keyboard. When you finish, hold down Ctrl (Windows) or Command (Mac) and click on an empty area of the page.

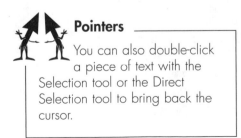

Pointers

You can also double-click a piece of text with the Selection tool or the Direct Selection tool to bring back the cursor.

Because a predefined type area doesn't bind the text, the line of type continues indefinitely. You can type off the edge of the imageable area. To begin a new line of type, you must manually press the Enter or Return key.

For this reason, typing directly into your illustration works best for short pieces of text, like labels and captions. If you want to insert a paragraph or more, a type area works better.

Click an existing piece of text with the Type tool, and the flashing cursor reappears, enabling you to add more text or edit the existing characters. Enter new characters at the insertion point by typing, or drag the cursor to select a string of characters, just like you would with a word processor. Remember, the line of type continues until you press Enter or Return. Don't expect the line to break automatically at the edge of the page.

It's easy to change the appearance of text that you type directly into your illustration. Click your text with the Selection tool to reveal its bounding box. Drag the handles of the bounding box to stretch or condense the type, as Figure 11.2 shows.

> **Drawing Perspectives**
>
> Even after you stretch or rotate a piece of text, you can still edit it freely with the Type tool. Any new characters that you insert automatically acquire the same degree of stretch and the same angle of rotation.

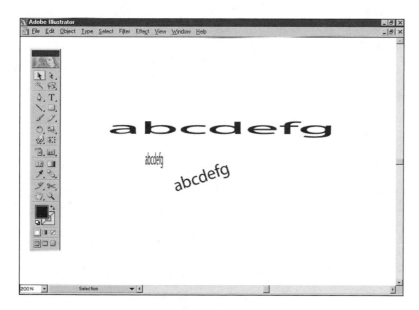

Figure 11.2

Use the Selection tool to stretch, condense, and rotate type. The type remains completely editable after these transformations.

You can also rotate the type by positioning the mouse pointer in the vicinity of one of the handles. Slowly move the pointer away from the handle until the pointer changes to a curved arrow. Then hold down the mouse button. Drag toward you to rotate the type clockwise. Drag away from you to rotate the type counterclockwise.

Defining a Type Area

When you need to add more text than just a word or two, think about using a type area. Unlike type that you insert directly, the type in a type area observes the boundaries of its container, which makes the type easier to manage.

To create a type area, grab the Type tool, and position the I-beam in the document window. Instead of just clicking the mouse button, hold it down and drag a rectangular area. When you release the button, the flashing cursor appears inside the rectangle.

Add characters by typing with the keyboard. Notice that the line of type automatically breaks when you reach the edge of the type area, as you can see in Figure 11.3. To finish, hold down Ctrl (Windows) or Command (Mac), and click an empty area of the document window. Deselecting the type area causes the rectangular border to become invisible. If you add more type than a type area can contain, the bounding box presents a small plus icon next to the last line of type. This is your signal to get out the Selection tool and resize the type area.

Figure 11.3

When you add characters to a type area, the line of type breaks automatically at the edge of the container.

When you click a piece of directly inserted text with the Selection tool, you gain the ability to transform it. Type areas, however, work a little differently. Click a type area with the Selection tool, and you can transform its shape and size without affecting the type that it contains. The type automatically *reflows*, or repositions itself, according to the new dimensions of the type area. If you rotate the type area, you can create interesting line-break effects, as Figure 11.4 shows. Notice that the type itself remains perfectly horizontal, even after you slant the container.

Figure 11.4

Rotating a type area with the Selection tool may angle the container, but the type itself remains perfectly horizontal.

Setting Type Properties

The Character palette and the Paragraph palette enable you to change the properties of the type. Look for these palettes under the Type menu, not the Window menu.

Character properties include the typeface, the type style, and the point size. Paragraph properties include alignment and indentation. As a general rule, the paragraph properties work best with type that sits in a type area. You can set the paragraph properties of freestanding type, but you may not see any noticeable effects, or you may get undesirable results. The character properties work equally well with both kinds of type.

Changing Character Properties

Call up the Character palette with Window → Type → Character. If your palette doesn't match the one in Figure 11.5, open the palette menu by clicking the triangle icon and choose Show Options.

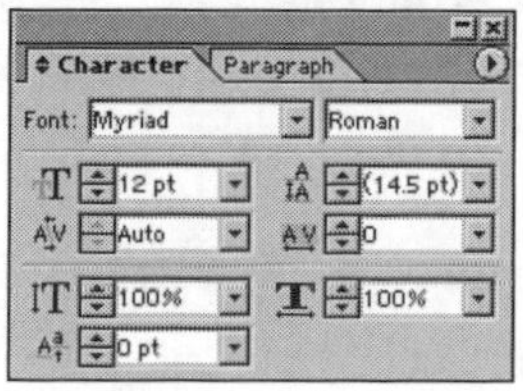

Figure 11.5

Use the Character palette to set character-level type properties, such as typeface and point size.

Now create a new type area with the Type tool, and insert a couple lines of type. Ctrl-click (Windows) or Command-click (Mac) to exit, and click your new type area with the Selection tool.

The Font drop-down list on the Character palette controls the typeface of the selected characters. Choose a new font from the list, and choose a new style—bold, italic, Roman, condensed, and so on—from the drop-down list to the right. Not all fonts have multiple styles, so the style list may not give you much of a choice. As you make your selections, all the type in the type area acquires the new typeface and style properties.

Under the Font list on the Character palette is the Font Size list. This list enables you to change the point size of the type in the type area. Naturally, the higher the point size, the larger the type becomes.

To the right of the Font Size list is the Leading list. *Leading* is the amount of space between lines of type. Increase this value to spread the lines farther apart. Decrease this value to pack them closer together. If you choose the Auto value, Illustrator calculates a standard amount of leading for the font.

Beneath the Font Size list is the Kerning list. *Kerning* is the amount of space between two characters in a line of type. To set the kerning, click an insertion point between two characters with the Type tool. Select a positive value from the list to increase the kerning, pushing the characters farther apart. Select a negative value to decrease the kerning, bringing the characters closer together. The Auto value gives you standard kerning for the selected font.

To the right of the Kerning list is the Tracking list. *Tracking* is like kerning, only it applies to every character in a selected area, not just the characters on either side of the cursor. To set the tracking, drag the cursor to select a few words, or click the type area with the Selection tool to select the entire piece of text. A positive tracking value pushes all the characters farther apart. A negative tracking value brings all the characters closer together. A value of zero indicates standard tracking for all the characters.

Under the Kerning list is the Vertical Scale list. Changing the vertical scale stretches or condenses the selected character's height. Likewise, the Horizontal Scale list next door stretches or condenses the selected character's width. In both cases, values of 100% give you normal, unscaled characters. Values less than 100% compress the characters, and values greater than 100% stretch out the characters.

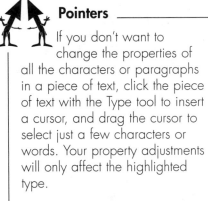

Pointers

If you don't want to change the properties of all the characters or paragraphs in a piece of text, click the piece of text with the Type tool to insert a cursor, and drag the cursor to select just a few characters or words. Your property adjustments will only affect the highlighted type.

Drawing Perspectives

The term *leading* comes from the early days of printing, when compositors would insert lead plugs between lines of type to separate them.

Finally, the Baseline Shift list enables you to change the position of the type relative to the baseline. The *baseline* is like the rule on a sheet of notebook paper. Most characters sit on top of the baseline. Some, like the lowercase letter p, have *descenders* that drop below it. You can see the baselines if you click a piece of text with one of the selection tools.

Choosing a positive value from the Baseline Shift list causes the selected characters to sit above the baseline in a line of type, as in a superscript. Choosing a negative value causes them to sit below the baseline, as in a subscript. A value of zero positions the line of type on the baseline precisely.

Perfecting Paragraph Properties

The Paragraph palette enables you to change the paragraph properties of type (see Figure 11.6). As I mentioned before, these options work best with type that sits in a type area. Click the Paragraph tab in the Character palette to call them up, or choose Window → Type → Paragraph from the menu.

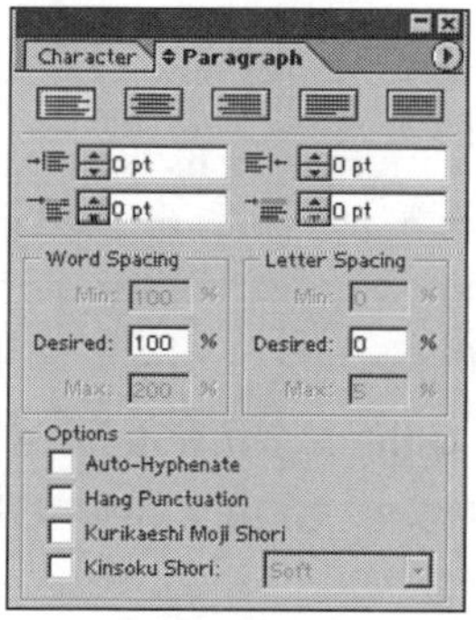

Figure 11.6

Use the Paragraph palette to set paragraph-level type properties, such as alignment and justification.

The first row of five buttons controls the alignment and justification of the text. You can align the text to the left margin, in the center of the type area, or to the right margin by clicking the first, second, or third button.

Justification creates lines of equal length by inserting space between words and sometimes between individual characters. Justified text has neat left and right margins. Unjustified text, or *ragged text*, has one neat margin and one uneven margin.

There are two justification buttons in Illustrator: Justify Full Lines and Justify All Lines. The Justify Full Lines button, which is the fourth button on the Paragraph palette, evens out the lines of type that reach all the way to the right margin. It does nothing to short lines, such as the last line of a paragraph. The Justify All Lines button, which is the fifth and last button, evens out every line of type, including the stumpy ones that fall at the end of the paragraph. Figure 11.7 shows an example of each type of justification.

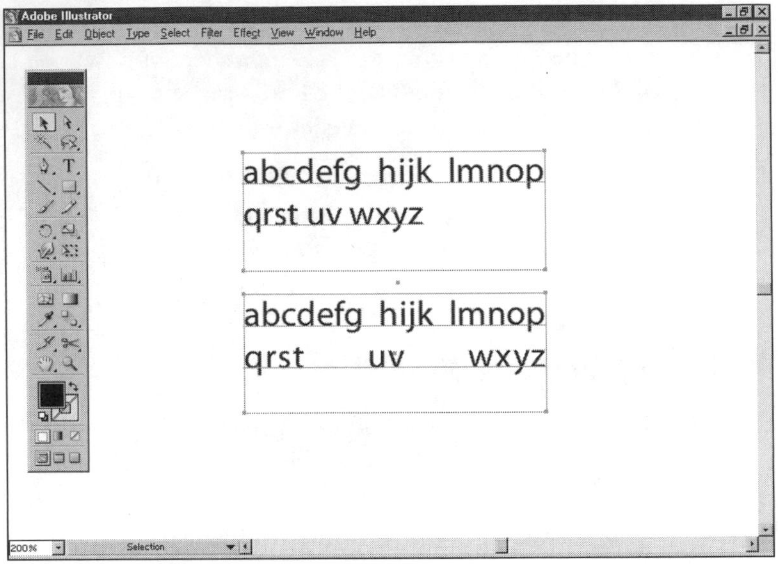

Figure 11.7

The Justify Full Lines button evens out only lines of type that extend all the way to the right margin, as in the type area on the top. The Justify All Lines button makes no such distinction, as in the type area on the bottom.

Each paragraph in a type area can have a different alignment or justification setting.

The first field under the alignment and justification buttons is the Left Indent field. Increase the left indent to push the beginnings of the lines farther into the type area. Notice that if you set the left indent to a negative value, the lines of type actually begin outside the left margin of the type area. Weird!

The field to the right, appropriately enough, is the Right Indent field. This field affects the end positions of the lines. Once again, a negative value pushes the line endings outside the type area.

Pointers

You can modify the degree to which Illustrator justifies lines of type by tweaking the values in the Word Spacing and Letter Spacing fields. Increasing the maximum values creates looser-looking lines of type.

Under the Left Indent field is the First Line Left Indent field. The value in this field affects the amount of extra space at the beginning of the first line of a paragraph.

To the right is the Space Before Paragraph field. The value in this field controls the amount of extra space between paragraphs in the type area. This value doesn't change the leading of the type area—that is, it doesn't affect the space between all the lines of type. It simply adds extra space between paragraphs.

You will note that at the bottom of the Paragraph palette you have options for automatic hyphenation and hanging punctuation. *Hyphenation*, of course, is the practice of breaking words at the end of a line of type with a hyphen (-) as a way to fit more type into the same amount of space. Illustrator's built-in dictionary knows how to hyphenate many, many words, so click the check box next to this option and give auto-hyphenation a try.

Hanging punctuation is punctuation that sits outside the margin of the type area. If you want punctuation characters such as periods, commas, and quotation marks to hang outside the margin, enable this option with a click. This feature only applies to punctuation characters that fall at the beginning or end of a line of type.

> **Drawing Perspectives**
>
> Only use hyphenation in paragraphs. Never use it in slogans, captions, titles, headlines, and so on.

Using Other Type Tools

Illustrator's Type toolset is especially bountiful, as Figure 11.8 shows. You get six tools in all. Have a look at the five hidden tools by holding down the mouse button on the Type tool.

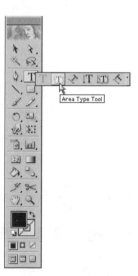

Figure 11.8

Illustrator gives you five hidden Type tools in addition to the original.

If you're feeling overwhelmed by Type tools at this point, don't be. These tools come easy, and they can help you to create some interesting effects like *area type*, which occupies the fill of a path, and *path type*, which runs along the stroke.

Creating Area Type

The Area Type tool is the first of the hidden tools. This one enables you to transform any closed path into a type area, like in Figure 11.9. Draw a closed path, and click along its stroke with the Area Type tool to make the switch.

When you convert a closed path into a type area, the path loses its appearance attributes. Click the path with the Direct Selection tool, though, and you can reapply the attributes.

Be careful that you don't click the text, or you will end up changing its appearance attributes instead. You will know you have the path when the fill-color square and the stroke-color square in the toolbox both contain the None value.

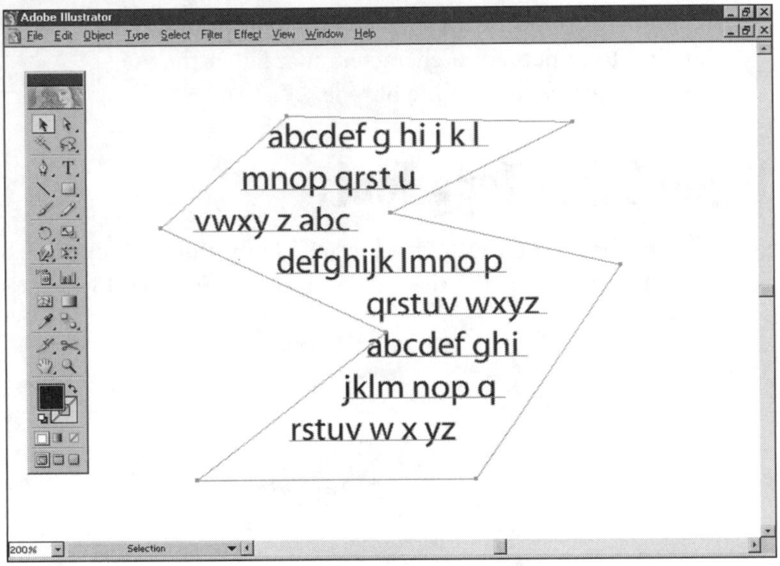

Figure 11.9

Convert any closed path into a type container with the Area Type tool.

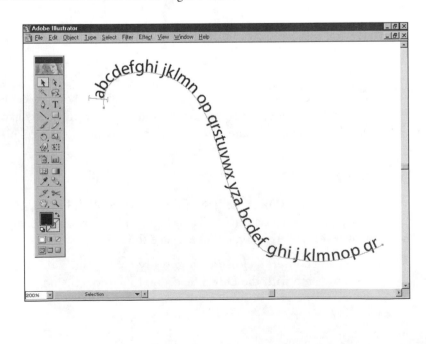

Attaching Type to a Path

The Path Type tool comes next. This tool enables you to attach type to any path, closed or open, creating an effect similar to the one in Figure 11.10.

Figure 11.10

The Path Type tool attaches type to a path.

Create a path with any of the drawing tools and click it with the Path Type tool to attach the text. The path loses its appearance attributes in the process, just like closed paths that get the Area Type treatment. Direct-select the path to reapply the appearance attributes.

Unfortunately, you cannot add area type and path type to the same path. However, you can create two identical paths. Attach area type to the one and path type to the other, and then superimpose them, as Figure 11.11 shows.

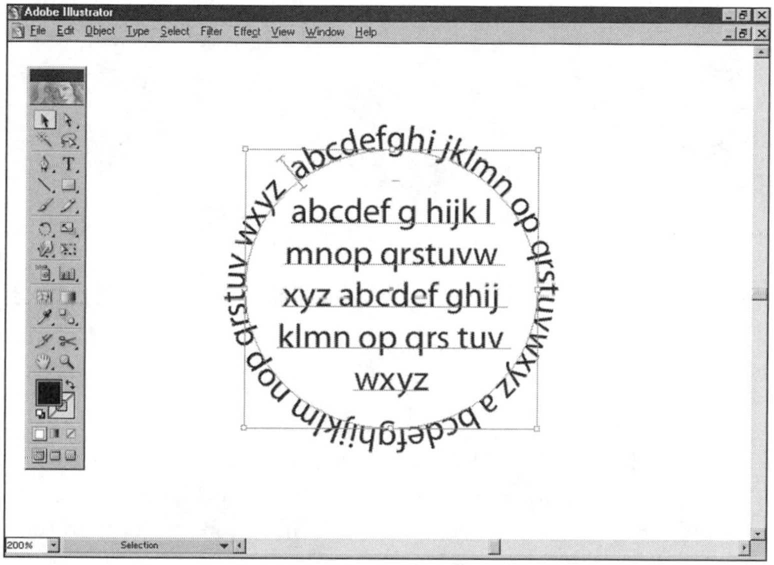

Figure 11.11

You cannot attach area type and path type to the same path. But you can create two identical paths and attach area type to the one and path type to the other. Superimpose the paths, and no one will know the difference.

Making Vertical Type

The last three hidden tools are Vertical Type, Vertical Area Type, and Vertical Path Type.

As Figure 11.12 demonstrates, a line of vertical type flows from top to bottom instead of left to right, and a new line begins to the left of the old line, not underneath it.

The Vertical Type tool works just like the regular Type tool. Click with the Vertical Type tool to insert vertical type directly into your illustration, or drag to create a vertical type area.

Similarly, the Vertical Area Type and Vertical Path Type tools work like their nonvertical counterparts. Click a closed path with the Vertical Area Type tool to convert the path into a vertical type area. Click any path with the Vertical Path Type tool to attach vertical type.

> **Drawing Perspectives**
>
> Vertical type is difficult to read in English and other Western languages, but it is essential to Eastern languages such as Chinese and Japanese.

Figure 11.12

The Vertical Type tool (left), the Vertical Area Type tool (middle), and the Vertical Path Type tool (right) work just like their nonvertical counterparts, only they create vertical type.

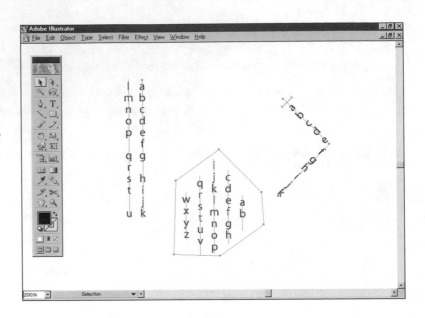

Coloring Type

When you click a piece of text with the Selection tool, or when you drag the type cursor to select a series of characters, you may notice that the color squares in the toolbox change to show a black fill and a transparent stroke. The black fill is none other than the black color of the type.

Pointers

When choosing color for type, lean toward high-contrast foreground/background combinations. If the type color is too close to the background color, the type becomes difficult to read, especially at small point sizes.

To change the color of the type, click the fill-color square in the toolbox. Then go to the Color palette and mix a new color, or pick one from the RGB Spectrum. You can also apply a swatch from the Swatches palette. Gradient swatches don't work, unfortunately, but pattern swatches do.

By adding a stroke color to type, you create an outline effect, like in Figure 11.13. Click the stroke-color square in the toolbox, and mix a new stroke color with the Color palette or apply an existing one with the Swatches palette. Adjust the weight of the stroke with the Stroke palette to complete the effect.

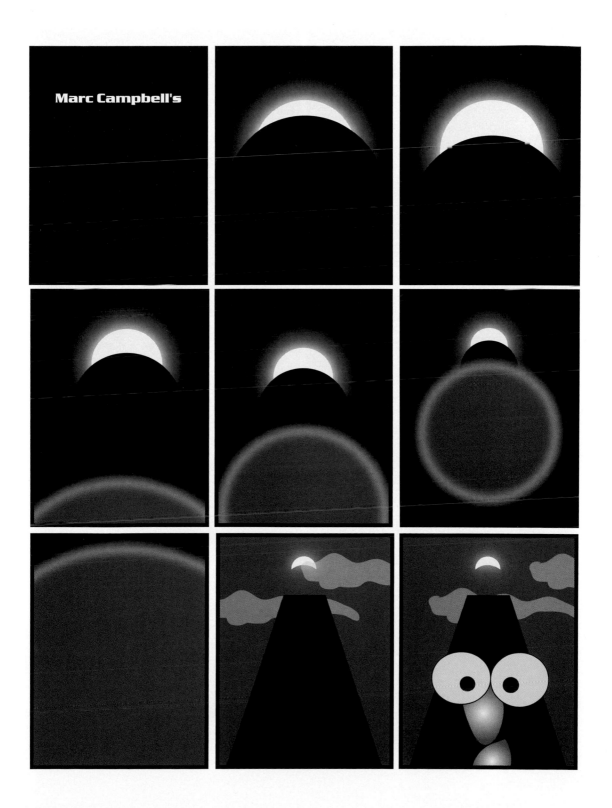

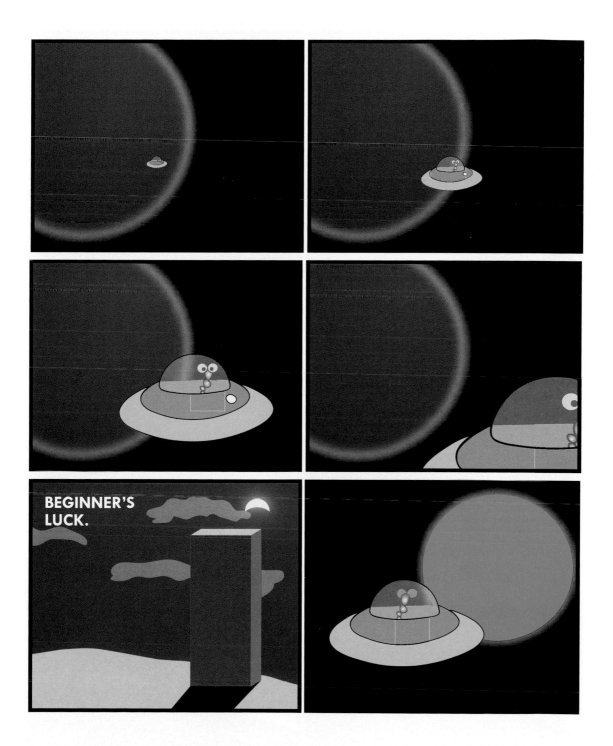

Figure 11.13

You can easily change the fill color of type and add a stroke color to create an outline effect.

Changing Type Into Paths

With all this changing of stroke and fill colors, you might get the impression that type is very much like any other path in your illustration.

Indeed it is. It's so similar, in fact, that you can transform type into a series of regular old paths with a single command. Clicking a piece of text with the Selection tool and choosing Type → Create Outlines does the trick.

Type that you convert in this way reads the same to a human. It still looks like text. However, Illustrator no longer recognizes it as text. You cannot edit it with the Type tool anymore. To the software, the paths are no different than those that you create with the drawing tools, even though they happen to look like letters and numbers.

Drawing Perspectives

Most of the fonts that you use on your computer every day are very, very similar to vector graphics. Windows TrueType fonts and Adobe PostScript fonts have the name *outline fonts* because they contain vector information about the shapes (outlines) of the characters. The opposite of an outline font is a *bitmap font,* which has no vector information and is therefore resolution-dependent. It should come as no surprise that pixels make up the characters of a bitmap font, just like pixels make up bitmap or raster graphics.

Why, then, would you ever want to change type into ordinary paths?

For one thing, it can help to resolve compatibility problems. If you share your .ai file with another computer illustrator, that person needs to have the very same fonts that you used in your work. Otherwise, Illustrator makes substitutions from the available fonts, which can significantly change the way your illustration looks.

Creating outlines of the type eliminates this problem completely. Because, by outlining, you convert all the letters and numbers to plain old paths, there are no fonts to miss, so there are no fonts to substitute. Your friend sees your work exactly as you intended.

There are other benefits. Converting type into paths enables you to process the type with all the path-editing tools at your disposal. You can achieve all kinds of tricky type effects this way. You will rely on some of these effects for the Astro Ape cartoon later in this book.

Remember, though, that creating outlines removes your ability to edit the paths as text. Make sure that the Type ➜ Create Outlines step comes at the end of the writing and editing process. You don't want to find spelling errors or typos after you have made the outlines, because there's no way of going back besides choosing Edit ➜ Undo.

Speak No Evil

With all this talk of type and letters fresh in your mind, you can create the word balloon for the last panel of the Astro Ape comic, when the monkey announces, "Reality is overrated." You can also finish what you started way back in Chapter 4, "Delivering Straight Lines," and add the words to the arrow sign.

Tackle the *word balloon* first. Launch Illustrator, open a new document window, and zoom in to 200% or so.

!#%@ **Word Balloon**

A **word balloon** is a shape, usually elliptical, that contains the dialogue or thoughts of a character in a comic strip. A triangular **pointer** extends from the balloon shape to the head or mouth of the speaking character.

The words in the word balloon sit in a type area, so get out the Type tool and drag a rectangular container. Make it big—about half as big as the viewable area of the screen. This is much larger than you need, but it will be easy to shrink the type area to the right size after you add the type.

Go to the Character palette and set the typeface and point size. I'm using Myriad as the font, which is the Illustrator default. It's a good, crisp, legible, general-purpose font. I'm also using 48-point type. Type the words **REALITY IS OVERRATED!** in all capital letters, and hold down Ctrl (Windows) or Command

(Mac) and click an empty area of the page. Now get out the Selection tool, click the type area, and resize it so that you get two lines of type, as shown in Figure 11.14.

Figure 11.14

Create a type area with the Type tool, add the text, and resize the container with the Selection tool so that the sentence breaks into two lines.

The space between the lines of type is just a touch too much, so go back to the Character palette and set the leading to the same value that you used for the letters. You specified 48-point type, so pull 48 from the Leading list. Make sure your baseline shift is set at 0 pt.

Drawing Perspectives

Before word balloons became the convention in comic strips, a character's dialogue or thoughts appeared on his shirt, coat, or hat. Political cartooning still uses this technique. The narration of a comic book story ("Meanwhile, back in Metropolis ...") used to appear in boxed captions, and occasionally it still does. Since the 1980s, though, the trend has been to let the art narrate itself. The caption boxes now belong to brooding superheroes, who share their ongoing internal monologues in this way.

Look under the Paragraph tab on the Character palette, and click the Align Center button. The words on your screen should now look similar to Figure 11.15.

Figure 11.15

Set the leading to the same value as the point size of the type, and click the Align Center button on the Paragraph palette.

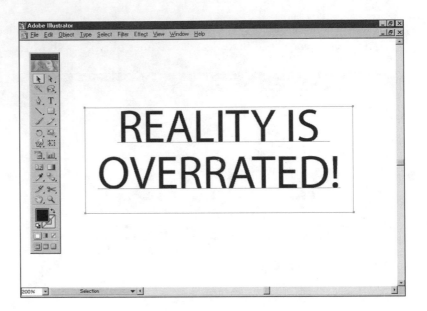

It's standard practice in the world of comics to use bold and italics on words that get emphasis. So take out the Type tool again, click at the beginning of the last word in the type area, and drag the cursor to select the entire word. Now return to the Character palette by clicking the tab, and set the type style to Bold Italic. (The Type Style list is to the right of the Font list.) A very comic-book-looking piece of text emerges, as Figure 11.16 shows.

Figure 11.16

Go back to the Character palette and make the last word Bold Italic.

So much for the word part. Now for the balloon part.

The balloon is an ellipse, so get out the Rectangle tool from the toolbox. (Just kidding with you there—you want the Ellipse tool, of course.) Instead of dragging the Ellipse tool, though, click once to call up the Ellipse dialog box. Enter a width of 350 points and a height of 167 points, and click OK to create the shape. While you're at it, choose Object → Arrange → Send To Back, so that the balloon sits behind the words in the stacking order. Also, turn off the fill color temporarily, but leave the black stroke. (The color of the word balloon doesn't have to be white, but it should be a pale, light color so as not to make the lettering hard to read.)

Snip a section from the lower right of the ellipse with the Scissors. Remove the clipping and delete it. Now click the ellipse with the Selection tool, and take the Pen from the toolbox. Attach a triangular pointer to the bottom of the path to create the word balloon, as in Figure 11.17.

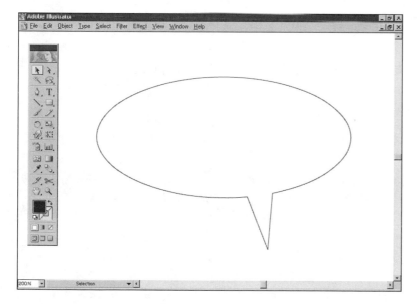

Figure 11.17

Draw an ellipse, snip off part of the bottom with the Scissors, and attach a pointer with the Pen to create the word balloon.

Specify white as the fill color of the balloon, and position the type area with the Selection tool. Astro Ape's commentary on the nature of reality is now ready for presentation, as Figure 11.18 shows.

Actual apes don't speak, of course, but some researchers believe that chimpanzees can learn sign language. Chimps seem most interested in using sign language to ask for food or to discipline their children.

Figure 11.18

Bring in the type, and you have a comic-style commentary on the nature of reality.

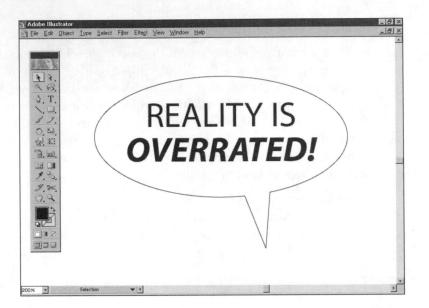

Save this file as *aa_wordballoon.ai* and close the document window. One down, one to go.

Open up the *aa_sign_color.ai* file that you created in Chapter 9, "Applying Brushes." The colored, brush-styled arrow sign appears.

The words on the sign should read "The Real World." You don't need a type area for this. You can enter the type directly into the illustration.

Grab the Type tool from the toolbox, and go to the Paragraph palette. Click the Align Left button. Now move the I-beam back into the document window, and click somewhere inside the arrow shape. The flashing cursor appears. Type the words for the sign. When you finish, hold down Ctrl or Command and click on an empty area of the page.

More likely than not, the words aren't the right size for the sign. Click the piece of text with the Selection tool, and choose a more fitting point size from the list on the Character palette. You might also take this opportunity to choose the typeface and type style. I'm using Myriad as the font again, and I like the way that the Condensed Bold Italic style looks for the sign letters.

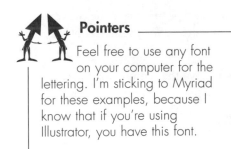

Pointers

Feel free to use any font on your computer for the lettering. I'm sticking to Myriad for these examples, because I know that if you're using Illustrator, you have this font.

In the interest of good form, you should also select the Auto value from the Leading list. You're correct in thinking that the leading value doesn't make any difference for this particular piece of text. You could set the leading to one million points, and the text would look exactly the same, because there is only one line of type.

Even still, get into the habit of putting away your toys after you play with them! You adjusted the leading when you created the word balloon, so it's a good idea to return the leading to its default value here, even if the leading doesn't matter one way or the other.

When you finish, your sign should look something like Figure 11.19.

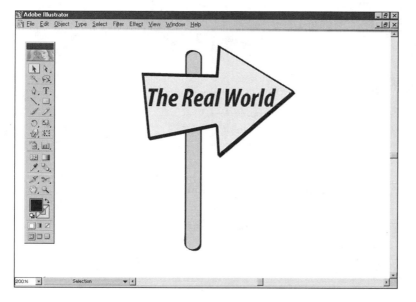

Figure 11.19

Add type directly to your illustration for the words on the sign.

Not bad, but my eyes tell me that the words could use a slight counterclockwise rotation. Click the piece of text with the Selection tool, and move the mouse pointer toward one of the handles on the bounding box. When the pointer changes to a curved arrow, hold down the mouse button and drag away from you. Release the mouse button when the words have the right amount of tilt, as shown in Figure 11.20. Fine-tune the position of the type with the Selection tool and the arrow keys, and you have a sign.

Choose File → Save As from the menu, and commit this file to your hard drive as *aa_sign_type.ai* to distinguish it from the other two sign illustrations.

You have come to the end of another chapter and the end of another part in this book. Now would be an excellent time to compose a new mockup scene for your refrigerator door.

Drawing Perspectives
Apes in captivity seem to be able to distinguish between complex shapes, such as Japanese characters and Arabic numerals. I should have asked you to create Japanese lettering for the sign.

Figure 11.20

For the best fit, rotate the words ever so slightly.

Keep *aa_sign_type.ai* open, and open the following other files: *aa_wordballoon.ai*, *aa_side_color.ai*, and *aa_background.ai*. For the sign, the word balloon, and the character design, choose Edit → Select All and Object → Group, just like you did at the end of Chapter 7, "Generating Shapes." Then copy the art, and paste it into the background illustration.

Adjust the relative sizes and positions of the groups, shuffle the stacking order as needed, and you get something like Figure 11.21.

Figure 11.21

Combine some recent illustrations for a more fleshed-out mockup scene.

Send this scene to your printer (that's with File ➜ Print, remember?) and save the file as *aa_mockup2.ai*. Compare the first mockup with the second, and I think you'll agree that you're turning out some fine work—maybe the best of your career.

The Least You Need to Know

- Click with the Type tool to insert type directly into your illustration.
- Click and drag with the Type tool to create a type area, or a special container for type.
- Use the Character palette and the Paragraph palette to set type properties.
- Area type occupies the fill of a path, whereas path type sits on the stroke.
- Vertical type flows from top to bottom, and new lines appear to the left.
- Apply fill and stroke colors to type like other paths.
- Convert type to regular paths with the Create Outlines command.

Part 4

Now You're Cooking

By now, you deserve to feel like a competent computer illustrator. You know all about anchor points. You understand strokes and fills. You're even getting the hang of that blasted Pen.

This part takes your skills to the next level. The next five chapters show you how to be clever with Illustrator menu commands, how to be efficient with organizational strategies, and how to make your illustrations work for you with well-placed transformations. You will create 3D effects with blend objects and explore color functions that have no equivalent in traditional illustration. The fun's just a page away.

Chapter 12

Manipulating Paths

In This Chapter

◆ Adding, deleting, and converting anchor points

◆ Averaging anchor points

◆ Simplifying paths

◆ Creating custom lettering for the Astro Ape comic

You're an art person. You prefer to do things visually. If somebody tells you to take a polygon and turn it into a rectangle, your first inclination (after asking why you have to do such a thing) is to reach for the Direct Selection tool and start dragging anchor points around. Slowly but surely, the desired shape emerges.

But if you think about art the way the computer thinks about it (that is, in terms of what each anchor point does), you can, quite literally, change any shape into any other with a few well-chosen techniques. Polygons become rectangles. Rectangles become ellipses. Ellipses become diagonal lines, and diagonal lines become perfectly horizontal or vertical.

The philosopher Heraclitus said that everything is in flux, that everything in the world is constantly changing. But not even Heraclitus dreamed of anything like this. In this chapter, you will learn how to make paths do your bidding by adding, deleting, converting, and otherwise processing the anchor points that make them up.

Using the Pen's Hidden Toolset

Everybody knows that anchor points define the shape of a path. If you change the position of the anchor points with the Direct Selection tool, the path changes shape. It's practically a law of nature.

> **Drawing Perspectives**
>
> Heraclitus lived in Greece before the time of Socrates, from about 535 to 475 B.C.E.

What happens, then, if you add anchor points to a path? What happens if you remove them? Or convert them from corner points to smooth points? The hidden toolset of the Pen has a tool for each of these functions, as Figure 12.1 shows. Are these tools just a needless bother, or can they save you time and effort? You can perform a few experiments to see.

Figure 12.1

The Pen's hidden toolset enables you to add and delete anchor points, as well as convert anchor points from one kind to another.

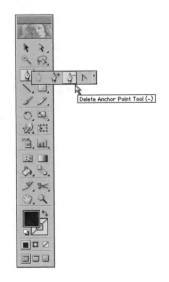

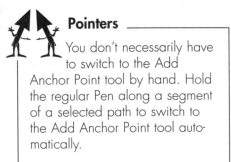

> **Pointers**
>
> You don't necessarily have to switch to the Add Anchor Point tool by hand. Hold the regular Pen along a segment of a selected path to switch to the Add Anchor Point tool automatically.

Adding Anchor Points

By adding anchor points to a path, you get more opportunities to alter the path's shape. One way to do this is to use the Add Anchor Point tool, which is the Pen with a plus sign in the upper-right corner.

To start, draw a rectangle with the tool of your choice. The rectangle has four anchor points—one in each corner of the shape. What if you want to manipulate the path at a point that isn't in a corner?

Look under the Pen for the Add Anchor Point tool. Select this tool, and move the mouse pointer onto the rectangle. Click to add an anchor point anywhere along the path. Then grab the Direct Selection tool and reposition the new anchor point. The entire path changes shape according to the new configuration of points, as Figure 12.2 shows.

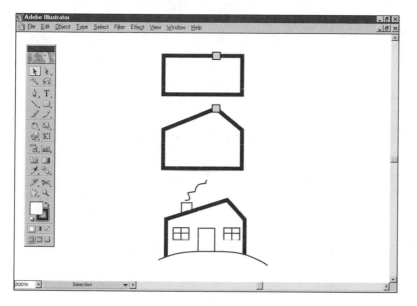

Figure 12.2

By adding an anchor point to a rectangle, you can modify the shape of the path at a location that isn't in one of the corners.

Add as many new anchor points to the path as you need. For instance, if you add two anchor points to a circle, one at the top left and another at the bottom right, you can squeeze the shape into an S by dragging the top anchor point downward and the bottom anchor point upward, as in Figure 12.3.

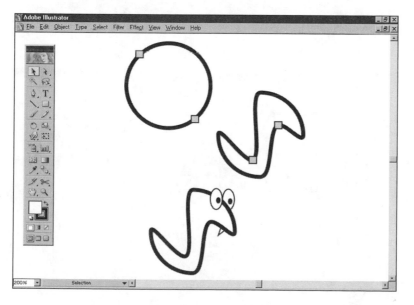

Figure 12.3

Add two anchor points to a circle to bend the shape into an S.

Art Alert _____

Adding anchor points doesn't change the shape of the path until you use the Direct Selection tool, but deleting anchor points can change the shape of the path significantly. Use Edit ➔ Undo to restore an anchor point that you would rather have back. This is usually easier than trying to replace the missing anchor with the Pen.

Pointers _____

The normal Pen becomes the Delete Anchor Point tool automatically when you position it over the anchor of a selected path, except when the anchor marks the start point or end point of an open path.

Deleting Anchor Points

What the Pen giveth, the Pen can taketh away. Use the Delete Anchor Point tool to remove anchor points from a path. The Delete Anchor Point tool is the Pen with the minus sign in the upper-right corner.

Remove anchor points when you want to simplify a shape. Changing a polygon into a rectangle qualifies here. A six-sided polygon has six anchor points, whereas a rectangle has only four. To get the rectangle, all you have to do is delete two of the anchors.

Give it a try. Use the Polygon tool to draw a six-sided path. Then pull out the Delete Anchor Point tool, and click the leftmost anchor point on the polygon. The six-sided path becomes a five-sided one. Click the right-most anchor point, and the rectangle appears, as in Figure 12.4.

You can also use this technique to smooth the kinks out of shaky Pencil or Paintbrush paths. Click the path with the Selection tool, and remove the anchor points that define the unintentional twists and turns, as Figure 12.5 shows.

Figure 12.4

Simplify a shape by removing anchor points. This is the most efficient way to change a polygon into a rectangle.

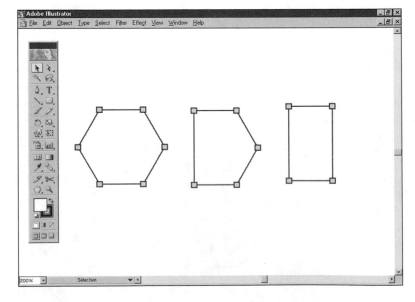

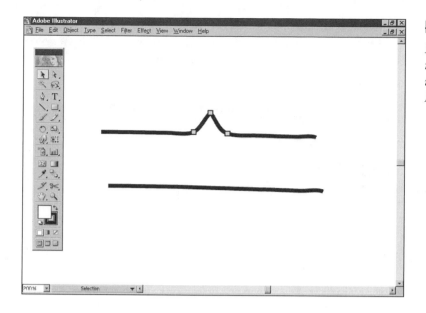

Figure 12.5

Remove anchor points to take the sting, or at least the unintended bumps, out of a Pencil or Paintbrush line.

Converting Anchor Points

Remember that there are two kinds of anchor points: corner points and smooth points. A corner point's segment comes out as a straight line, and a smooth point's segment comes out as a curve. By changing a corner point to a smooth point or a smooth point to a corner, you can drastically alter the shape of a path.

Consider a circle and a square. To outward appearances, these shapes don't have much in common. But in terms of anchor points and paths, they are virtually identical. A circle has four smooth points, and a square has four corner points. In theory, if you could get in there and change the circle's smooth points into corner points, you could make a square.

Put the theory to the test. Draw a circular path, and grab the Convert Anchor Point tool from the Pen's hidden toolset—the tool that looks like a caret (^).

Click one of the circle's anchor points. The anchor changes from a smooth point to a corner point. Convert the three remaining smooth points, and the square appears, as Figure 12.6 demonstrates.

You can also convert corner points into smooth points. This comes in handy for drawing smooth curves without fussing too much with the Pen.

Begin with a straight path. By now, you can draw this in your sleep. Take the Pen, plot two anchor

Drawing Perspectives

It is easier to change a circle into a square than it is to change a square into a circle. Converting the four corner points of the square into four smooth points with the same degree of slope takes practice.

points, and you're done. Now take out the Convert Anchor Point tool, and position the mouse pointer over one of the anchor points. Instead of clicking and releasing, hold down the mouse button and drag a pair of direction lines. The corner point changes to a smooth point, and the straight path begins to curve.

Figure 12.6

Convert a circle's four smooth points into corner points, and you get a square.

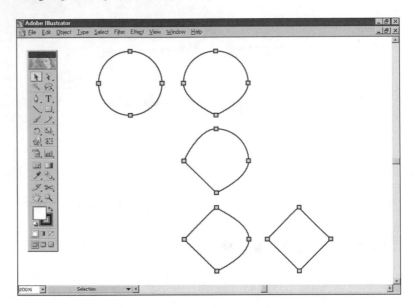

Go to the other anchor point, and drag another pair of direction lines. The Convert Anchor Point tool follows the same kooky logic as the Pen. Create a C-shaped curve by dragging in the opposite direction as you did for the first anchor. Create an S-shaped curve by dragging in the same direction.

The advantage of using the Convert Anchor Point tool to create curves is that you see the effects of this tool immediately. With the Pen, the curve doesn't appear until after you plot the second anchor point. The Convert Anchor Point tool makes it easier to shape a curve by eyeballing, which is never a bad thing for illustrators.

Automatically Adding Anchor Points

The Add Anchor Point tool gives you precise control over where the new anchor point goes. Sometimes, though, you may want to distribute new anchor points evenly across a path, like in the middle of each side of a rectangle. For times like these, leave the Add Anchor Point tool in the toolbox and use Illustrator's Add Anchor Points command instead.

Click a path with a Selection tool, and choose Object → Path → Add Anchor Points. Illustrator drops a new anchor point in the middle of each segment on the path. If you use this command on a straight path, for instance, one new anchor point appears in the middle of the path. But if you use this command on an ellipse, four new anchor points appear: one in the middle of each segment, as Figure 12.7 shows. To add more anchor points to the same path, simply repeat the command.

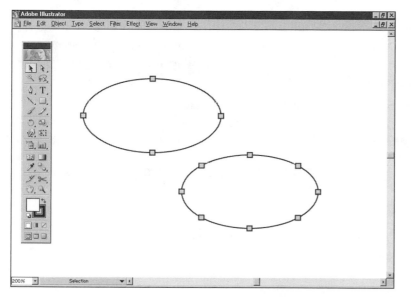

Figure 12.7

The Add Anchor Points command drops a new anchor point in the middle of each segment on a path.

This operation doesn't alter the shape of the path by itself, but you can use the Direct Selection tool to adjust the new anchors to your liking. You can also use the Delete Anchor Point tool to get rid of any new anchor points that you don't need.

Averaging Anchor Points

Illustrator's Average command takes two or more anchor points and lines them up. The anchors can be on the same path, but they don't have to be.

The simplest way to see how this command works is to try it on a diagonal line. Draw one with the Pen, and then grab the Direct Selection tool. Click one of the anchors, hold down Shift, and click the other anchor. This selects them both, as you know.

Now choose Object → Path → Average. The Average dialog box appears and asks you to choose an axis: horizontal, vertical, or both.

Pointers

If you average anchor points on different paths, the paths seem to twist and bend together, but they remain separate paths.

Select the Horizontal option and click OK. The anchor points line up horizontally but keep their vertical positions, creating a perfectly horizontal line. Choose Edit ➔ Undo, and try Object ➔ Path ➔ Average again. This time, select the Vertical option. The anchor points line up vertically but keep their horizontal positions. As you probably expected, you get a perfectly vertical line.

Try the Average command again, selecting the Both option, and the path seems to vanish. It is still there, believe it or not, but the points that make it up now share the same horizontal and vertical position. Unless you want to collapse a line into a single point, use the Both option only on paths with more than two anchors.

The Average command is useful for straightening out lopsided figures. Consider, for instance, the not-quite-rectangular rectangle in Figure 12.8. By selecting the anchor points on the right and averaging them on the vertical axis, the rectangle snaps into shape.

Figure 12.8

Averaging these anchor points on the vertical axis straightens out this lopsided rectangle.

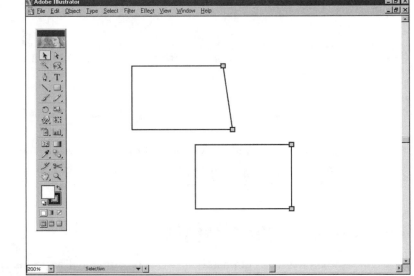

Simplifying Paths

Illustrator's Simplify command removes anchor points from a path without changing the path's general shape. Use this command to clean up *extraneous anchor points,* or anchors that the path doesn't need to define its shape. Illustrator is clever enough not to give you extraneous anchor points without your asking, but you can add them accidentally (or on purpose) by way of the Pen or the Add Anchor Points command.

Draw a rectangle, and then use Object ➔ Path ➔ Add Anchor Points to create some extraneous anchors on the path. Choose Object ➔ Path ➔ Simplify, and the Simplify dialog box appears. Check the option for Straight Lines at the bottom of the dialog box, because you want the rectangle to keep its straight segments. Also check the Preview box.

Now adjust the Angle Threshold slider until the extraneous anchor points disappear on the path. You shouldn't have to nudge the slider much. A single degree should do the trick. Click OK, and the path casts off its needless burden.

Try the same trick with an ellipse. Add a bunch of extra anchor points, and then get rid of them with Object → Path → Simplify. Check the Preview box as needed in the Simplify dialog box, but uncheck the Straight Lines option this time, because you want the ellipse to have curved segments. Drag the Curve Position slider until the extra anchor points disappear. You shouldn't need to touch the Angle Threshold slider. Then click OK to clean the path.

!#%@   Word Balloon

Extraneous anchor **points** are anchors that a path doesn't need to define its shape.

Oversimplifying complex paths can create some interesting effects, as a certain tailed ape can attest in Figure 12.9.

Figure 12.9

The Simplify command can clean up extraneous anchor points, but oversimplification has unusual results.

A Logo with Simple Needs

In honor of Astro Ape's conversion to the cubist movement, you can begin to create the logo for the comic strip with some intentional oversimplification.

You may recall from Chapter 11, "Inserting Type," that I discussed creating type outlines, or changing pieces of text into paths. This enables you to adjust the shapes of the letters with the usual path-editing tools and commands. When I mentioned this, you probably thought that I meant the Direct Selection tool, and you may have anticipated a practice exercise in which I asked you to change the letter b into the symbol for infinity or some such nonsense. To be honest, I had something far more nefarious in mind.

Drawing Perspectives

Cubism as an art movement lasted from 1907 to 1914. Its goal was to break down natural, three-dimensional shapes into abstract, two-dimensional forms. The picture of Astro Ape in Figure 12.9 is not a good representation of the cubist aesthetic.

Art Alert

Remember, converting text to paths is a one-way trip, unless you use Edit ➔ Undo.

When you create type outlines, you get very complex paths with all kinds of anchor points. And the more anchor points a path has, the more interesting effects you can achieve by oversimplifying it. You can start with a solid, all-purpose font like Myriad, the Illustrator default, and end up with some strange, futuristic-looking letters as befitting the Astro Ape logo.

With that thought to tempt you, open a new document window and adjust the magnification to 200%. Also, bring up the Character palette with Window ➔ Type ➔ Character if you don't see this palette on your screen already.

Take the Type tool from the toolbox, and select Myriad from the Font list on the Character palette. Set the type style to Roman, and adjust the type size to 48 points.

You don't need a type area for this, so click once with the Type tool to summon the flashing cursor. Key in the words *astro ape.* Press the Enter or Return key after the word *astro* so that the words appear on two lines of type. I'm using all lowercase letters, as you can see in Figure 12.10. Proofread your work, and then hold down Ctrl (Windows) or Command (Mac) and click a blank area of the screen.

Figure 12.10

Use the Type tool to key in the words of the logo.

Now click the piece of text with the Selection tool, and choose Type → Create Outlines. (If you have a two-button mouse, right-clicking the selection also gives you the Create Outlines command.) The letters change into ordinary paths. Look at all those anchor points in Figure 12.11! This is going to be fun.

Figure 12.11

Choose Type → Create Outlines to convert the text to paths. As you can see, typographical paths are rich with anchor points.

Choose Object → Path → Simplify, and start dragging sliders. Notice how the letters change shape as you remove anchor points. After much experimentation, I'm settling on a curve precision of 60% and an angle threshold of 91 degrees. The angle threshold keeps the letter *t* in shape. I didn't use the Straight Lines option to preserve the roundness of the vowels and the *s*. Have a look at my results in Figure 12.12.

You have the beginnings of something here. There is much more fun with the logo to come, but for now, save your work as *aa_logo.ai*. Somewhere, I'm sure, the philosopher Heraclitus is smiling.

Drawing Perspectives

If you had kept the words on the same line of type, or if you had centered them instead of aligning them to the left, the results of the Simplify command would have been different! As you try out this technique on the characters of different fonts, as I'm sure you will, experiment also with altering the alignment settings.

Figure 12.12

A little controlled oversimplification creates fun, futuristic letters in the proper spirit of Astro Ape.

The Least You Need To Know

- Add anchor points to create more opportunities for the Direct Selection tool.
- Delete anchor points to simplify a shape.
- Create flowing curves more easily by converting corner points to smooth points.
- Average anchor points to create perfectly horizontal and vertical lines or segments.
- Simplify paths to remove extraneous anchor points.
- Oversimplifying paths can create interesting effects.

Organizing Objects

In This Chapter

- ◆ Working with groups
- ◆ Aligning and distributing objects
- ◆ Working with layers
- ◆ Creating groups for the Astro Ape comic

Technical people like to make up their own names for things, and computer programmers are no exception. Computer programmers don't turn their computers on and off. They "boot up" and "power down" instead. They would rather "create a data asset" than save a file. So when these people talk about "objects," you can bet there is an understandable idea lurking somewhere beneath the jargon.

In computer illustration, an *object* is simply a thing unto itself, like an item on a shelf. When you click part of your illustration with the Selection tool, the object is what you select, and the object is what you can move around the document window. Therefore, every time you create a path with a drawing tool, you add a new object to your illustration.

Depending on how you organize these objects, you can make your life happier and easier. This chapter explores some of the methods for organizing objects and the advantages of doing so.

Making Groups

A *group* is an object that contains other objects. When you click a group with the Selection tool, you automatically select all the objects in the group. If you move the group around the document window, all the objects in the group move in exactly the same way. The group behaves like a single path, in other words, even though it might contain a dozen paths.

The great advantage to making groups, of course, is that it saves you time and effort. In vector graphics, as you know well by now, a single illustration is hardly ever a single path. Group together the paths that form a figure, and you can move the figure around the document window as a whole. You can scale it, rotate it, and change its appearance attributes collectively as if it were a single path.

Demonstrating this concept is easy. Draw a few paths with different fill colors and arrange them to form a simple figure, like the alien life form I created in Figure 13.1. Even this basic drawing has 10 paths. Now, if you want to move the alien to a different position on the screen, you can move all 10 paths individually, one at a time, or you can create a group.

Figure 13.1

This alien may look friendly, but he is difficult to work with unless you group the 10 component paths.

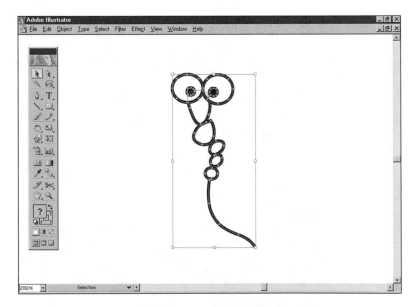

To create the group, first select all the paths that you want to group together. You can hold down Shift and click each path with the Selection tool, as you have done before, or you can drag a marquee. A *marquee* is a rectangular selection zone that selects everything that falls inside it. This is the quickest way to select a large number of paths. To make a marquee, hold down the mouse button and drag with the Selection tool. A thin rectangle appears. Adjust the size and shape of the marquee as you go. When you release the mouse button, you select everything inside the area of the rectangle.

After you select all the paths, choose Object → Group. If you have a right mouse button, you can right-click the selection and pull the Group command from the context menu. You have now inserted a new object into the illustration—a group object that, in the case of the alien, contains 10 path objects. Click the alien group with the Selection tool, and you can move it anywhere you like. Drag the handles of the group's bounding box, and the group changes size.

Let me direct your attention to the toolbox or the Color palette, where you will note that the fill-color and stroke-color squares have gray question-mark patterns instead of color values. This signifies that the paths in the group have different colors. The color squares speak the truth. The eyeballs of the alien have black fills, and the other paths have white fills.

If you want to give all the paths in the group the same fill and stroke colors, proceed as if you were coloring a single path. Therefore, to change the fill of all the paths in the group to pure blue, click the fill-color square on the Color palette, drag the blue slider to 255, and drag the other sliders to zero. To change the stroke color of the paths to white, click the stroke-color square and drag all the sliders to 255. Every path in the group promptly changes color, saving you the hassle of applying the same color scheme to each path, as Figure 13.2 shows. Notice also that the question marks have disappeared; the color squares now show blue and white, meaning that all the paths in the group have the color scheme.

> **Pointers**
>
> Marquees aren't always precise. If you select more paths than you want with a marquee, hold down Shift and click the paths that you want to exclude from the selection.

> **Drawing Perspectives**
>
> Normally, when you drag the handles of a type area's bounding box, the container for the type changes size, but the type itself doesn't. If you group a type area with a path and then resize the group, however, the type inside the container stretches.

Selecting Group Members

You will not always want to make changes to all the paths in a group. For instance, in Figure 13.2, you may decide to change the bottom path so that it has a blue stroke and no fill but keep the other paths as they are.

Figure 13.2

After you group the paths, you can change the fill and stroke colors for all the paths in the group as if you were coloring a single path.

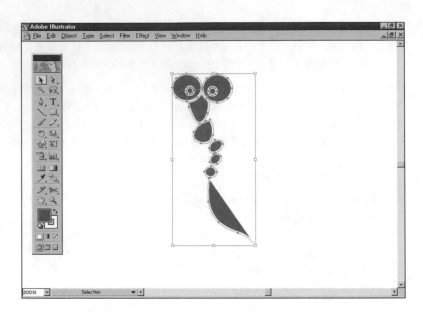

There's an easy way to do this. As a matter of fact, there's a dedicated tool for the job. It's the Group Selection tool, and it's hiding underneath the Direct Selection tool in the toolbox, as you can see in Figure 13.3.

Figure 13.3

Use the Group Selection tool to select individual paths within a group.

This tool's name is slightly misleading. It doesn't select groups, as you might guess. The regular old Selection tool does that. Instead, the Group Selection tool selects an individual path within a group and enables you to make changes to that path alone.

Using the Group Selection tool, click the bottom path of the alien drawing. Then go to the toolbox or the Color palette, apply blue to the stroke, and turn off the fill. The bottom path changes accordingly, leaving the other paths of the group as they were. Figure 13.4 shows the results.

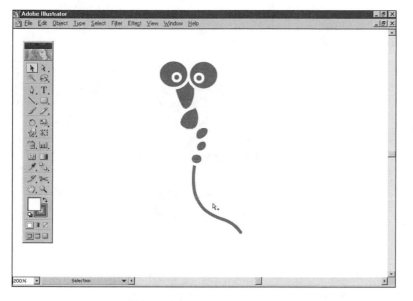

Figure 13.4

By clicking the bottom path with the Group Selection tool, you can change the attributes of that path alone without affecting the other paths in the group.

You can change more than just the color. Change the position of a path by dragging it with the Group Selection tool. To scale the path, first click it with the Group Selection tool, and then switch to the regular Selection tool. A bounding box appears around the path. Drag the handles, and the path changes size.

To select multiple objects in the group without picking up the whole thing, you can hold down Shift and click with the Group Selection tool, or you can drag a marquee.

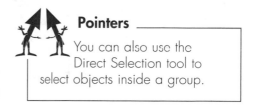

Pointers

You can also use the Direct Selection tool to select objects inside a group.

Ungrouping Groups

Sometimes groups outlive their usefulness, like when you want to make many different kinds of changes to the component paths. True, you could use the Group Selection tool, but that can get clumsy if you need to do scaling.

The best thing to do in these cases is to ungroup the paths. To do so, select the group, choose Object ➔ Ungroup from the menu, and click a blank area of the page. You can also right-click the selection for the Ungroup command.

It goes without saying that you're free to regroup the paths after you make your changes.

Aligning and Distributing Objects

At times, you need objects to fall on a perfectly horizontal or vertical line. At other times, you need to space out objects evenly. Sure, you could eyeball it, but why waste your time nudging paths around with the arrow keys? It's quicker and more precise to use the Align palette, which comes up when you choose Window → Align (see Figure 13.5).

Drawing Perspectives

Macromedia FreeHand has a dedicated button on the main toolbar for aligning and distributing objects.

The Align palette gives you buttons for aligning and distributing the objects in your illustration. *Aligning* objects means arranging them in a straight line. *Distributing* them means spacing them evenly within a given area. You have six choices for each operation. The little diagram on each button shows you what the button does.

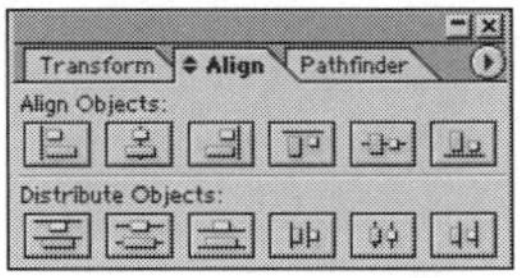

Figure 13.5

Use the Align palette to align and distribute objects.

Try out the Align palette by drawing a few random paths. Select the paths and click the second button from the left in the top row of the palette. The paths fall into a straight line, as Figure 13.6 shows.

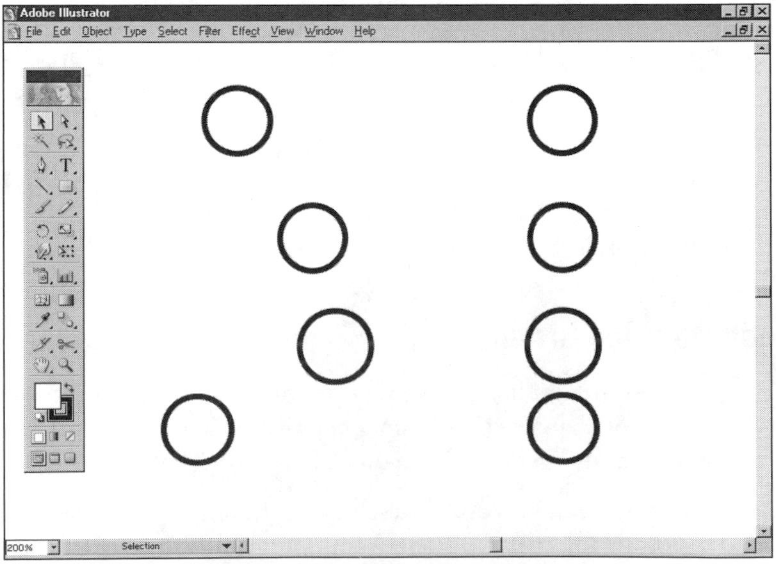

Figure 13.6

Illustrator aligned these circles on their center points.

Now, to space the paths out evenly, go back to the Align palette and click the second button from the left on the bottom row. Illustrator distributes the paths on their center points, as Figure 13.7 shows.

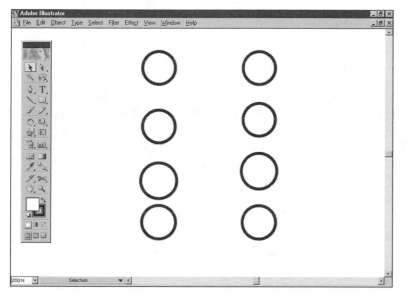

Figure 13.7

Illustrator distributed these circles on their center points.

Using Layers

In Illustrator and other graphics programs, a *layer* is like a clear sheet of plastic that you place over the artboard. You can draw directly on the layer, or you can cut objects from the artboard and paste them there. Objects that you place on the layer cover up objects on the artboard, but otherwise the layer remains perfectly transparent. You can add as many layers to your illustration as you want.

Illustrator's Layers palette makes working with layers easy (see Figure 13.8). Call up the Layers palette under Window → Layers.

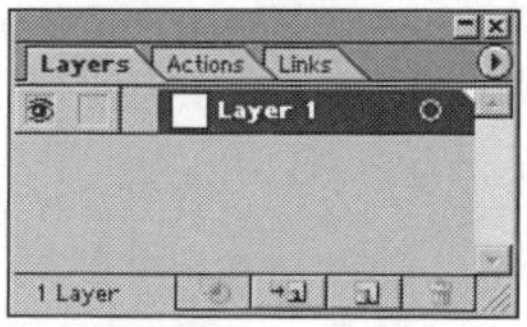

Figure 13.8

You can use the Layers palette to manage the layers of your illustration.

As you can see, your illustration already has a layer. You may not have realized it, but you have been using a layer all along! Layer 1 is the artboard itself. To prove it, grab some drawing tools and create a few multicolored paths. The little thumbnail image for Layer 1 in the Layers palette makes a faithful, if small, representation of the artboard art.

Now click the small triangle icon to the left of the thumbnail image. This shows the objects that the layer contains. Go back to the artboard and group the paths. The object list in the Layers palette changes from several individual path objects to a single group object. The group object also gives you another triangle icon, which you can click to see the individual members of the group.

These object lists are actually very useful. Remember changing the stacking order under Object → Arrange? You may have bad memories of this process if you had a number of paths to arrange, and you may have wondered whether there was an easier way to reorder the stack. As a matter of fact, there is. All you have to do is drag around the objects in the list. Click an object in the list and hold down the mouse button. Roll the mouse away from you to place the object higher in the stacking order, or pull the mouse toward you to place the object lower. Release the mouse button when the object occupies the correct position in the stack.

Pointers

You will find billions of uses for the object lists on the Layers palette. Here's a good one: You can add a path to an existing group by dragging the path object from its place in the list and dropping it into the group object's list. You can just as easily remove a path from a group by dragging the path object outside the group object's list, and you can change the stacking order of the objects within the group by shuffling their positions in the list. Illustrator doesn't give you menu commands for some of these actions, so keep the Layers palette handy when you work with groups.

But I digress. Click the triangle icons again to close the object lists until only the Layer 1 object shows. Now click the third button from the left at the bottom of the Layers palette. This adds a new layer, Layer 2, to your illustration, with a white thumbnail image beside it.

If you glance at the artboard, you will note that your illustration looks exactly the same. You cannot tell that you have added a layer. This is as it should be. Layers themselves are completely transparent. The white thumbnail image in the Layers palette doesn't mean that Layer 2 is white, like an opaque piece of paper. Instead, the white in the thumbnail signifies transparency.

Grab a drawing tool and create a path. You have added an object to the new layer. Again, looking at the illustration, you cannot really tell a difference. You could have drawn this object in Layer 1, and the art would have looked exactly the same.

Click the new path with the Selection tool, and notice the red bounding box. Red signifies that the object resides on Layer 2. Click one of the other objects, and the bounding box turns blue. Blue is the color of Layer 1. This color-coding helps you keep track of which objects are on which layers.

With the Selection tool, move the objects so that they sit on top of each other. Now go to the Layers palette, click on Layer 2, and hold down the mouse button. Drag the mouse toward you, so that Layer 2 drops below Layer 1 in the list, and release the mouse button.

Now, at last, you can see a difference in the illustration! The Layer 2 object disappears behind everything in Layer 1. Drag Layer 1 back to the bottom of the list, and the object in Layer 2 returns to the foreground.

So it goes, no matter how many layers you add to your art. Objects in the uppermost layer always sit on top of objects in the lower layers. This is sort of like shuffling the stacking order, with one important difference. If you click an object in a lower layer and choose Object ➜ Arrange ➜ Bring To Front, the object only goes as far as the top of its layer. Objects in the higher layers remain farther up in the illustration. In other words, every layer has its own stacking order. If Layer 2 is on top of Layer 1 in the Layers palette, then the lowest object in Layer 2 will always sit above the highest object in Layer 1, no matter what you do with the stacking order.

What's the advantage to using multiple layers, you might wonder. Because Layer 1 has a perfectly good stacking order, you can put objects in front of other objects without the bother of adding new layers. As always, you make a good point.

Many times, the usefulness of layers lies in what you don't see. The little eyeball icons to the left of the layers control visibility. Click an eyeball, and all the objects on the corresponding layer disappear. Click the empty box, and the eyeball icon comes back, along with the objects of the layer.

> ### Drawing Perspectives
>
> Illustrator's color-coding of layers is arbitrary, and you are free to change it. To do so, double-click a layer on the Layers palette and choose a new color from the drop-down list. You can also change the name of the layer this way.

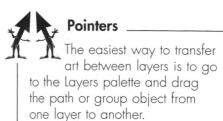

Pointers

The easiest way to transfer art between layers is to go to the Layers palette and drag the path or group object from one layer to another.

Use this feature to try out different combinations of the foreground and background in your illustration. For instance, if you were creating a scene of a monkey in a space suit walking across a cartoon landscape, you could start out by drawing the landscape in Layer 1. Create a second layer for the monkey, and draw away, making sure to group the monkey paths when you finish. Then click the monkey group with the Selection tool and choose Edit ➜ Copy from the menu. Add a third layer to the illustration, and choose Edit ➜ Paste. This places an identical copy of the monkey onto Layer 3. Position the two monkey illustrations as you desire. By alternating the visibility of the second and third

Art Alert

Don't bother trying to add objects to a locked layer, because Illustrator won't stand for it. The drawing tool icons appear with slashes through them when you move them into the document window. Unlock the layer first, and you can draw in it normally.

layers, you can determine which design works best for the illustration. Finally, delete the layer that you don't need by highlighting it on the Layers palette and clicking the button with the trashcan icon.

You can also lock a layer by clicking the empty square to the right of the eyeball icon. A padlock icon appears in the square. Locked layers are completely frozen. You can still see their objects in your illustration, but you cannot select the objects or change them in any way. This prevents you from accidentally messing up a design or editing an object that you didn't mean to edit. If you need to change an object on a locked layer, click the padlock icon. The padlock disappears, and the layer reopens for business.

Creating Type Layers

In the professional world, it's not unusual for computer illustrators to place all the type for an illustration into a single layer, which you can call a *type layer* for obvious reasons. Type layers make it easier for editors and art directors to work with the piece after it leaves the artist's desk.

Type layers can also help you, and you don't even need to be a professional designer. All you need are Adobe Illustrator and Adobe Photoshop.

I haven't talked much about Photoshop yet, but that shouldn't matter. You may recall that Photoshop is an image editor, which means that it works best with pixels, not paths. Photoshop and Illustrator make a good team in spite of their differences, and you can load artwork that you created in one for use in the other. With this in mind, if you place all the text of an Illustrator file on a single layer, you can edit the text freely when you bring the file into Photoshop.

Here's how the process works. Before you use the Type tool in Illustrator, create a new layer and position it wherever you want in relation to the other layers of your illustration. Then grab the Type tool and add text. If you already have type on other layers, simply drag the existing type objects to the new layer.

When you're ready to go to Photoshop, save your work, but don't choose File ➔ Save. Choose File ➔ Export instead, and pick Photoshop from the Save As Type dropdown list. When you click the Save button, the Photoshop Options dialog box appears. Put a check mark in the box for Editable Text, and click OK. Now, when you launch Photoshop and open the exported artwork, you can modify all the text with the Photoshop Type tool.

Of course, if you don't plan to work with the text in Photoshop, you don't have to export your artwork in Photoshop format. Save your drawing as an Illustrator file under File ➔ Save as you normally would. You will still be able to load the Illustrator file into Photoshop for processing, although you will not be able to use the Photoshop Type tool to edit the text.

In Part 6, "Applying Finishing Touches," I talk about processing Illustrator art with Photoshop.

Locking Objects

Here's the situation. You have an object that you want to lock down. You don't want to change it anymore, and you're happy with its position in the illustration. However, this object sits in a layer with other objects that you do want to edit. If you lock the layer, you lose the capability to edit the other objects. But if you leave the layer unlocked, you might accidentally change the object that you don't want to touch.

Fortunately, Illustrator enables you to lock down individual objects, not just layers. Click the object in question with the Selection tool, and choose Object ➔ Lock. The object stays put, enabling you to work freely with other objects on the layer.

Unlocking the object is a bit trickier. You can choose Object ➔ Unlock All from the menu, but as the name of the item suggests, this operation unlocks every locked object in your illustration, which you might not want. The best way to unlock objects is to use the Layers palette. Click the triangle icon next to the layer that contains the locked object, and note that the locked object has a padlock icon. Click this icon to remove the padlock and thereby unlock the object.

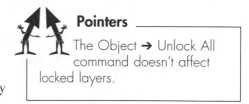

Pointers

The Object ➔ Unlock All command doesn't affect locked layers.

The Order of the Monkey

The Astro Ape exercise for this chapter is low-key, but it's important. It won't be long now before you begin combining the various files, and you can save yourself a good deal of time and aggravation if you group the paths that make up each illustration.

I'll bet you saw this one coming. You may recall that, when you created the mockup illustrations for your refrigerator door, I pointed out that grouping the paths would make your life easier. Now that you know something more about groups, I'm sure you agree wholeheartedly.

So far, five files will benefit from the grouping treatment: *aa_side_color.ai*, *aa_rear_color.ai*, *aa_sign_type.ai*, *aa_background_ai*, and *aa_wordballoon_ai*.

Drawing Perspectives

What about the *aa_logo.ai* file from Chapter 12, "Manipulating Paths"? Doesn't anything in that file require grouping? Not in this case. If you open the file and click the letter paths with the Selection tool, you will see that Illustrator automatically grouped them when you issued the Create Outlines command. In fact, you can ungroup the letters if you want and rearrange them with the Selection tool. If you do this, just make sure to group them back up again before saving your work.

Go ahead and open these files in Illustrator. For each one, choose Edit ➔ Select All to select all the paths, and then choose Object ➔ Group to group them. Save your work under File ➔ Save, and close the document window. You're done!

The Least You Need to Know

- An object is what you select with the Selection tool.
- A group is an object that contains other objects.
- Drag the Selection tool to create a marquee.
- Use the Group Selection tool to modify objects within a group.
- Use the Align palette to line up and distribute objects.
- Organize your illustration into layers to try out different combinations of the foreground and background.
- Put all your type into a layer of its own if you plan to edit text in Photoshop.
- You can lock layers as well as individual objects.

Applying Transformations

In This Chapter

- ◆ Using the transformation tools
- ◆ Transforming paths mathematically
- ◆ Creating a running pose for the Astro Ape comic

You know that paths are easy to change. You can stretch and rotate the bounding box of a path with the Selection tool. You can get at the segments and anchor points of a path with the Direct Selection tool. You can process a path with commands like Object → Path → Average and Object → Path → Simplify.

But there's more! Much more. Illustrator offers a host of tools for just this sort of thing. These are the transformation tools. This chapter looks at the transformation tools and shows you how to use them for more than just special effects.

Anatomy of a Transformation

Let me define a term here before I get too carried away. A *transformation*, in the broadest sense, is any kind of modification to a path. When you push anchor points around with the Direct Selection tool, you are, in essence, applying a transformation. However, when most computer illustrators talk about transformations, they mean specifically the transformations that come from Illustrator's dedicated tools and commands, not necessarily the transformations that you create manually.

!#%@ Word Balloon

A **transformation** is any kind of modification to a path, especially when the modification comes from a transformation tool or command. Transformations have two kinds of controls: the bounding box and the point of origin.

Drawing Perspectives

In Adobe Illustrator, the transformation controls are the bounding box and the point of origin. In Macromedia FreeHand, they are the transformation handles and the fixed point or centerpoint.

Some transformations happen by way of the *bounding box*. You know this control well. This is the rectangle with handles that appears around a shape when you click it with the Selection tool. In fact, every time you dragged the handles of a bounding box, you were applying a transformation, even if you didn't realize it.

Many transformations have a different control: the *point of origin*. Unlike the bounding box, the point of origin doesn't automatically appear when you click an object with the Selection tool. If you want to set the point of origin, you have to use the transformation tools.

What is the point of origin? Think of it as the reference point for the transformation. When you apply a transformation tool to an object, the point of origin is where the transformation happens. In a rotation, for instance, the point of origin acts like the hub of a wheel. The object rotates around this point.

If this isn't quite clear, don't fret. You will see exactly how the point of origin works when you try a few examples.

Scaling

Scaling is nothing new. You have scaled so many paths by now that you could be a professional. All you have to do is click an object with the Selection tool and drag a handle. The path scales, or changes size, at your whim. Hold down the Shift key, and the object maintains its proportions.

This is scaling at its quickest and dirtiest. For more precise control over the scaling process, use the Scale tool. This is the tool directly under the Pencil in the toolbox, as Figure 14.1 shows.

Give the Scale tool a try. First, draw a path, and then grab the Scale tool from the toolbox. Notice that a bounding box doesn't appear around the path that you drew. Instead, if you look at the center of the path, you will find a circular icon with four spokes, like in Figure 14.2. This is the point of origin. By default, the *point of origin* is always dead center. You can easily change it, but leave it where it is for now.

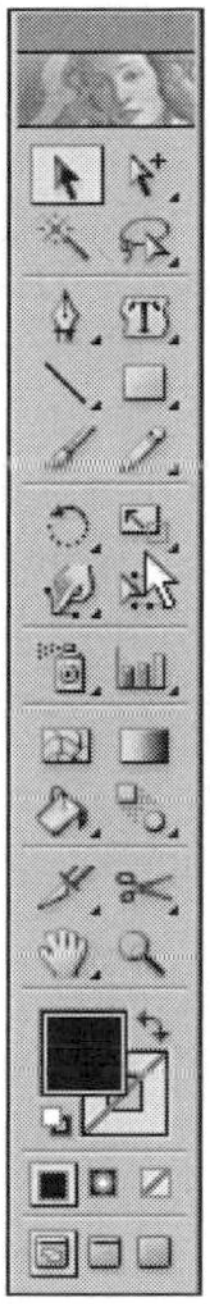

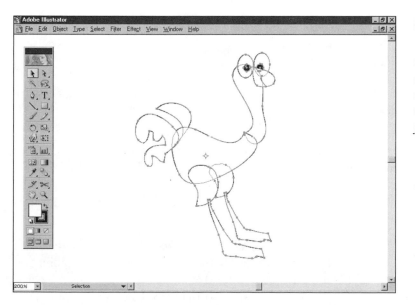

Figure 14.1

Use the Scale tool to change the size of an object.

Figure 14.2

When you use a transformation tool, you get a circular icon with four spokes. This is the point of origin, or the reference point of the transformation.

Move the mouse pointer into the document window, and the pointer becomes crosshairs. This is your signal that the transformation is ready to go. For fine control, keep the crosshairs away from the point of origin. For quicker going, bring the crosshairs toward the point of origin. Just don't place the crosshairs on top of the point of origin—at least not yet.

Position the crosshairs anywhere on the path, and hold down the mouse button. Drag left and right to scale the path horizontally, or drag toward you and away from you to scale the path vertically. If you press Shift while you drag, the object scales uniformly. To finish, release the mouse button, and you get something like Figure 14.3.

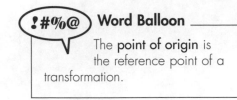

Word Balloon

The **point of origin** is the reference point of a transformation.

Figure 14.3

Taking the Scale tool to the path on the left gives you something like the path on the right.

Now move the crosshairs on top of the point of origin, hold down the mouse button, and drag. The point of origin follows. You can drop it anywhere inside the document window by releasing the mouse button. Then reposition the crosshairs, and scale the object from the new point of origin.

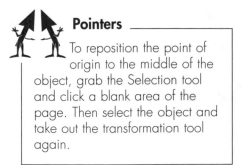

Pointers

To reposition the point of origin to the middle of the object, grab the Selection tool and click a blank area of the page. Then select the object and take out the transformation tool again.

The point of origin works like a thumbtack or the tip of your finger. It holds the object in place at that point, and the object scales around it. If you don't notice a difference in the way that the path scales, try moving the point of origin to the lower-left corner of the object, and then scale up and to the right. Then move the point of origin to the top-left corner and scale the object down and to the left.

Rotating

You can rotate objects with the Selection tool. Click the object and move the mouse pointer in the vicinity of one of the corner handles until the pointer changes to a curved arrow. Hold down the mouse button and drag, and the object rotates. This is old news.

As an alternative, you can use the Rotate tool, which sits to the left of the Scale tool in the toolbox (see Figure 14.4). Much like the Scale tool, the Rotate tool gives you better control over the transformation by enabling you to change the point of origin. As I mentioned before, the point of origin in a rotation is like the hub of a wheel. It's the point around which the object rotates.

Figure 14.4

Use the Rotate tool to rotate objects with greater precision than the Selection tool allows.

Here's how the process works. Draw a new path or click an existing path with the Selection tool, and then grab the Rotate tool. Note the point of origin in the middle of the path. Now move the mouse pointer anywhere inside the document window. As with the Scale tool, the farther you keep the pointer from the point of origin, the greater the precision of the Rotate tool.

To rotate the object, hold down the mouse button. Drag toward you to rotate clockwise, or drag away from you to rotate counterclockwise. Hold down Shift to constrain the angle of rotation to multiples of 45 degrees. To finish, release the mouse button. You get something like what you see in Figure 14.5.

Art Alert

Don't try to rotate a featureless circle! The transformation works just fine, but you will not be able to tell the difference.

Figure 14.5

The Rotate tool takes objects like the one on the left and gives you objects like the one on the right.

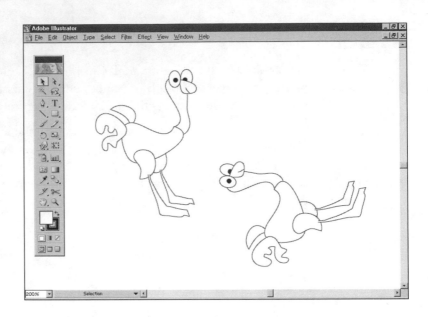

Now try repositioning the point of origin. Move the crosshairs directly on top of the point, and drag it anywhere inside the document window. Then move the crosshairs to a blank area of the page, hold down the mouse button again, and rotate the object. You should notice a difference in the transformation right away. The object rotates around its new point of origin instead of its center.

Reflecting

Reflecting an object means to change the object into its mirror image. Use the Reflect tool to achieve this effect. The Reflect tool is under the Rotate tool in the toolbox, as you can see in Figure 14.6.

Figure 14.6

The Reflect tool transforms an object into its mirror image.

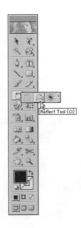

This tool works a bit differently than the Rotate tool and the Scale tool. I will step you through the procedure.

First, draw a path or select an existing path, and pick up the Reflect tool. The mouse pointer changes into crosshairs. Move the crosshairs into the document window, click the point of origin, and release the mouse button. Do not hold down the button or drag the mouse. Just click once and let go. The mouse pointer changes from crosshairs to a solid black arrowhead.

To reflect the object horizontally, move the arrowhead anywhere above or below the point of origin and click the mouse. To reflect the object vertically, move the arrowhead to the left or right of the point of origin and click. If you hold down the mouse button and drag instead of clicking and releasing, you can rotate the reflected object into position. See Figure 14.7 for an example.

Pointers

If you want to use the existing point of origin in a reflection, you don't have to click the point while the mouse pointer is in the form of crosshairs. Just hold down the mouse button and drag to reflect the object. This shortcut isn't always so short, because it requires you to rotate the reflected object into place.

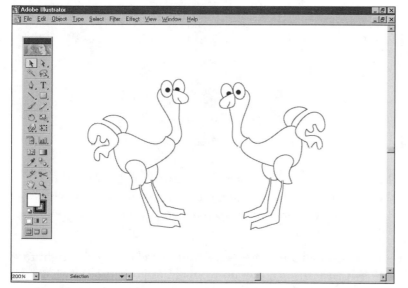

Figure 14.7

Create evil twins, opposite numbers, and antiheroes with the Reflect tool. (The evil one is the one on the right.)

Give it another try. Notice that the mouse pointer has changed back into crosshairs. This time, instead of clicking exactly on top of the point of origin, click elsewhere in the document window. The point of origin jumps from the middle of the path to the location you specified, and the mouse pointer once again turns into an arrowhead. Reflect away, following the same guidelines. Click above or below the point of origin to reflect the object horizontally, click to the left or right of the point of origin to reflect vertically, or hold down the mouse button and drag to rotate the reflected object.

The point of origin in a reflection is like the surface of a mirror. The farther the point of origin from the object, the farther inside the mirror the reflection appears.

Shearing

When you *shear* an object, you slant it horizontally or vertically. Use the Shear tool for this sort of thing. The Shear tool hides under the Scale tool in the toolbox, as Figure 14.8 shows.

Figure 14.8

Use the Shear tool to slant or skew an object along an axis.

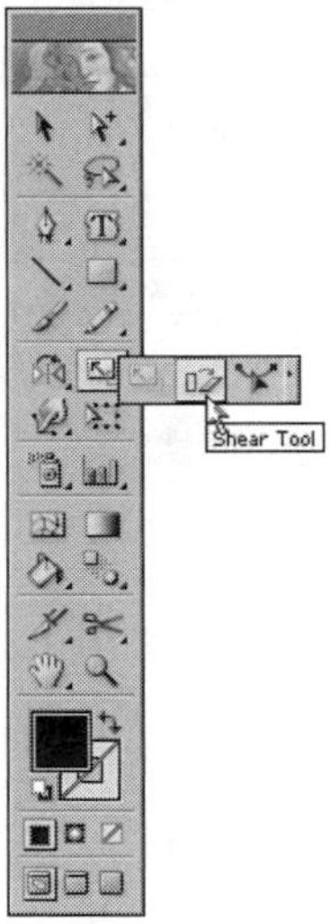

The Shear tool works like the Reflect and Scale tools. Draw or select an object, choose the Shear tool, and set the point of origin by dragging it to the desired location. Then position the crosshairs. Like before, the farther you keep the crosshairs from the point of origin, the more precise the transformation.

Drawing Perspectives
In other drawing programs, shearing goes by the name of *skewing*.

Hold down the mouse button and drag left or right to shear the object horizontally, as in Figure 14.9. Drag toward you or away from you to shear the object vertically. Hold down Shift to constrain the transformation to multiples of 45 degrees.

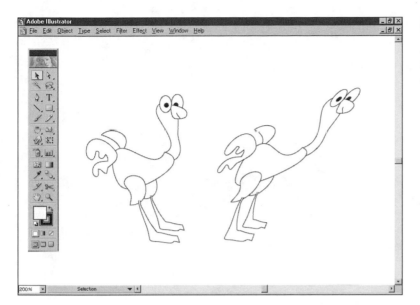

Figure 14.9

Put a horizontal slant on things by dragging with the Shear tool.

Shearing is especially useful for creating shadows. Allow me to demonstrate.

Start with an object. Select it, and grab the Shear tool. Drag the point of origin to the vicinity of the object's base. In the case of the ostrich I've been using for these examples, the base is the feet. Then shear the object along both axes by dragging diagonally. Trust your eyeballs here. When the shadow looks about right, hold down Alt (Windows) or Option (Mac) and release the mouse button. Holding down Alt or Option creates an identical copy of the object and applies the transformation to the copy instead, leaving the original object as it is. This trick works for all the transformation tools, by the way.

All you have to do now is make the shadow look like a shadow. Select it, call up the Color palette, and specify a black fill and stroke. Choose Object ➔ Arrange ➔ Send Backward to put the shadow behind the object that's casting it, and fine-tune the shadow's position with the arrow keys. See Figure 14.10 for the results.

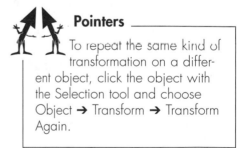

Pointers

To repeat the same kind of transformation on a different object, click the object with the Selection tool and choose Object ➔ Transform ➔ Transform Again.

Figure 14.10

With a few simple steps, the Shear tool creates serviceable shadows. Nice!

Distorting

Distorting an object enables you to reposition the handles of the object's bounding box as if the handles were anchor points. This repositioning causes the object to change shape. Use the Free Transform tool for distortions. This tool sits under the Scale tool in the toolbox, as Figure 14.11 shows.

Figure 14.11

The Free Transform tool enables you to distort the shape of an object.

The Free Transform tool isn't like the other transformation tools, in that it gives you a bounding box instead of a point of origin—a bounding box that you can scale and rotate. In this regard, the Free Transform tool is like the Selection tool. But you can also distort the Free Transform tool's bounding box—a feature that the Selection tool's bounding box doesn't have.

To distort an object, click the object with the Selection tool. Then grab the Free Transform tool from the toolbox. When you click the Free Transform tool, the object's bounding box switches to the kind that you can distort. The bounding box doesn't look any different, but it behaves differently, as you will soon see.

Move the mouse pointer to one of the corner handles. The pointer changes to a diagonal arrow. Hold down the mouse button and begin to drag the handle. The object begins to scale. Now hold down Ctrl (Windows) or Command (Mac). Scaling stops abruptly, and you find that you can move the handle as if it were an anchor point. The object distorts as you change the shape of the bounding box that contains it. Release the mouse button to finish.

> **Drawing Perspectives**
>
> Look under Effect ➔ Distort & Transform for a number of specialty distortion commands. I talk about these commands in Chapter 19, "Adding Effects."

Distort the object as much as you want. Remember to start out by dragging one of the corner handles, and only press Ctrl (Windows) or Command (Mac) after you start dragging. After a few permutations, your object may look something like the one in Figure 14.12.

Figure 14.12

By distorting with the Free Transform tool, life becomes a carnival funhouse.

You can also use the Free Transform tool to distort an object in *perspective*, as shown in Figure 14.13. That is, you can create the illusion that the object is sitting in three-dimensional space. Keep in mind that Illustrator objects are two-dimensional, so they will always look flat, regardless of the perspective.

To distort in perspective, begin by dragging one of the corner handles of the Free Transform tool's bounding box, just like before. Then, instead of holding down Ctrl or Command, hold down Ctrl, Shift, and Alt for Windows or Command, Shift, and Option for the Macintosh. Continue dragging the mouse, and release the mouse button to finish.

> **!#%@ Word Balloon**
>
> **Perspective** is an illustration technique that creates the illusion of depth by shortening and lengthening certain lines of a drawing in a uniform way.

Figure 14.13

Distorting in perspective makes it seem like the object is sitting in three-dimensional space.

Transforming by Number

Remember in Chapter 7, "Generating Shapes," when you used the dialog boxes of the shape tools? You used these boxes to enter numerical values for the width and height, which gave you precise control over the size of your shapes. I bring this up only because the transformation tools offer the same kind of control.

If you need to transform an object to a fixed degree or by a known quantity, such as scaling an object to two and two-thirds its current size or reflecting an object perfectly vertically, the transformation dialog boxes are the way to go. To use them, select the object you want to transform. Then double-click the transformation tool of your choice. The corresponding dialog box appears, which is similar to the one shown in Figure 14.14.

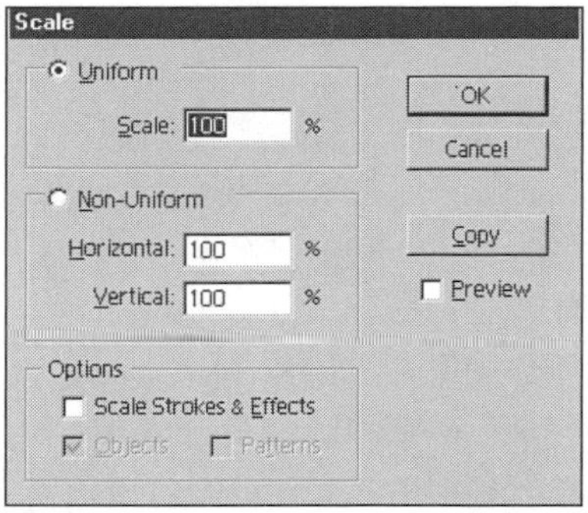

Figure 14.14

Use the transformation dialog boxes to transform an object according to precise numerical values.

Pointers

Another way to call up the transformation dialog boxes is to look under Object → Transform and select the name of the transformation that you want to apply. And another way to make transformations numerically is to use the Transform palette, which appears when you choose Window → Transform. In the Transform palette, use the X and Y fields to move the selected object to a new position on the artboard. Use the W and H fields to scale the object. Rotate and shear the object by typing values into the fields at the bottom of the palette. Open the palette menu, and you find commands for flipping the object as well as an option for scaling the object's stroke.

All the transformation dialog boxes have a Preview check box in the lower right corner. It's a good idea to check this box. That way, you can see the effects of the transformation before you commit to it.

Describe the transformation by typing values into the fields. If you checked the Preview box, press the Tab key to see what the transformation will look like. If all is to your liking, click OK to set the transformation.

The Scale dialog box has an extra option for scaling the stroke of the selected object. If you check this option, the weight of the stroke increases or decreases in proportion to the change in size. For instance, scaling an object with a 4-point stroke to twice its normal size changes the weight of the object's stroke to 8 points. If you aren't sure whether you should scale the stroke, use the Preview option and test the transformation both ways.

I should mention that the Free Transform tool doesn't have a dialog box, in case you go looking for it.

See Ape Run

Here follows a dirty rotten trick. This trick is so dirty and rotten that I'm almost ashamed to show it to you. It goes against everything that creative people ought to stand for, and it makes a compelling case for doing things the quick-and-easy way. But it works, and I use it all the time, and I'm going to show it to you.

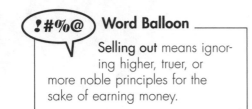

Word Balloon

Selling out means ignoring higher, truer, or more noble principles for the sake of earning money.

This trick falls under the heading of "repurposing content." I mentioned this subject once before, in Chapter 7, and if memory serves, my words were rather harsh. Repurposing content has to do with taking existing material, such as an illustration, and using it in a slightly different way to avoid the cost and labor of creating something new. In general, the bean counters love to repurpose content, but everyone else, including the audience, regards it with suspicion, and rightly so.

I might as well just come out and say it. In this section, you're going to take the existing Astro Ape side view and, using a few simple transformations, create a brand new pose of Astro Ape bounding happily along. Then, with a single command, you will make Astro Ape walk the opposite way. You will end up using both of these repurposed illustrations in the finished comic strip. And no one but the most acute observer will be able to tell the difference. That's what's so sneaky about this particular exercise. It's repurposed content, but most people will never catch on. The bean counters are going to love you for this.

Start out by opening *aa_side_color.ai*. You grouped the paths of this illustration at the end of Chapter 13, "Organizing Objects," so the first order of business is to ungroup the paths here. This is the best way to work with the individual paths.

Drawing Perspectives

If you rotate the foreground limbs inward and the background limbs outward, the illustration doesn't look quite as animated. You will use this design in the Astro Ape comic before you're through, but in a way that you might not expect. More on this in Chapter 20, "Putting the Pieces Together."

Click the leg path in the foreground with the Selection tool, and then grab the Rotate tool. Drag the point of origin to about the middle of the hip, and rotate the leg clockwise so that the toes are just about vertical to the ground. Then rotate the foreground arm. Put the point of origin in the middle of the shoulder, and rotate the path counterclockwise. Finally, rotate the background leg a few degrees counterclockwise and the background arm a few degrees clockwise, and you get something like Figure 14.15. You may need to fine-tune the position of the limbs with the Selection tool so that the pose looks more natural.

Figure 14.15

Rotate the limbs, and Astro Ape is on the move.

Choose Edit ➔ Select All and then Object ➔ Group to regroup the paths, and save your work as *aa_side_running1.ai*. Finished! If you thought that was easy, wait until you see the next one.

Click the group with the Selection tool, and double-click the Reflect tool. The Reflect dialog box appears. Choose the Vertical option under Axis, and then click the OK button. Astro Ape does a quick about-face, as Figure 14.16 shows.

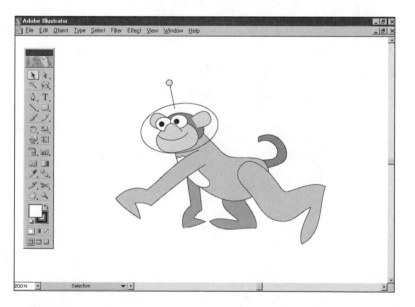

Figure 14.16

Send Astro Ape back to where he came from by using the Reflect tool.

There's no need to regroup these paths, because you never ungrouped them. Just save this file as *aa_side_running2.ai*, and try to put the cheap business of repurposing content behind you. Your muse may be throwing a temper tantrum right now, but look at it this way. You have three times as many Astro Ape side views as you did when you started this chapter, and as everyone knows, the quantity of a thing determines its quality.

The Least You Need to Know

- You can transform any object with Illustrator's dedicated set of tools.
- The transformation controls in Illustrator are the bounding box and the point of origin.
- The point of origin is the reference point of the transformation.
- Use the Shear tool to create shadows.
- For precise control, open the transformation dialog boxes or use the Transform palette.
- Apply transformations to copies of existing illustrations as a sneaky way to create "new" art.

Chapter 15

Creating Blend Objects

In This Chapter

◆ Using blends to create transitions in color and shape

◆ Adjusting the number of intermediate objects

◆ Working with the spine

◆ Adding a 3D effect to the Astro Ape logo

Imagine, if you will, an illustration with two objects: a circle in the upper left corner and a square in the lower right corner. Now imagine a series of intermediate shapes between them. These shapes start out round, like the circle, and gradually become more angular until they look just as square as the object at the bottom of the document window. Figure 15.1 illustrates exactly what I'm talking about.

This isn't just a bizarre thought exercise. It's the premise behind *blend objects* in Illustrator. Much as a gradient is a gradual shift between two or more colors, a blend object is a gradual shift in characteristics between two or more objects.

This chapter shows you how to make blend objects and gives you some ideas for using them to whet your creative appetite.

Figure 15.1

A blend object is a gradual shift in characteristics between two or more objects.

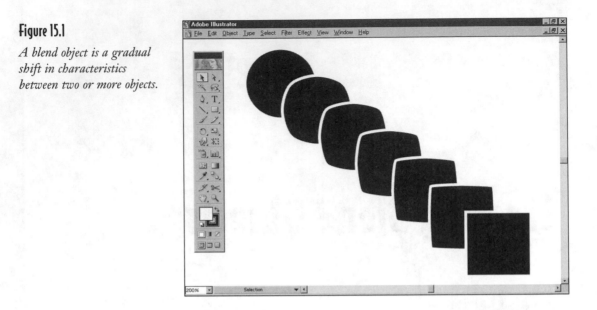

Getting the Blends

A blend object is a strange thing. It has two or more component objects, which act as the start point and end point, like the circle and square in Figure 15.1. Call the start point the *back* of the blend and the end point the *front*. A blend object also has a *spine*, which is the path that determines the direction of the blend. The intermediate shapes fall along this path.

The quickest way to create blend objects is to use the Blend tool. The Blend tool sits under the Gradient tool in the toolbox, as Figure 15.2 shows.

Figure 15.2

Create blend objects with the Blend tool.

The most common blends come in three different kinds. The first kind gives you intermediate steps in shape. The second kind gives you intermediate steps in color, and the third kind blends shape and color simultaneously. The procedure for creating all three is essentially the same, but the results are often different.

Creating Shape Blend Objects

In a shape blend, Illustrator draws variations in shape between the back and front objects, much like in Figure 15.1.

Art Alert

Creating blends puts your computer's processor through a workout. Don't be alarmed if you have to wait a few seconds before anything happens.

To create a shape blend, you need two different objects of the same color—say a triangle and circle. Draw these shapes as you normally would. Just to make things interesting, give the triangle a stroke weight of 6 points, and give the circle a stroke weight of 1 point. Then take out the Blend tool. The mouse pointer changes to the blend icon.

Move the pointer to the middle of the triangle, and watch for an X to appear next to the blend icon. When the X appears, click the mouse button. This defines the triangle as the back, or the start point of the blend.

Then move the mouse pointer to the middle of the circle, look for a plus sign to appear next to the icon, and click again. The circle becomes the front of the blend, and Illustrator automatically draws the intermediate shapes, as shown in Figure 15.3. Depending on the characteristics and the placement of the objects, you may get more intermediate steps than shown in Figure 15.3, or you may get fewer. I explain how to set the number of steps a bit later in this chapter. But notice in particular the gradual decline in stroke weight as the blend goes from a 6-point triangle to a 1 point circle.

Now grab the Selection tool and click the blend object. See the path that stretches from the back to the front? That's the spine. It's essentially a path like any other, although it doesn't have a stroke color or a fill color, which makes it invisible. Because the spine is just a regular path, you can adjust it with the Direct Selection tool, thereby changing the direction of the blend, as I demonstrate a bit later.

A blend requires at least two objects, but it can have more than two objects. Add a rectangle with a 10-point stroke to your illustration somewhere below the circle, and get out the Blend tool again.

Pointers

If you start out with more than two objects, click the Blend tool on each object in order of back to front. That is, the first object you click should be the start point in the blend. Proceed to the next object in the blend, and the next one, and so on, and finish by clicking the object that you want to have in front.

This time, click the circle first, and then move the mouse pointer to the rectangle. Watch for the plus sign to appear next to the blend icon, and click. The blend now passes from the triangle to the circle and from the circle on to the rectangle, as Figure 15.4 shows.

Figure 15.3

A shape blend object goes from one shape to another.

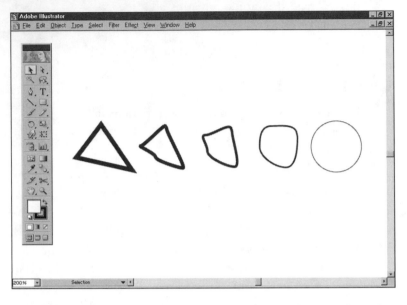

Figure 15.4

A blend can have more than two objects. Here the blend goes from the triangle to the circle and then from the circle to the rectangle.

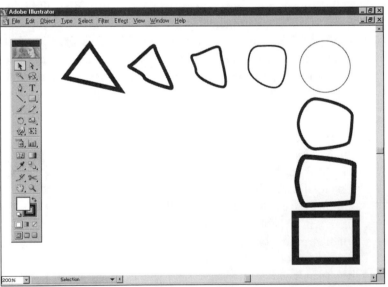

Creating Color Blend Objects

If a shape blend is a gradual transition between different shapes of the same color, it stands to reason that a color blend is a gradual transition between differently colored objects of the same shape. The intermediate objects don't have different shapes. Instead, they have different colors.

Here's how to create a color blend. Start off with an object—make it a circle. Select the circle, choose Edit → Copy, and then choose Edit → Paste. Position the copy of the circle elsewhere in the document window. Now give the first circle a purple fill, and give the second circle a green one. Turn off the strokes for both objects so that you can see exactly what happens when you make the blend.

Grab the Blend tool. Click the purple circle first, and then click the green circle. The result is something like Figure 15.5. This is a *smooth color blend.* There are so many intermediate steps between the two components that the blend object appears to be a continuous shape.

!#%@ Word Balloon

A **smooth color blend** is a blend object with so many intermediate steps that it appears to be a continuous shape.

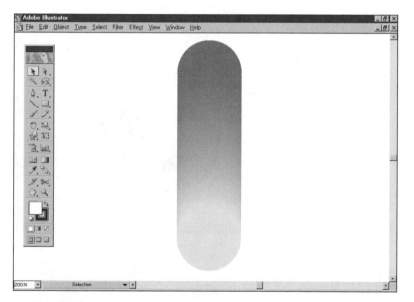

Figure 15.5

A smooth color blend includes so many intermediate steps that the blend object appears to be a continuous shape.

If you select the blend object, you can see the front and back objects clearly, along with the spine. But when you deselect the object, the blend looks more like a smear of color. It's difficult to pick out the component objects. Because the intermediate objects are so close together, you usually need to turn off either the fill color or the stroke color of the component objects to get the right effect.

Art Alert

If you create a smooth color blend between objects that have both a fill and a stroke color, usually only the change in the stroke color is visible. You can reduce this effect by changing the weight of the strokes to less than 1 point.

Turning off the fill can create some interesting possibilities. Try this one: Draw a circle with a black stroke and no fill. Copy this shape, paste the copy so that it partially covers the original, and change the stroke color of the copy to some other value.

Now take the Selection tool and draw a marquee around both shapes so that the center points appear. Then grab the Blend tool and click the center points, one after the other. Illustrator creates a smooth color blend, and you achieve what appears to be a three-dimensional tube, as Figure 15.6 shows.

Figure 15.6

Apply a smooth color blend to two circles with different stroke colors and no fill colors, and you can make a three-dimensional tube.

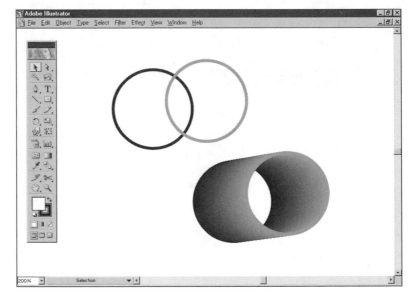

You may be wondering why I specifically asked you to click the center points. It's because the overall appearance of the blend object depends on where you click with the Blend tool. If you want to blend to a specific anchor point on an object, click that point with the Blend tool. (You know you have an anchor point when the square of the blend icon changes color.) By mixing combinations of sides and anchors, you can create all kinds of shapes. See Figure 15.7 for some examples.

Drawing Perspectives

Remember that only circles, ellipses, squares, and rectangles have built-in center points.

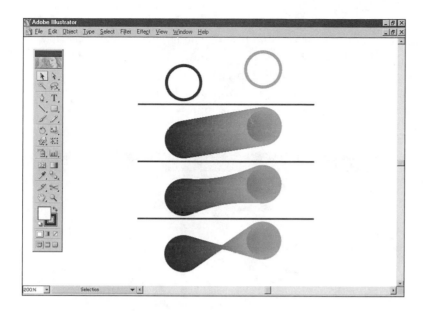

Figure 15.7

Depending on where you click with the Blend tool, the overall shape of the smooth color blend changes. From top to bottom: No blend, center point to center point, bottom anchor to left anchor, lower right side to top anchor.

Blending Shape and Color

Of course, you can also create a blend from two completely different objects. They don't have to be the same color or the same shape, as Figure 15.8 shows. Simply draw the shapes, and then click them with the Blend tool as you have been doing. I should point out that this often results in a smooth color blend, unlike the example in the figure, but you can easily reduce the number of intermediate steps, as I explain in the next section.

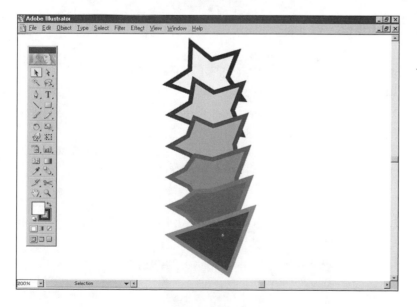

Figure 15.8

You can also create blends from objects of completely different shapes and colors. Here a yellow star with a black stroke blends into a dark blue triangle with a red stroke.

Create subtle shading effects with smooth color blends between similar objects. As an example, draw an oval with a light blue stroke and no fill. Then, below it, draw another, larger oval—this one with a dark blue stroke and no fill. Draw a marquee around the shapes to reveal their center points, and then click these points with the Blend tool. The result looks something a like a lampshade or an overturned bucket, as you can see in Figure 15.9. The gradation of the blues gives the impression of light on a three-dimensional surface.

Figure 15.9

Blend similar objects for shading effects.

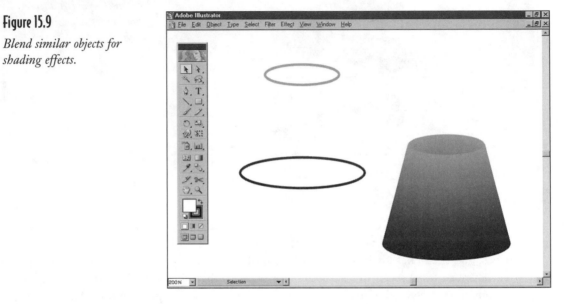

Controlling the Steps

When you create a shape blend, Illustrator usually gives you only a few intermediate objects. On the other hand, when you create a color blend, unless you're using complex objects like groups, Illustrator usually gives you smooth color, so that the blend object looks like a continuous shape.

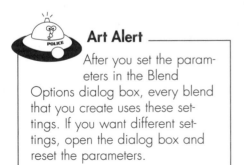

Art Alert

After you set the parameters in the Blend Options dialog box, every blend that you create uses these settings. If you want different settings, open the dialog box and reset the parameters.

In either case, the Blend tool provides two ways for you, the artist, to control the number of intermediate objects. You can enter the precise number of steps that you want, or you can specify the distance interval between each object. Set these parameters in the Blend Options dialog box, which appears after you double-click the Blend tool (see Figure 15.10).

To demonstrate, draw a few paths and then group them together. Copy and paste the group object, recolor the copy, and then create a blend between it and the original. This should give you just a few intermediate objects.

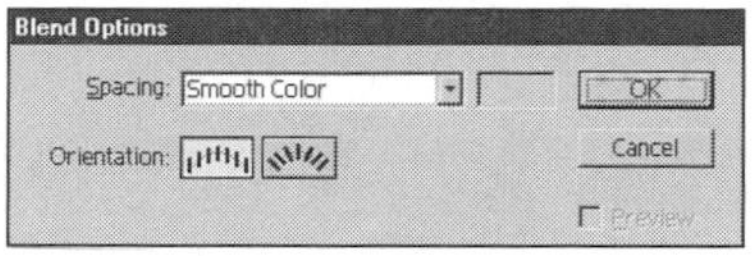

Figure 15.10

Use the Blend Options dialog box to control the number of intermediate objects.

Click the blend object with the Selection tool, and then double-click the Blend tool to open the Blend Options dialog box. Choose Specified Steps from the Spacing drop-down list, type **10** into the field, and click OK. Illustrator draws 10 intermediate objects between the back and the front, as Figure 15.11 shows.

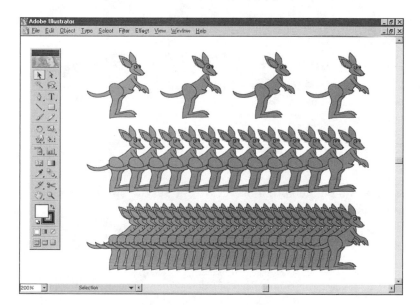

Figure 15.11

The default blend (top) becomes more populous when you specify 10 steps (middle), and it gets downright crowded when you specify 12-point spacing (bottom).

Double-click the Blend tool again, and this time choose Specified Distance from the drop-down list. Illustrator draws an intermediate object at whatever interval you specify in the field. Try 12 points, and click OK. (Refer to Figure 15.11 for an example.)

Just as you can increase the number of intermediate objects in a shape blend, you can reduce the number of intermediate objects in a smooth color blend. To prove it, double-click the Blend tool, reset the spacing to Smooth Color, and click OK.

Pointers

If you choose Smooth Color from the Spacing drop-down list and Illustrator doesn't oblige, try Specified Steps instead, and type **250** into the field. You may need to wait a few moments as Illustrator calculates and draws these steps, especially if the blend uses complex objects.

Then draw a red polygon and a blue rectangle, both without strokes, and create a blend between them. Select the blend, and double-click the Blend tool again. Choose Specified Steps from the Spacing list, type **5** into the field, and click OK. The blur of color becomes more distinct, as in Figure 15.12.

Figure 15.12

With smooth color (top), this blend is a blur. But with five specified steps (bottom), you can see the shape changing.

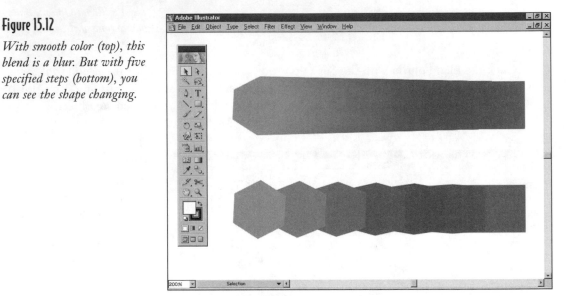

If you know precisely how you want a blend to look, feel free to set the options before you take up the Blend tool. The Blend Options dialog box remembers your settings. However, it's usually easier to modify a blend after you create it, when you can see what's going on, even if it takes some trial and error.

Repositioning the Spine

I mentioned earlier that the spine is just a path. It's normally invisible because it doesn't have a stroke or fill color, but you can see the spine clearly when you click a blend object with the Selection tool. The spine is the straight line that stretches from the back object to the front, as Figure 15.13 shows.

Because the spine is a path, you can modify it. Use the Direct Selection tool for the job. Deselect everything by clicking an empty area of the page, and then bring the Direct Selection tool into the blend object. The spine becomes visible. Move the pointer to the spine, and click to select it. Notice that the spine has two

Drawing Perspectives

Cutting the spine with the Scissors doesn't shorten the blend object or split it in two, unfortunately. Drag the anchors of the spine with the Direct Selection tool to change its size.

anchor points—one at either end. Now click one of these anchors, hold down the mouse button, and drag. The spine changes size and direction. When you release the mouse button, the blend object reconfigures itself accordingly, as Figure 15.14 shows.

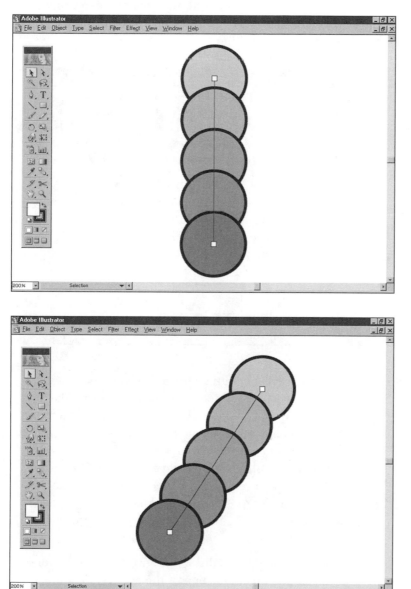

Figure 15.13

The spine is normally invisible, but it appears as a straight path that stretches from the back object to the front when you click a blend object with the Selection tool.

Figure 15.14

By dragging the anchor points of the spine with the Direct Selection tool, you can change the size and direction of the blend object.

You can make other changes to the spine, too. To curve it, click the path with the Direct Selection tool. Then grab the Convert Anchor Point tool from the toolbox. (This is the tool with the caret-shaped icon that hides under the Pen, remember?) Roll the mouse pointer onto an anchor point, hold down the mouse button, and drag a pair of direction handles. The spine curves, as does the direction of the blend object, as Figure 15.15 shows. To finish the curve, use the Convert Anchor Point tool on the other anchor, dragging in the same direction for an S-shaped curve or in the opposite direction for a C-shaped curve. Ah, yes, it's all coming back to you now.

Figure 15.15

Use the Convert Anchor Point tool on the anchors of the spine to create a curved blend object.

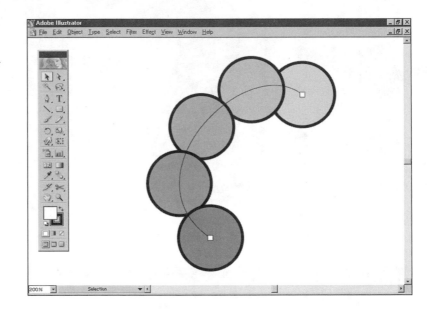

To give the spine a more complex shape, click it with the Direct Selection tool, and then plot new anchors along it with the Add Anchor Point tool. This is the Pen with the plus sign next to it—you just knew these hidden Pen tools would come in handy one day, right? After you plot the new anchors, feel free to drag them with the Direct Selection tool, change their type with the Convert Anchor Point tool, remove them with the Delete Anchor Point tool, and so on. The blend object bends and contorts with the spine as you go. Figure 15.16 shows an example.

Pointers

Here's a wild trick. Click the spine with the Direct Selection tool and get out the Pencil. Position the Pencil anywhere along the path, hold down the mouse button, and drag to redraw the spine. Here's another one. Direct-select the spine and trace over parts of it with the Erase tool. This creates transparent gaps in the blend object.

The Blend Options dialog box gives you two buttons for setting the orientation of the objects along the spine. To experiment with these controls, select a blend object, and then double-click the Blend tool. The second button, Align To Path, causes the objects in the blend to reorient themselves according to the shape of the spine, as in Figure 15.17. The first button, Align To Page, restores the objects to their default position, which is relative to the page, not the shape of the spine.

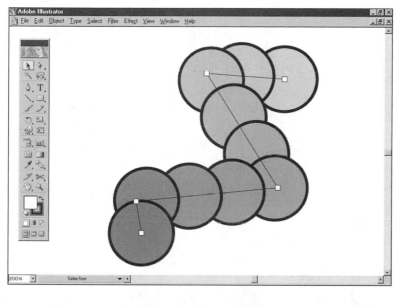

Figure 15.16

Add anchor points to the spine and then reposition them with the Direct Selection tool to create blends with complex shapes.

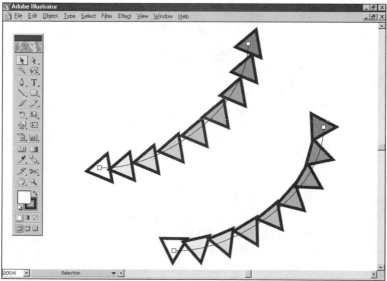

Figure 15.17

The Blend Options dialog box lets you change the orientation of the objects in the blend. With the Align To Page option (top), the objects sit on the spine relative to the page. With the Align To Path option (bottom), the objects reorient themselves according to the shape of the spine.

Blending Along a Path

If the spine is just a path, as you have now proven to yourself, is there any good reason why you can't take an ordinary path and turn it into a spine?

Drawing Perspectives

By the way, you can also create a blend without the Blend tool. Simply select the component objects and choose Object ➔ Blend ➔ Make. The blend flows from the lower object in the stacking order to the higher object.

Of course not. Here's how to do it. Begin by drawing a path with the Pencil. Set it aside for a moment, and create a blend between two other objects as you normally would. Now select the blend object, hold down Shift, and select the Pencil path. Choose Object ➔ Blend ➔ Replace Spine, and the blend object discards its original path and attaches itself to the path that you drew.

You aren't limited to Pencil paths. Feel free to use any drawing tool at your disposal, including the shape tools, like I did with the spiral in Figure 15.18. Note, though, that the shape of the blend follows the stroke of the path, not the fill.

Figure 15.18

Use Object ➔ Blend ➔ Replace Spine to trade an ordinary path for something more intrinsically interesting, like this spiral.

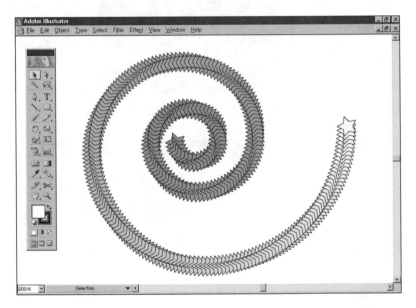

Editing Blend Objects

A blend object, strange as it is, is an object. You can click it with the Selection tool and move it around the document window. By selecting the blend, you can also apply appearance attributes such as stroke color, stroke weight, and fill color, which all the objects in the blend acquire. For instance, to change the strokes of all the objects in a blend to 4-point black, click the blend object with the Selection tool, call up the proper palettes, and set the desired attributes, just like you would for any other object. (The proper palettes, of course, are the Stroke palette for the weight and the Color palette for the color.)

If you need to *reverse the spine*—that is, if you need to switch the front and back objects—you need look no further than the Object menu. Click the blend object, and choose Object ➔ Blend ➔ Reverse Spine. The blend object flows in the opposite direction, from the new back object to the new front object.

⁈#%@ Word Balloon

Reversing the spine means switching the front and back objects of a blend.

Changing Component Objects

By using the Direct Selection tool, you can change the shapes of the objects in the back and front of the blend. Click an anchor point or segment with the Direct Selection tool, hold down the mouse button, and drag as you will. The blend automatically reconfigures itself according to the new shape of the component object. Likewise, after direct-selecting an object, you can add new anchor points, remove existing anchor points, and convert anchor points with the hidden Pen tools. You can process the anchors with the Object ➔ Path commands. You can use the transformation tools. You can change the stroke and the fill. The blend reflects everything that you do to the component object.

You cannot use the Direct Selection tool on the intermediate objects—these, Illustrator creates automatically from the shapes and colors of the components. You can, however, expand the blend. By doing so, you remove the blendness of the blend, as it were, much like the Create Outlines command removes the typeness of type. The blend doesn't behave as a blend anymore, in other words. You cannot adjust the shape of the blend by moving the spine, and you cannot change the number of the intermediate objects by double-clicking the Blend tool. You can freely modify the intermediate objects, but any changes you make don't affect the other objects.

Art Alert

After you expand a blend, the blend object is gone for good. The only way to restore it is to invoke Edit ➔ Undo.

With that in mind, if you want to proceed, choose Object ➔ Blend ➔ Expand. Illustrator replaces the blend object with a group. Ungroup the objects to modify them at will.

Releasing the Blend Object

Releasing a blend means getting rid of all the intermediate objects. To do this, click the blend with the Selection tool and choose Object ➔ Blend ➔ Release. The intermediate objects disappear, leaving only the front and the back objects. Use Edit ➔ Clear to delete the components.

Journey to the Third Dimension

It's time to polish off that Astro Ape logo you started in Chapter 12, "Manipulating Paths," with some three-dimensional effects courtesy of the Blend tool.

Begin, then, by opening the file *aa_logo.ai* and zooming in a good bit—all the way to 600% if you have the screen space. As you recall, you created outlines of these letters and then oversimplified them intentionally to get the distinctive shapes. Although you may not have realized it at the time, you also automatically created a group object around the letters.

The first order of business is getting rid of this group. Click the letters with the Selection tool, and choose Object → Ungroup from the menu. Click a blank area of the page to deselect the letters.

On to arranging the words. With the Selection tool, draw a marquee around the word *astro* and choose Object → Group. Then draw a marquee around *ape* and do the same thing. The words are much easier to move around when you group them like this. Otherwise, you would have to move each letter independently.

Now position the words one on top of the other with a healthy amount of space between them, and center them in the document window. There's no need to be too precise about it yet. You will knock the words into perfect alignment with the Align palette shortly.

After you move the words, select both groups and open the Color palette. Change the fill color from black to web-safe RGB red 102, green 255, and blue 51 for a bright shade of green. Don't apply a stroke color. When you finish, your screen should look something like Figure 15.19.

Deselect everything by clicking a blank area of the page, and select the word *astro*. Choose Edit → Copy and then Edit → Paste. Select the copy you just made and double-click the Scale tool. The Scale dialog box appears. Choose the Uniform option and type **10** into the Scale field. Click OK to make the change. The copy should shrink drastically. Move the copy to the middle of the document window, and repeat this procedure for the word *ape*.

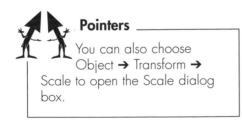

Pointers

You can also choose Object → Transform → Scale to open the Scale dialog box.

When you finish, draw a marquee around both scaled-down words, and go back to the Color palette. Change the fill to web-safe RGB red 153, green 0, and blue 153. The small logo changes to a shade of purple. Now arrange these words in the middle of the document window, one on top of the other, only don't leave much space between them.

Figure 15.19

Position the words of the Astro Ape logo and color them a bright shade of green.

Now for the alignment. Choose Edit ➔ Select All, and open the Align palette under Window ➔ Align. Click the second button from the left in the top row to align the words. Now deselect everything, and draw a marquee around the small words in the middle. Pull Object ➔ Ungroup from the menu, followed by Object ➔ Group. This replaces the two separate groups, *astro* and *ape*, with a single combined group.

Choose Edit ➔ Select All again, go back to the Align palette, and click the second button from the left in the second row. Illustrator evenly distributes the three remaining groups. As you might have guessed, combining the small words into a single group prevented the Distribute command from splitting them apart and adding more space between them than you want.

Invoke Edit ➔ Select All one last time, and choose Object ➔ Ungroup. This gets rid of all the group objects in the illustration. You will not need groups again until the very end of this exercise. Deselect everything, and compare your work with Figure 15.20.

At last, you're ready to do some blending. Double-click the Blend tool first, and make sure that Smooth Color appears in the Spacing list. Click OK to proceed.

Now, with the Blend tool, click the letter *a* in the smaller *astro*. Then click the corresponding letter *a* in the larger word, and a smooth color blend appears between the two letters. Move the mouse pointer to a blank area of the page, hold down Ctrl (Windows) or Command (Mac), and click.

Create a blend between the small *o* and large *o* in the same way, remembering to Ctrl-click or Command-click afterward. Continue with the letters *s*, *r*, and *t*, in that order. Don't forget to Ctrl-click or Command-click after each one! Use Edit ➔ Undo to amend mistakes.

Figure 15.20

Create copies of the words, scale them down, change their color, and arrange them like so.

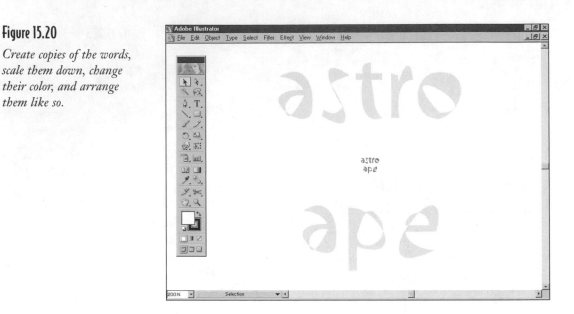

You may be wondering why you don't just create the color blends from left to right, going from *a* to *s* to *t* to *r* to *o*. The answer is the stacking order. As you know, Illustrator adds the most recent object to the top of the stack. This is true when you create objects with the drawing tools, and this is also true when you create blend objects. In order for the 3D effect to look right, the middle letter, *t*, needs to seem like it is closest to the viewer, and the letters on either end of the word, *a* and *o*, need to seem like they're farthest away. By creating the blends for *a* and *o* first, you ensure that they sit lower in the stack than the other letters. Likewise, by creating the blend for *t* last, you ensure that it sits higher in the stack than the others.

Art Alert

If you don't Ctrl-click or Command-click after creating each blend, Illustrator may get confused and think that you want to continue the blend that you just made.

With that in mind, create the blends for the word *ape*. The order of the letters should be *a*, *e*, and *p*. Click the smaller letter first, followed by the larger letter, and Ctrl-click or Command-click after you make each blend. When you finish, your screen should look like Figure 15.21.

The *3D* effect works nicely—a bit too nicely. As with other smooth color blends, it's hard to tell the shapes of the component objects, which is a problem when the shapes are letters that the audience is supposed to be able to read.

This is a problem, all right, but it's a problem that you can handle. Take up the Direct Selection tool, hold down the Shift key, and click each of the front letters. Now choose Edit ➔ Copy and Edit ➔ Paste In Front. This creates a copy of the letters and pastes them directly on top of the letters in the blend.

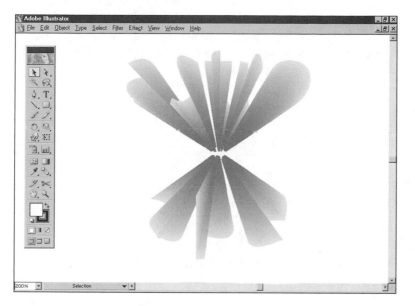

Figure 15.21

Use the Blend tool to make smooth color blends between the smaller letters in the back and their larger counterparts in the front.

With the copies selected, go to the Color palette and change the fill color to web-safe RGB red 0, green 0, and blue 102 for a dark shade of blue. Finally, choose Edit → Select All and then Object → Group, deselect everything, and have a look at your logo at last. You should notice a strong similarity between yours and the one in Figure 15.22.

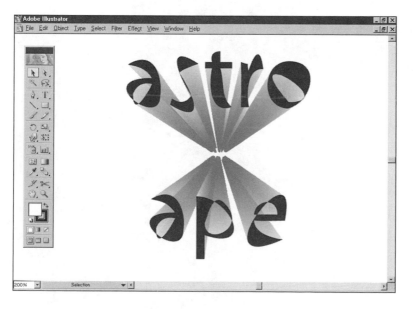

Figure 15.22

Copy the topmost letters, paste them in front, and recolor them to complete the logo.

Good job! So ends your journey to the third dimension. Save your work as *aa_logo_blends.ai*.

By the way, if you had modified the fill of the front letters without creating copies first, you would have only changed the colors in the blend, and the letters wouldn't have been any easier to read. The copies aren't part of the blend, so you can change their colors as often as you want without affecting the blend at all.

The Least You Need to Know

- ◆ A blend object is a gradual shift in characteristics between two or more component objects.
- ◆ Use the Blend tool to create blend objects.
- ◆ A smooth color blend has so many intermediate objects that the blend appears to be a continuous shape.
- ◆ Use smooth color blends to create 3D and shading effects.
- ◆ Double-click the Blend tool to adjust the parameters of a blend object.
- ◆ The spine is a path that you can easily modify.
- ◆ When you edit the characteristics of the component objects, the blend reconfigures itself.
- ◆ Expand a blend to edit the intermediate objects.

Chapter 16

Modifying Colors

In This Chapter

◆ Uniformly adjusting component colors

◆ Creating in-between shades for a series of objects

◆ Saturating and desaturating color

◆ Converting colors to grayscale

◆ Using blending modes in the Astro Ape comic

It makes perfect sense, if you think about it. There are probably a billion ways to modify a path and manipulate an object. Why wouldn't Illustrator complement these features with a handy set of color-editing and color-processing commands?

Some of these commands save you time and effort. Some help you to make sound aesthetic decisions. Others create unique color effects. This chapter explores a number of ways to modify color to the benefit of art and artist alike.

Adjusting Component Colors Evenly

Here's a quick review. You may recall from Chapter 8, "Coloring Fills and Strokes," that every color in your illustration is actually the product of its component colors. These components come together in various combinations to create the shades you see on screen or in print. In the RGB color model, the components are red, green, and blue. In CMYK, they are cyan, magenta, yellow, and black.

Drawing Perspectives

Remember, RGB is the color model for onscreen graphics, and CMYK is the color model for print media.

As you know, you can adjust the component colors of a stroke or fill easily enough. Simply drag the sliders on the Color palette. To increase the amount of blue in a purple fill, for instance, you would select the object that uses the fill, click the fill-color square on the Color palette, and drag the blue slider toward the right.

But what if you want to increase the blue component uniformly in all the objects of your illustration? You could drag the blue slider for each individual object, taking pains to adjust the level the same amount each time, or you could spare yourself the agony and use the Adjust Color command.

The Adjust Color command works very much like the tint knob on a television. It increases or decreases the levels of the component colors evenly for as many objects as you select. If you don't want to adjust the color of a particular object, then, hey, don't select it.

To demonstrate, draw three objects, and give each of them different stroke and fill colors. Then select any two of them and choose Filter → Colors → Adjust Colors. The Adjust Colors dialog box appears, as in Figure 16.1.

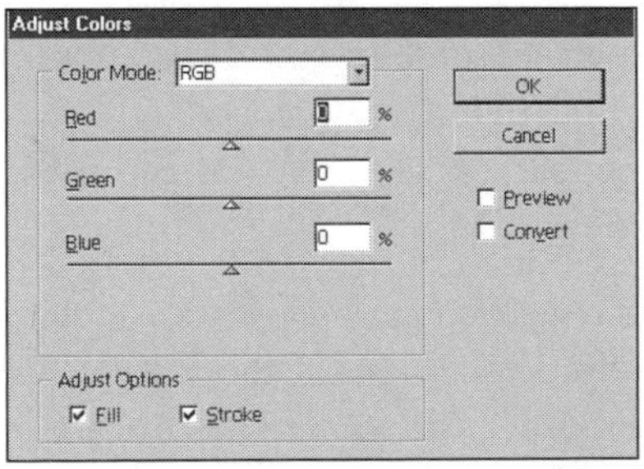

Figure 16.1

Use the Adjust Colors dialog box to increase or decrease the levels of the component colors uniformly, just like turning the tint knob on a television.

Before you start dragging sliders, check the Preview option on the right so that you can monitor your progress. Also, at the bottom of the dialog box, you will find options for adjusting the fill and stroke. If you only want to adjust the fill colors of the selected objects, uncheck the Stroke option, and vice versa. For the sake of this example, keep both options checked, but feel free to experiment with these at your leisure.

Now, to adjust the component colors of the selected objects, drag the sliders. Dragging the red slider to the right increases the amount of red in the objects. Dragging the green slider to the left decreases the amount of green, and so on. You're using the Preview option, so keep your eye on the document window. After you drag a slider, the colors of the objects change.

After you adjust the colors to your liking, click OK to accept the change. Click Cancel to close the dialog box without changing anything.

Pointers

To make the entire illustration darker, select all the objects, and decrease all three colors by the same degree. Conversely, to make the entire illustration lighter, increase all three colors by the same degree.

Blending Color

Assume that you have an illustration with five different objects in a row. The leftmost object has a red fill. The rightmost object has a blue fill. You're trying to fill the middle objects with in-between shades that get progressively bluer, but your color theory is a little rusty, your eyes are tired, and your head hurts. If you ever find yourself in this predicament, Illustrator can get you out with the Blend commands.

Be careful here. The Blend commands aren't the same as the blends from Chapter 15, "Creating Blend Objects." These blends aren't independent objects at all. They're simply commands for processing color. What they do is apply in-between shades to a series of objects, like in the earlier hypothetical example.

The Blend commands need at least three objects to work, and all the objects need to have fill colors. The first object's fill represents the starting color. The last object's fill represents the ending color. The middle objects receive in-between shades as their fills.

The starting and ending objects depend on which Blend command you use. There are three commands: Blend Front To Back, Blend Horizontally, and Blend Vertically. With Blend Front To Back, the starting object is the one highest up in the stacking order, and the ending object is the one farthest down. With Blend Horizontally, the starting and ending objects are the ones at the left and right of the series, and with Blend Vertically, they are the ones at the top and bottom.

To blend the colors of a series of objects, select the objects, and look under Filter ➔ Colors for the Blend command of your choice. See Figure 16.2 for an example.

I should point out that the Blend commands only change fill colors. They don't affect stroke colors at all.

Art Alert

If one of the middle objects doesn't have a fill color, the Blend commands ignore it. Give this object a generic fill such as white or black before you blend. If the starting or ending object doesn't have a fill color, Illustrator beeps at you when you try to blend the colors, and nothing else happens.

Figure 16.2

The Blend Horizontally command filled the middle objects in this series (top) with in-between shades (bottom).

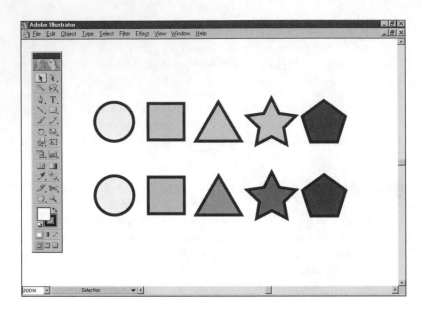

Inverting Color

Select an object and choose Filter → Colors → Invert, and the object's colors *invert*, or switch to their opposites. An inverted image looks like the negative on a roll of film, as Figure 16.3 shows.

Figure 16.3

Use Invert Color to change an object (top) into its photonegative (bottom). A color and its inverse often make a pleasing color scheme.

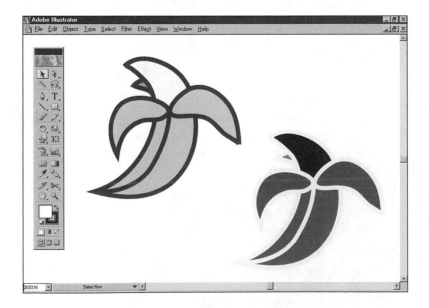

What good is the Invert command, you might wonder, if you don't really need to create photonegatives of your objects? To answer, the inverse of a color is its *complement* in the RGB color model. Complementary colors tend to match. They work well together. If you're in the process of drawing something and you don't know what color scheme to use, try making all the objects the same color. Then bring in the complementary color by using the Invert command on some of the objects.

Saturating and Desaturating Color

The Saturate command increases or decreases the intensity of an object's stroke and fill colors. Fully saturated colors appear vivid and pure. Desaturated colors seem fainter and washed out, as you can see in Figure 16.4.

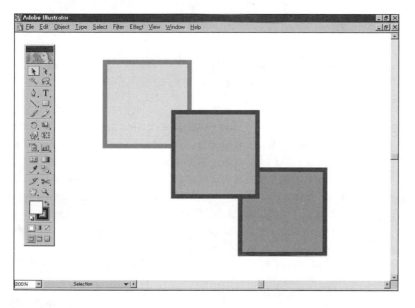

Figure 16.4

The Saturate command decreases (top) or increases (bottom) the intensity of an object's color.

To use this command, select the object that you want to saturate or desaturate, and choose Filter → Colors → Saturate. The Saturate dialog box appears, as Figure 16.5 shows.

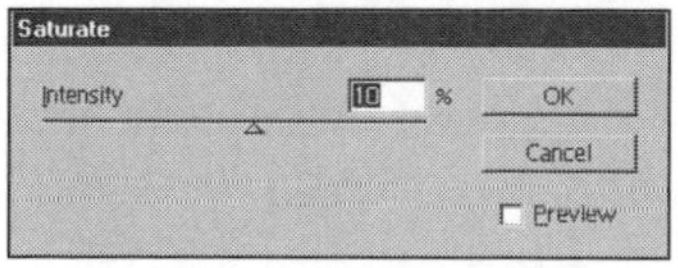

Figure 16.5

Drag the Intensity slider in the Saturate dialog box to adjust the saturation of a selected object's color.

Drawing Perspectives

If you're saturating or desaturating many colors at once, some colors might seem to stop changing before others do. When a particular color stops changing, it has become either fully saturated or fully desaturated.

Check the Preview option, and then drag the Intensity slider to change the saturation. Dragging to the right increases saturation, and dragging to the left decreases it. Click OK to finish the deal.

There isn't much room in the Astro Ape comic for desaturated colors. In fact, if you open *aa_side_color.ai* and increase the saturation to 100%, you don't see much of a difference. The colors are fairly saturated as they are, which is a good thing. If you're too subtle in a comic strip, you risk losing your audience. But if you're going for an understated, classy, or antique look, try desaturating the entire illustration.

Going Gray

The Convert To Grayscale command transforms an object's colors into shades of gray, like in a black-and-white photo. Darker colors appear blacker, and lighter colors appear whiter.

To make the switch, select an object, and choose Filter ➜ Colors ➜ Convert To Grayscale. If you open the Color palette, you will note that a single K slider has replaced the three RGB sliders. This is K as in CMYK, and the K stands for black. Adjust the intensity of the gray by dragging this slider. Click an RGB object with the Selection tool, and the Color palette switches back to the familiar three sliders that you know and love. But if you leave the Color palette in grayscale mode, the next object you draw will be in grayscale as well.

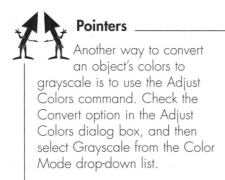
Pointers
Another way to convert an object's colors to grayscale is to use the Adjust Colors command. Check the Convert option in the Adjust Colors dialog box, and then select Grayscale from the Color Mode drop-down list.

To change a grayscale object back to RGB, select the object and open the Color palette menu. Choose RGB from the list. Then pick a color from the RGB Spectrum, or mix a color of your own with the sliders.

Using Blending Modes

To the computer, colors, like paths, are just a bunch of numerical relationships. You demonstrate this fact every time you mix a new stroke or fill on the Color palette. As the numerical values change, the color changes.

Where there are numbers, mathematics is sure to follow. It should come as no surprise that Illustrator can take two color values and process them mathematically. Unless you're a scientist, I'm sure this sounds dull. But this very procedure creates some of the most interesting color effects in computer illustration.

Call these mathematical operations *blending modes*. There's that blending word again. I won't apologize for the terminology, because I didn't make it up, but I fully sympathize with any confusion that it may cause.

For the sake of clarity, here is what blending modes are not. They aren't blend objects, like the kind from Chapter 15. They aren't commands for creating in-between shades of color, like in the "Blending Color" section earlier in this chapter. To tell you the truth, blending modes don't have much in common with either of these, except of course, their name.

Blending modes tell the computer what to do when the colors of two objects overlap. In the Normal blending mode, for instance, nothing unusual happens. The object that occupies the higher position in the stacking order appears to be on top, and the colors of the objects don't combine in any way. But in the Multiply blending mode, the situation changes. Illustrator multiplies the color values of the upper object with the color values of the lower one, and a new color, the product, appears in the overlapping area, as shown in Figure 16.6.

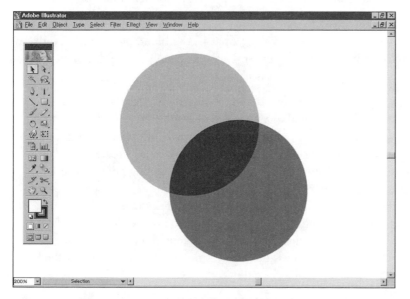

Figure 16.6

In the Multiply blending mode, Illustrator displays the product of the top color and the bottom color wherever the two colors overlap.

You can apply blending modes to the objects in your illustration by way of the Transparency palette, which opens after you choose Window → Transparency from the menu. The Transparency palette's drop-down list controls the blending mode of an object, as Figure 16.7 shows.

Figure 16.7

The Transparency palette's drop-down list controls the blending mode of an object.

With the Transparency palette at the ready, simply select an object and choose a blending mode from the drop-down list. The colors of this object will now blend with the colors of everything underneath it, as you can see when you place this object on top of another. You may need to adjust the stacking order so that the object with the blending mode is higher up in the stack.

Blending modes, like rivers, always flow downhill. That is, the blending operation only affects objects that are lower in the stacking order. If you're trying to decide which object to click to apply a blending mode, the answer is clear. It's always the object in front.

Art Alert

Certain blending modes may not appear to work on certain objects, especially if the objects are mostly black or white. Try a different blending mode, or consider changing the color of the object to a comparable shade of gray.

Illustrator offers 15 blending modes, not counting Normal, which is the default. These modes affect different objects in various ways, but you can count on a few rules of thumb. Multiply mode creates a darker color than either of the overlapping colors, whereas Screen mode, which multiplies the inverse of the overlapping colors, creates a lighter shade. Color Dodge brightens the color of the top object in the overlapping area, and Color Burn darkens the color. The degree of brightness or darkness depends on the value of the bottom object's color.

The best way to see what the blending modes can do is to experiment with them.

Through Rose-Colored Glasses

Speaking of blending modes, you can use one of these modes to achieve a special effect that I've been saving. (No, not coloring the helmet. That's coming up shortly.)

This trick is about switching the point of view of the comic for one panel. The *point of view* is the eye through which the audience sees the story. So far, the audience has watched from the *third person*, or the point of view of a spectator. By switching to the *first person*, the audience sees the events from the point of view of Astro Ape himself. It's a handy technique for focusing the audience's attention on whatever the main character is thinking.

Here's what I propose. Astro Ape activates his space goggles in one panel, and the audience sees the arrow sign from his point of view in the next.

Start by opening *aa_side_color.ai*. Click the illustration with the Selection tool and choose Edit → Ungroup.

Now you need some space goggles. Start by defining the fill color. Open the Color palette, click the fill-color square, and mix web-safe RGB red 255, green 51, and blue 153 for a vivid shade of pink. Set the stroke to 1-point black, and you're ready to draw the goggles. Pick a convenient, empty area of the document window. Use the Rounded Rectangle tool, and rotate the shape a few degrees clockwise, as Figure 16.8 shows.

Position the goggles on Astro Ape's face. Use the Selection tool to scale the goggles if they don't quite fit, and adjust the angle of rotation as required. Then send the goggles backward in the stacking order until the nose sits in front of them, as in Figure 16.9.

You have to admit, it's a bold fashion statement. Even still, the comic strip should try to explain where the goggles came from, because the reader sees Astro Ape without goggles at the beginning of the strip. Having Astro Ape press the secret buttons on either side of his helmet should do the trick, because everyone knows that pressing secret buttons on a space helmet causes space goggles to appear.

❗#%@ Word Balloon

The **point of view** is the eye through which the audience experiences a story. The **first person** is the point of view of a character in the story. The **third person** is the point of view of an uninvolved spectator.

Drawing Perspectives

The Apollo astronauts used gold-plated visors to filter the rays of the sun.

Figure 16.8

Use the Rounded Rectangle tool to draw some space goggles, and rotate the shape a few degrees clockwise.

Figure 16.9

Position the goggles and send them backward in the stacking order so that the nose sits in front.

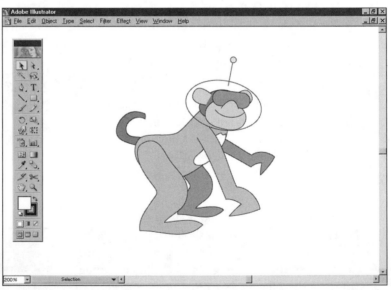

Pressing secret buttons requires new arm designs. Grab the Pencil and draw the arms off to the side. Use the Eyedropper or the Paint Bucket to color them. See Figure 16.10 for the finished designs.

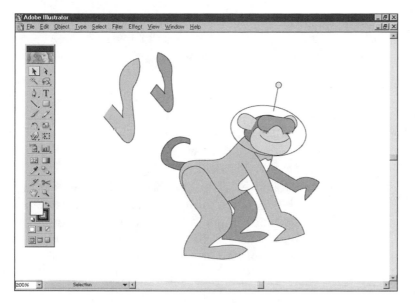

Figure 16.10

Draw new arms with the Pencil and color them with the Eyedropper or Paint Bucket.

Now get rid of the old arms by selecting them and choosing Edit → Clear or pressing the Delete key. Move the new arms into place. Keep the foreground arm at the top of the stacking order, but send the other arm all the way to the back. Adjust the size of the arms if you need to, and you have a goggle-activating monkey, as Figure 16.11 shows.

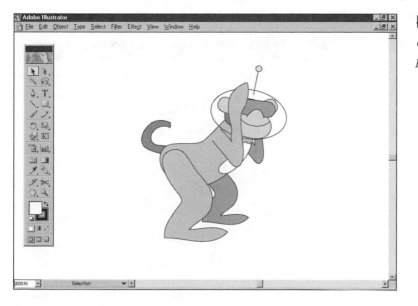

Figure 16.11

Get rid of the old arms and position the new ones.

Choose Edit → Select All and then Object → Group, and save this file as *aa_side_goggles.ai*. Congratulations! You successfully modified some art. I hope this goes down better than that shameless repurposing from Chapter 14, "Applying Transformations."

You're ready to tackle the first-person point of view. Close this file, choose File ➔ New, and then open *aa_background.ai* as well as *aa_sign_type.ai.* You should now have three open files in Illustrator. Choose Window ➔ Tile so that you can see all your files simultaneously.

You opened the background and sign illustrations so that you could borrow objects from them. Grab the Group Selection tool from under the Direct Selection tool, and click an empty area of the background's document window. The window activates. Now click the sky portion of the background with the Group Selection tool. This selects the sky object from the group. Hold down Shift, and select a star or two. Then choose Edit ➔ Copy, move the mouse pointer into the empty document window, and click. Paste the sky and the stars into this window. Close *aa_background.ai*, and when Illustrator asks whether you want to save the changes, click No.

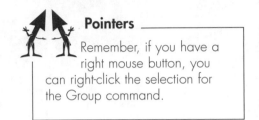

Pointers

Remember, if you have a right mouse button, you can right-click the selection for the Group command.

Tile the windows again to make them bigger, and copy the sign to the new document window. You should use the regular Selection tool for the job, because you want the entire sign and not just a few objects that belong to the group. After you paste the sign, close *aa_sign_type.ai* without making changes.

Maximize the new document window, and zoom in so that you can see what you're doing. Then resize and position the objects to match Figure 16.12.

Figure 16.12

Arrange the sign, sky, and star objects something like this.

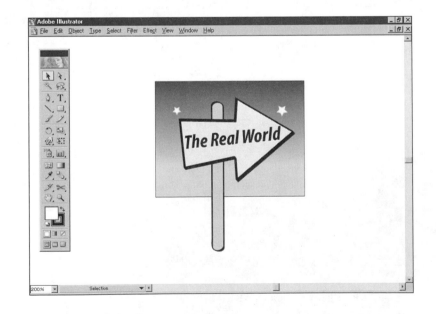

Now click the sky and choose Edit ➔ Copy and Edit ➔ Paste. Drag the copy of this object to a blank area of the document window. You may want to zoom out a bit if you don't have enough room. Give the copy of the sky a black fill. Draw a rounded rectangle with a white fill, and line up the center points of this object and the black rectangle, like in Figure 16.13.

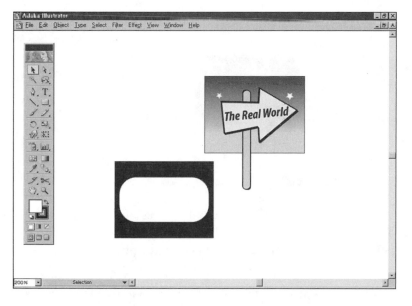

Figure 16.13

Copy the sky, color the copy black, and draw a rounded rectangle on top of it for the view through the space goggles.

The next step calls for a command that you haven't used before—at least not in this book. Click the rounded rectangle, and choose Object ➔ Path ➔ Slice from the menu. This command makes the rounded rectangle work like a cookie cutter. It punches a space-goggle-shaped hole in the black rectangle. The rounded rectangle is still there, even though it has turned black.

By the way, if you want to prove that the Slice command works as advertised, grab the Selection tool, click a blank area of the screen, and then drag the rectangle onto the sky. The sky should show through the hole. Choose Edit ➔ Undo to return the rectangle to its original position.

Click a blank area of the page with the Selection tool, and then select the rounded rectangle. Make its fill color the same as the space goggles (red 255, green 51, and blue 153). Then go to the Transparency palette and choose Multiply as the blending mode. Group these objects, and check your progress in Figure 16.14.

Pointers

If the sky keeps poking out from behind the goggle group no matter which way you nudge, just scale the goggle group up a little.

Figure 16.14

Punch a hole in the black rectangle with the Slice command and apply the pink fill to the rounded rectangle.

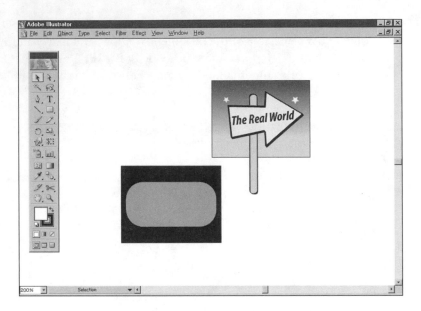

Drag this group so that it sits directly on top of the sky, and you get a first-person view through space goggles. Thanks to the blending mode, the rounded rectangle multiplies every color behind it by space-goggle pink, creating the effect of the proverbial rose-colored glasses.

Move the goggles away, and adjust the size and position of the sign and the stars as you like. Also, take this opportunity to cut off the bottom part of the signpost with the Knife. Reassemble the pieces, nudge the goggle group into perfect alignment, and group everything together, as in Figure 16.15.

Figure 16.15

Bring the elements together and tidy up, and you see through the eyes of the ape.

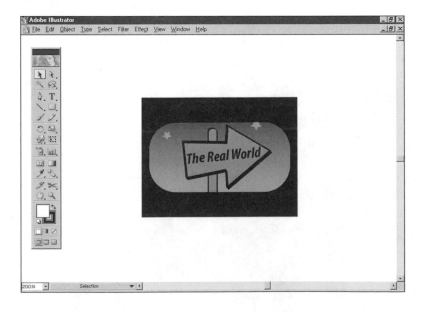

You're done! Congratulations again. Save your work as *aa_sign_pov.ai*—that's *POV*, as in *point of view*. You're coming into the home stretch now, and you're doing great. Very soon, you will have a comic strip to prove it.

The Least You Need to Know

- The Adjust Color command works much like the tint knob on a television
- The Blend commands create in-between shades of fill color in a series of objects.
- Inverting a color produces its complement in the RGB color model.
- A color and its complement usually match.
- Use the Saturate command to intensify or wash out the colors of an object.
- The Grayscale command converts color information to shades of gray, like in a black-and-white photo.
- Blending modes are mathematical operations between two color values.
- Use blending modes to produce interesting color effects.

Part 5

Getting Fancy

Your computer illustration is approaching critical mass. Are you looking for just the right catalyst to complete the reaction? Maybe you want to experiment with semitransparent objects. Maybe you want to explore masking techniques. Maybe you want to choose a few pieces of eye candy from Illustrator's rich suite of effects and filters. If so, the next three chapters are for you. This part shows you how to bring your creative efforts to fruition.

Working with Transparency

In This Chapter

- ◆ Applying transparency to objects
- ◆ Making opacity masks
- ◆ Mixing transparency and opacity
- ◆ Coloring the helmet in Astro Ape

To make an object completely clear, you turn off its fill. To make the object disappear entirely, you turn off its fill and its stroke.

But what if you want to make an object partially disappear? You still want to be able to see the object, but you want the objects underneath to show through. This is where *transparency* comes in. Illustrator supplies a number of ways to make an object transparent, and this chapter shows you how to use them.

Applying Transparency to Paths

Remember the Transparency palette? You used it in Chapter 16, "Modifying Colors," to specify blending modes. Not surprisingly, you will use it again in this chapter.

Few procedures in computer illustration are easier than making a path transparent. Simply select the path, open the Transparency palette under Window → Transparency, click the arrow icon next to the *Opacity* field, and drag the slider control that pops up.

The farther you drag the slider to the left, the less opaque—and the more transparent—the path becomes. If you don't want to bother with the slider on the Transparency palette, you can type a percentage value directly into the Opacity field.

A path with less than 100% opacity reveals the shapes and colors of the objects beneath it, as Figure 17.1 shows. These objects can be on lower layers, or they can be farther down in the stacking order of the same layer. As common sense suggests, an object that sits on top of a transparent path isn't affected at all, just like a piece of cake doesn't become see-through when you place it on a glass plate.

> **!#%@** **Word Balloon**
>
> **Transparency** is an appearance attribute that makes an object partially invisible. **Opacity** is the opposite of transparency, and you measure it on the same scale. For instance, if an object is 75% opaque, then it is 25% transparent.

Figure 17.1

If a path is less than 100% opaque (right), you can see the objects beneath it.

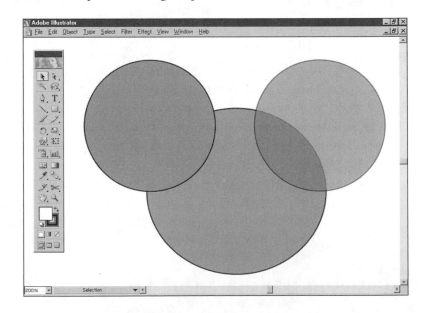

Opacity is an appearance attribute, much like fill color, stroke color, and stroke weight. You can apply opacity settings with the Eyedropper and the Paint Bucket.

Applying Transparency to Groups

The plot thickens somewhat when you apply transparency to a group instead of a single path. To see what I mean, draw a couple of overlapping objects, group them together, and reduce the opacity to 66%. Notice that the members of the group show through each other, like in Figure 17.2.

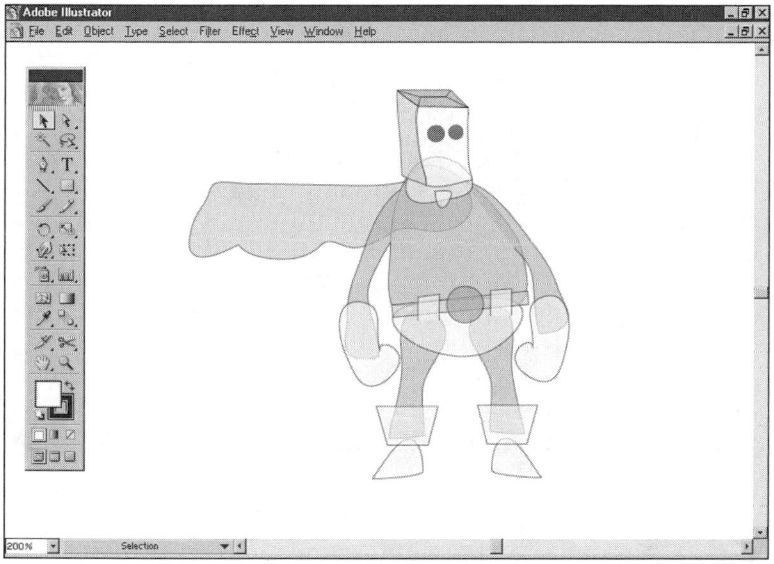

Figure 17.2

By default, when you apply transparency to a group, the objects in the group show through each other.

If this is the effect you want, then great. But if you would rather have the group become transparent as a whole, you need to alter the procedure slightly.

Drag the opacity back to 100% and call up the Layers palette under Window → Layers. Then click the arrow icon in the current layer to see its list of objects. One of the objects, if not the only object, is the group that you created.

Look to the right of the group object in the palette, and you find a small circle. This circle is the target of the object. Click the target. Now go back to the Transparency palette and set the opacity to 66%. The group becomes transparent as if it were a single path, as Figure 17.3 shows.

To edit the transparency of the group after using this trick, click the group's target in the Layers palette again. Don't click the group itself with the Selection tool. If you do, you will find that adjustments to the opacity create the see-through effect that you were trying to avoid.

Similarly, by clicking the target of a layer, you can apply transparency to all the layer's objects without the objects showing through each other.

Figure 17.3

Click the target of the group in the Layers palette, and you can apply transparency evenly, as if the group were a single path.

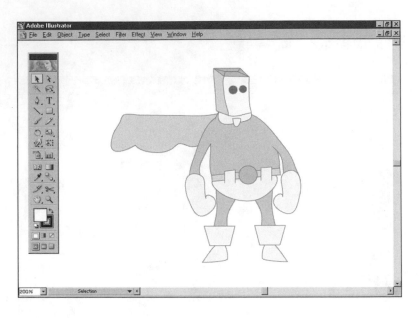

Creating Opacity Masks

So far, the level of transparency across an object has been consistent. That is, when you reduce the opacity of an object, the entire object acquires the same level of transparency. But with an *opacity mask*, you can apply different levels of transparency to the same object.

An opacity mask begins life as an object like any other. It's usually a path with a stroke or fill value that sits on top of another object. When you change this path into an opacity mask, it disappears, but its color values determine the levels of transparency on the object underneath.

!#%@ Word Balloon

An **opacity mask** is an object that creates different levels of transparency on another object.

Here's a quick exercise to show you how opacity masks work. Start by drawing a rectangle. Then add an ellipse that partially covers the rectangle. Give the ellipse the fill color of your choice, but make its stroke black, and bump up the stroke weight to 4 points. Select the ellipse, and choose Edit → Copy and then Edit → Paste. Move the copy so that it covers both shapes. Now open the Swatches palette by way of Window → Swatches, and apply the Camouflage pattern swatch to the fill of the second ellipse.

To create the opacity mask, select both ellipses. Click the triangle icon at the top of the Transparency palette, and choose Make Opacity Mask from the menu that slides out. The second ellipse disappears, but its fill-color bands determine the levels of transparency on the first ellipse, as shown in Figure 17.4. Notice that the black stroke of the opacity mask is completely transparent, but the different camouflage colors of the fill create different levels of opacity.

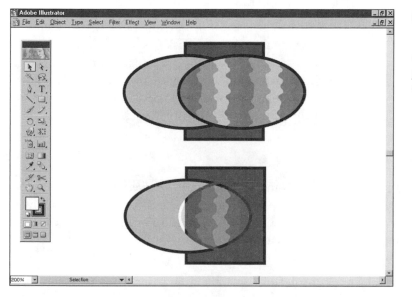

Figure 17.4

The colors of an opacity mask determine the levels of transparency on the object underneath it.

Have a look at the thumbnail images on the Transparency palette. If you don't see them, choose Show Thumbnails from the palette menu. The thumbnail on the left shows the *masked object*, or the object that receives the transparency. The thumbnail on the right shows the *mask*, or the object whose colors determine the levels of transparency. The chain icon between them indicates that the masked object and the mask are linked—that is, they move around the document window like a group.

To reposition the masked object under the mask, click the chain icon to unlink the objects. Then drag the masked object with the Selection tool. The mask remains in place, but the masked object changes position. After you have made the proper adjustments, click the empty space between the thumbnail images to link the masked object to the mask again.

If you want to edit the mask instead, click the mask's thumbnail on the Transparency palette and unlink the objects. You can now reposition the mask with the Selection tool, and you can add

Drawing Perspectives

The luminosity of a color determines the level of transparency that color confers in an opacity mask.

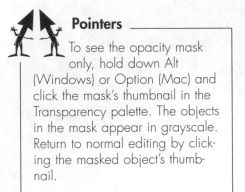

Pointers

To see the opacity mask only, hold down Alt (Windows) or Option (Mac) and click the mask's thumbnail in the Transparency palette. The objects in the mask appear in grayscale. Return to normal editing by clicking the masked object's thumbnail.

new objects to the mask by drawing them. Change the colors of the mask to alter its levels of transparency. After you finish, be sure to click the thumbnail of the masked object. If you don't, you will only be able to edit the objects in the mask itself.

To turn off an opacity mask temporarily, select it and choose Disable Opacity Mask from the Transparency palette menu. The effects of the opacity mask disappear, and the mask's thumbnail appears with a red X through it. Turn the mask back on by opening the palette menu and choosing Enable Opacity Mask.

Inverting the Opacity

Checking the Invert Mask option on the Transparency palette produces inverse levels of transparency on the masked object—that is, previously opaque areas become transparent, and previously transparent areas become opaque. This option also makes the masked object itself perfectly transparent, except where the mask overlaps. Restore the opacity mask to normal by unchecking this option.

To work with inverted opacity masks by default, open the Transparency palette menu and choose New Opacity Masks Are Inverted.

Releasing the Mask

To get rid of an opacity mask entirely, select it and choose Release Opacity Mask from the Transparency palette menu. The mask regains its fill and stroke color values. Delete these objects by selecting them and choosing Edit ➔ Clear or pressing the Delete key.

!#%@ Word Balloon

A **compound path** is an object that contains two or more ordinary paths. By default, the areas where these paths overlap become perfectly transparent.

Creating Compound Paths

A *compound path* is a special kind of object that lets you mix transparent and opaque areas. As its name suggests, a compound path contains two or more ordinary paths that behave as a single unit, much like a group. Unlike a group, though, a compound path becomes transparent by default in the areas where the component paths overlap, as you can see in Figure 17.5. Notice also that the compound path has only one set of appearance attributes—the color of the circle in Figure 17.5 changes to match the color of the square when the two shapes become a compound path.

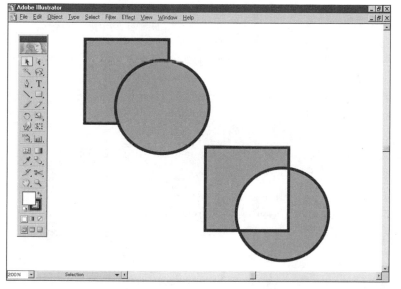

Figure 17.5

In a compound path, the component paths create perfectly transparent areas where they overlap.

To create a compound path, arrange the paths that you would like to combine. Select them all, and choose Object → Compound Path → Make from the menu. If you have a right mouse button, you can right-click the selection and choose Make Compound Path from the context menu. The areas where the objects overlap become transparent, and the appearance attributes of the bottommost object apply to the compound path as a whole.

If you want to adjust the arrangement of the components in a compound path, use the Direct Selection tool. Click a blank area of the page to deselect everything, and then click the opaque area of the component path that you want to move. Drag the path to its new position, and release. You can also use the Direct Selection tool to manipulate the anchors and segments of the component paths.

For more complex editing, or to delete the compound path entirely, you need to release the compound path. Select it, and pull Object → Compound Path → Release from the menu, or right-click the compound path and choose Release Compound Path from the context menu. The compound path spits out its component objects. Change them as you will, and then re-create the compound path.

Notice that, when you release a compound path, the component objects retain the appearance attributes of the compound path. They don't revert to their original appearance. Unfortunately, those original attributes are long gone. You may be able to reclaim them by undoing your actions until just before you created the compound path in the first place.

Feathering

Feathering an object causes its edges to become transparent gradually, like in Figure 17.6.

To feather an object, select it and choose Effects ➔ Stylize ➔ Feather from the menu. The Feather dialog box appears. Type a value in the Feather Radius dialog box, or click the arrow buttons to step the value up or down in increments of one. The feather radius determines the scope of the effect. The larger the value, the farther from the edge of the object the feathering begins.

Figure 17.6

A feathered object (bottom) has edges that become gradually transparent.

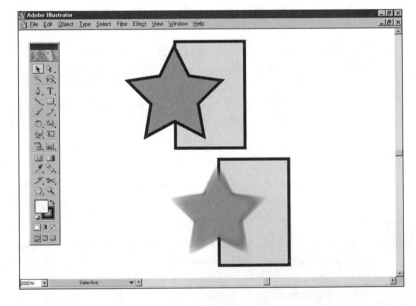

Check the Preview option to see the effect as you tweak it. Click OK to feather the object, or click Cancel to leave the object as it is.

To remove a feathering effect from an object, select the object and open the Appearance palette under Window ➔ Appearance. You haven't used the Appearance palette yet. It makes its official debut in Chapter 19, "Adding Effects," but I will give you an exclusive advance preview here.

The Appearance palette lists the appearance attributes of an object. In the list for the object that you selected will be an item labeled "Feather." Click this item, and then click the trashcan icon at the bottom of the palette. The attribute disappears from the list, and the object returns to its unfeathered state.

Clearer Vision

I'm sure you have heard the old saying, "Monkey see, monkey do." The subtitle for this section could have been "You do, monkey see." You're going to color Astro Ape's space helmet at last, and by what you do with the transparency, you will allow the monkey to see out of the helmet.

It's weak, I know, but the hour is late, and I hope you will excuse me.

No matter what you call it, this is another straightforward Astro Ape exercise. All you have to do is open the various Astro Ape illustrations that you created so far, click the helmet, give it a fill value, and then reduce the opacity.

Art Alert

If you feather a stroked object and then turn off the object's stroke, the feathering effect reconfigures itself. The same thing happens when you feather an object without a stroke and then supply a stroke color. To compensate for this, you may need to adjust the feather radius manually. Call up the Feather dialog box by double-clicking the Feather item in the Appearance palette's list.

Drawing Perspectives

The saying "Monkey see, monkey do" is Jamaican in origin, as is the expression "monkey business."

Five Astro Ape illustrations require helmet coloring: *aa_side_color.ai*, *aa_rear_color.ai*, *aa_side_running1.ai*, *aa_side_running2.ai*, and *aa_side_goggles.ai*. Open these and tile the document windows by way of Window → Tile.

Start with *aa_side_color.ai*. You grouped these paths, so get out the Group Selection tool instead of the regular Selection tool, and click the edge of the helmet. Now take the Eyedropper tool and click the antenna bulb. This transfers the appearance attributes of the antenna bulb to the helmet, as you well know.

So far you did, but the monkey can't see. Correct this by going to the Transparency palette and setting the opacity to 25%. As Figure 17.7 shows, Astro Ape has a clear view through his aqua-tinted helmet.

One down, four to go. Save this file as *aa_side_color_t.ai*—*t* for transparency—and close the document window. Retile the remaining windows with Window → Tile, and proceed with *aa_rear_color.ai*. Use the Group Selection tool and the Eyedropper just like you did before, and reduce the opacity to 25%. Save this file with the _t suffix if you can, retile the document windows, and continue.

Figure 17.7

Apply the fill color of the antenna bulb to Astro Ape's helmet, and then reduce the opacity to 25% so that the poor ape can see.

When you finish, you should have five transparent blue helmets and five new files on your hard drive: *aa_side_color_t.ai*, *aa_rear_color_t.ai*, *aa_side_running1_t.ai*, *aa_side_running2_t.ai*, and *aa_side_goggles_t.ai*. These are the completed Astro Ape designs—the illustrations that you will use in the comic strip.

The Least You Need to Know

◆ Transparency is an appearance attribute like stroke weight and fill color.

◆ Use the Transparency palette to adjust the opacity level of an object.

◆ Target a group in the Layers palette before applying transparency.

◆ Use an opacity mask to apply different levels of transparency to the same object.

◆ Create compound paths to make objects with opaque and transparent regions.

◆ Use the feathering effect to make the edges of an object gradually transparent.

Chapter 18

Working with Masks

In This Chapter

◆ Creating clipping masks

◆ Modifying the appearance of a mask

◆ Making the panel border for the Astro Ape comic

In Chapter 17, "Working with Transparency," you saw that an opacity mask is a special kind of object. It is a path, but its stroke and fill values don't determine its color. Instead, these values determine the level of transparency on the object that it masks.

A *clipping mask* is the same kind of thing. Its properties affect the object that it masks. Instead of creating different levels of transparency, however, a clipping mask determines which portions of its object are visible. This chapter shows you how to create and modify clipping masks.

Creating Clipping Masks

A clipping mask is like a window that you place on top of your art. You can see through the window to the illustration underneath, but everything outside the window becomes hidden from sight.

When you talk about clipping masks, you use the same terminology that you do with opacity masks. The *mask* is the object that acts like the window. Its shape determines what you can see of the *masked object*, or the underlying art.

You can illustrate this concept with a few clicks of the mouse. Pick a shape tool and draw a path, and then draw another path that partially covers the first. Assign stroke and fill values to both.

Drag a marquee around the objects with the Selection tool, and choose Object → Clipping Mask → Make from the menu. If you have a two-button mouse, you can right-click the selection and choose Make Clipping Mask from the context menu.

The result is much like Figure 18.1. The object on the top becomes the mask, or the window. Its stroke and fill colors disappear entirely. The object on the bottom, the masked object, also disappears, except where the two paths overlap. The masked object is only visible though the window of the mask.

Figure 18.1

By changing the circle into a clipping mask, you limit the visibility of the polygon to the area in which the two paths overlap.

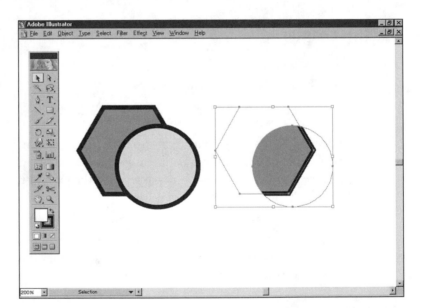

When you drag the clipping mask with the Selection tool, the object that it masks goes with it. These objects behave like a group, in other words.

The mask itself can be a regular path, like in the previous example, or it can be a compound path like the kind you created in Chapter 17. A compound path, as you recall, is a combination of regular paths. The areas where these paths overlap become transparent by default. Use compound paths as clipping masks when you want to create more sophisticated effects, as in Figure 18.2.

You can mask more than one object. As a matter of fact, you can mask as many objects as you like. The mask itself is always the uppermost object in the stacking order.

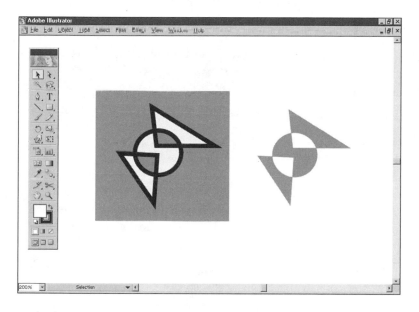

Figure 18.2

Compound paths used as clipping masks allow for more than one window to the art underneath.

Adding Objects to the Mask

After you create a clipping mask, adding masked objects is easy enough. The best way to do it is to use the Layers palette, which you can summon with Window → Layers.

You will recall from Chapter 13, "Organizing Objects," that the Layers palette lists all the objects that belong to each layer. A clipping mask and its objects appear in this list as a group. To see for yourself, open the Layers palette and click the triangle icon next to the current layer, which is probably Layer 1. If you still have the clipping mask that you created in the preceding section, there will be a group object in the list that represents the mask and its underlying art. Click the triangle icon next to this object, and you see the mask itself under the label *clipping path* at the top of the list, followed by all the masked objects.

Now, to add a new masked object, click the current layer in the Layers palette and draw a path. Position the path in front of the clipping mask with the Selection tool, and go back to the Layers

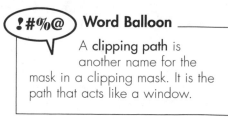

Word Balloon

A **clipping path** is another name for the mask in a clipping mask. It is the path that acts like a window.

palette. You should find a new entry in the list for the path that you just drew. Click this object, and drag it underneath the entry for the clipping path. The new path now sits behind the mask, as you can see when you look back at the document window.

Art Alert

Make sure that you grab the correct object in the Layers list. If you drag the entry for the clipping path outside the clipping-path group, the clipping mask disappears. Use Edit ➔ Undo to rectify this situation.

You can change the stacking order of the masked objects in much the same way. Drag their entries in the Layers list to arrange them. The object just under the clipping path is the uppermost object in the stack, and the object at the bottom is the lowest.

If you want to remove an object from the mask, simply drag this object's entry anywhere outside the clipping-mask group.

Moving the Mask

By moving a clipping mask, you move the window through which you see the underlying art. You could use the Direct Selection tool for the job, but the process can be unwieldy. Your best bet is to use Edit ➔ Select ➔ Masks.

Pull this command from the menu, grab the Selection tool, and drag the mask by its edge to reposition it. Your view of the underlying art changes accordingly when you release the mouse button.

Be careful, though! Edit ➔ Select ➔ Masks selects all the masks in the illustration. If you have more than one mask, you probably don't want to move them all in precisely the same way. Before dragging the edge of the mask that you want to move, hold down Shift, and with the Selection tool, click the edges of the masks that you don't want to move. This deselects them. When the selection includes only the mask that you want, proceed with the Selection tool as usual.

Adjusting the Mask

Because the mask is just a path with anchor points and segments, you can change its shape with the Direct Selection tool. As you might expect, changing the shape of the mask changes the shape of the window.

Begin by grabbing the Direct Selection tool and deselecting everything. Then move the mouse pointer onto the edge of the mask so that the outline of the path appears, but don't click just yet. Position the pointer on the segment or anchor point that you want to move, and then hold down the mouse button and drag. Release the mouse button to see the effect.

To work with the mask's bounding box, invoke Edit → Select → Masks and grab the Selection tool. Feel free to scale and rotate the bounding box as you see fit. After you select the mask, you can also apply the transformation tools, such as Reflect and Shear.

Applying Appearance Attributes

When you create a clipping mask, the stroke and fill values of the mask disappear, but there's nothing stopping you from putting them back. Applying appearance attributes to a mask makes the shape of the window clearer, as Figure 18.3 shows.

Pointers

By clicking the edge of the mask with the Direct Selection tool, you can use the hidden Pen tools to add, remove, and convert the mask's anchor points.

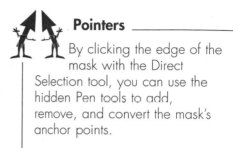

Figure 18.3

Add appearance attributes to the mask to make its shape easier to see.

All you have to do is click the mask with the Direct Selection tool. Then pull out the Color palette and the Stroke palette, and assign fill and stroke color values to your liking. The fill color of the mask appears behind its masked objects, so you will only see it in the areas that the objects don't cover.

You can also adjust the opacity of the mask, like in Figure 18.4. The mask's stroke and fill colors become transparent, but the masked objects retain their original levels of opacity.

Figure 18.4

Adjust the opacity of a clip-ping mask to make the mask's colors transparent.

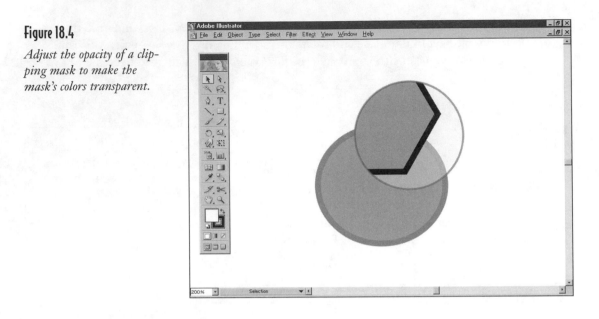

Releasing Clipping Masks

To unmake a clipping mask, click it with the Selection tool and choose Object → Clipping Mask → Release from the menu. If you have a right mouse button, you can right-click the selection and choose Release Clipping Mask from the context menu. When you do, the masked objects come fully into view.

The mask itself is still there, even if you cannot see it. It's a path without a stroke or fill value. Roll the Selection tool into the vicinity of where the mask used to be, and you will find it. You can delete this path if you like by selecting it and choosing Edit → Clear or pressing the Delete key.

If you applied appearance attributes to the mask, you will have a much easier time finding it. Illustrator releases the mask as a regular path with the same appearance attributes.

> ### Drawing Perspectives
>
> The Layers palette also gives you a way to make and release clip-ping masks. To make a clipping mask, drag a marquee around the objects that you want to use, and click the first button on the left at the bottom of the Layers palette. To release a clipping mask, select the mask and click the same button.

Paneling the Strip

What good is all this masking to computer illustrators, you might wonder. For one thing, clipping masks make great frames. Remember that vector illustration of the cat that I showed you in Chapter 2, "Of Pixels and Paths"? I used a clipping mask on it to clean up the edges and fit the paths into a neat, rectangular package, as Figure 18.5 shows.

Figure 18.5

Without the clipping mask acting as a frame, this illustration spills all over the place.

You can use the same principle to create the panel for the main scene in the Astro Ape comic. The panel is nothing more than a rectangular clipping mask that crops the edges of the underlying art.

The first step is to combine the arrow sign with the cartoon background. Open *aa_background.ai* and *aa_sign_type.ai*. Use Window ➜ Tile to fit both document windows on the screen.

Take up the Selection tool and click the sign group. Choose Edit ➜ Copy and close *aa_sign_type.ai*. You don't want to save the changes, so click No when Illustrator asks. Use Window ➜ Tile again to resize the remaining document window.

Paste the sign into the background illustration. Hold down the Shift key, and scale the sign to the right size with the Selection tool. Arrange the sign on the background like in Figure 18.6. When you finish, group everything together by choosing Edit ➜ Select All and then Object ➜ Group.

As I mentioned before, the panel itself is a rectangle. Grab the Rectangle tool, and draw a shape that nearly covers the combined illustration. Leave a little room on all four sides, as Figure 18.7 shows. This breathing space will help you out in Chapter 19, "Adding Effects," when you color the hills. Also be sure to reduce the opacity of the rectangle before you create the clipping mask to preview the window effect.

Figure 18.6

Combine the sign and the background in preparation for paneling.

Figure 18.7

Use the Rectangle tool to draw the shape that will become the panel.

Choose Edit ➔ Select All again, and follow it with Object ➔ Clipping Mask ➔ Make. The edges of the illustration disappear behind the mask, as in Figure 18.8.

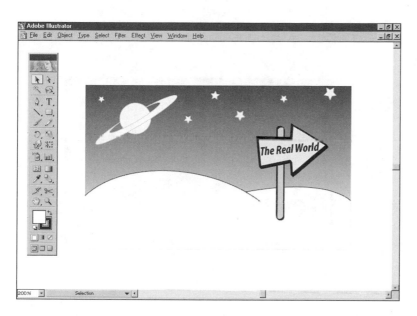

Figure 18.8

Apply a clipping mask to the rectangle and its underlying artwork.

A comic strip panel is usually a black outline. To achieve the same effect here, use Edit → Select → Masks to highlight the clipping path, and then give the mask a 4-point black stroke. Don't bother specifying a fill color, because you will not be able to see it anyway. The mask doesn't extend beyond the borders of the art.

Now is the time to look at the illustration with a critical eye. You assembled it piecemeal, so in all probability, there will be a few things about it that you will want to tweak. Use the Group Selection tool to highlight the objects that you want to adjust. If you look at Figure 18.9 very carefully, you will see that I nudged the rightmost star down a few hairs so that it doesn't sit so close to the panel border.

> **Drawing Perspectives**
>
> In comics, the shape of the panels and their arrangement on the page influences the way the audience reads the story.

Save this file as *aa_panel.ai* and consider the main scene paneled. You will use this piece for three of the eight panels in the strip.

Figure 18.9

Give the mask a 4-point black stroke, and make adjustments to the illustration elements as needed.

The Least You Need to Know

◆ A clipping mask determines which parts of its objects are visible.

◆ Use the Layers palette to arrange the masked objects.

◆ Choosing Edit ➔ Select ➔ Masks is the fastest way to select a mask.

◆ Rearrange the anchor points and segments of a mask with the Direct Selection tool.

◆ You can apply fill and stroke attributes to a mask.

◆ Clipping masks make excellent frames.

Chapter 19

Adding Effects

In This Chapter

◆ Enhancing your illustration with effects

◆ Comparing effects and filters

◆ Using effects in the Astro Ape comic

This chapter wraps up the discussion about vector graphics by showing you how and when to add effects to your work. I saved effects for last, because they belong in the last position. Not that they aren't useful. Not that they aren't particularly good in Illustrator. As a matter of fact, Illustrator's effects are some of the best around.

Effects, though, are like hot peppers in chili. You only need a few sprinkles to get the point across. Effects should enhance an illustration, not cover for it or overpower it.

You have lived up to your end of the bargain. You've worked hard to make your illustrations pleasing enough without effects. Now sit back and get ready for some well-earned magic.

Creating Drop Shadows

A *drop shadow* can increase the depth of your illustration by making it appear as though an object sits above the page. Illustrator's default drop shadows aren't just good. They are incredible. Figure 19.1 doesn't do them justice.

Figure 19.1

Add a drop shadow to an object, and the object appears to sit above the page. The drop shadow gives depth to the bottom diagram.

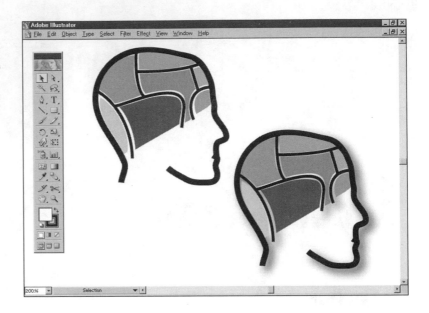

Take the opportunity here, at the top of the chapter, to open a new document window and draw a few objects. Make them as simple or as complex as you like. Use these objects to test the various effects as they come up.

Now, to add a drop shadow, click one of the objects with the Selection tool, and choose Effect → Stylize → Drop Shadow from the menu. The Drop Shadow dialog box appears, as shown in Figure 19.2. Use this dialog box to set the options of the effect. Check the Preview option, and begin playing with the controls.

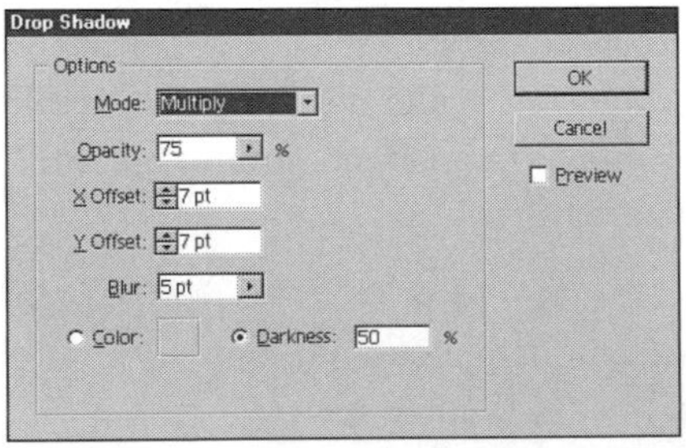

Figure 19.2

The Drop Shadow dialog box enables you to set the options for the drop shadow.

The Mode list offers different blending modes for the drop shadow. These are the same blending modes from Chapter 16, "Modifying Colors." Normally, you will want to keep this option on Multiply mode, its default. But feel free to experiment with different blending modes to get the right look.

You can also modify the opacity of the shadow, which affects how heavily the shadow falls upon objects underneath.

Change the distance of the shadow from its object under X Offset and Y Offset. Negative numbers in these fields cause the shadow to appear to the left and above the object, as if the source of light were down and to the right.

Set the overall fuzziness of the shadow with the Blur slider. The higher the value, the more diffuse the shadow.

By default, the shadow is black, but if you want to choose a different color, set the Color option and click the swatch beside it.

When you get the shadow that you want, click OK to apply it to the object.

Effects like drop shadows are appearance attributes, much like stroke and fill colors. To prove it, go back to the menu and choose Window → Show Appearance to open the Appearance palette, shown in Figure 19.3.

Drawing Perspectives

Remember that Illustrator objects are two-dimensional, so the drop shadow effect will always emphasize the flatness of the object. Don't rely on this effect to create natural-looking shadows in perspective.

 **Art Alert**

If you set the blur of the drop shadow too high, the effect may become so diffuse that you can't see it. To avoid this, increase the blur gradually, just a few points at a time. Check the Preview option on the Drop Shadow dialog box, and keep your eye on the art as you go.

Figure 19.3

The Appearance palette lists the appearance attributes of an object.

The Appearance palette lists the appearance attributes of the currently selected object. Sure enough, if you look in the list, you should see an entry for Drop Shadow.

To change the properties of the drop shadow, double-click its entry in the list, and the Drop Shadow dialog box reappears. Make the changes and click OK. To remove the drop shadow entirely, click its entry once to select it, and then click the trashcan icon at the bottom of the Appearance palette.

Now group a couple of your sample objects, and apply a drop shadow to the group. Notice that every object in the group acquires a drop shadow, like the group on the left in Figure 19.4. If you want the effect to apply to the group as a whole, like the object on the right, simply target the group on the Layers palette.

Figure 19.4

Normally, when you apply an effect to a group, every object in the group gets the effect (left). By targeting the group on the Layers palette, you can apply an effect to the group as a whole (right).

You have targeted groups before, in Chapter 17, "Working with Transparency," to be precise. The same procedure applies here. Open the Layers palette under Window ➔ Show Layers, and click the triangle icon of the current layer to reveal the list of objects. Find the entry for the group, and click the circle after its name to target it. Now, when you apply the drop shadow, the effect treats the group like a single path.

Making Glows

Glows create the appearance of hazy light, which helps to bring out dark objects when they sit against a dark background. There are two kinds of glows in Illustrator: inner glows and outer glows. An inner glow puts the glow effect inside the object, like a neon sign. An outer glow puts the effect outside the object, like a halo. Figure 19.5 shows examples of both types of glows.

Drawing Perspectives
An object can have both an inner and an outer glow. In fact, an object can have as many effects as you care to apply.

Adding glows is as easy as adding drop shadows. Select an object, open the Effect menu, and choose Stylize ➔ Inner Glow or Stylize ➔ Outer Glow. Either way, you get a dialog box of options.

In an inner glow, the Mode option represents the blending mode of the light. Use the default Screen mode for most purposes. The swatch to the right of the Mode list gives the color of the light. Click the swatch to change the color. You also have options for setting the glow in the center or along the edge of the object. If you choose the Center option, the glow appears in the fill of the object. If you choose the Edge option, the glow appears in the stroke.

You have fewer choices in an outer glow. Set the blending mode, the color of the light, the opacity, and the blur. Much like with drop shadows, the greater the blur, the more diffuse the glow.

Click OK in the dialog box to set the effect. You can modify your object afterward or remove it entirely by way of the Appearance palette, and you can apply the glow to a group as a whole by targeting the group in the Layers palette.

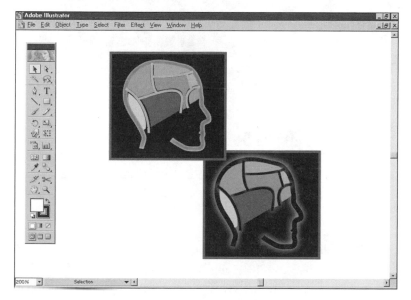

Figure 19.5

An inner glow (top) creates the effect of a neon sign. An outer glow (bottom) creates the effect of a halo.

Causing Distortion

Distortion changes the shape of an object. Unlike the transformation tools, which let you control exactly how the object transforms, the distortion effects apply mathematical operations to the anchor points and segments of the object. Some of these effects, such as scribbling, use random functions. See Figure 19.6 for a healthy cross-section of distortion effects. From left to right in the top row, the effects are pucker, bloat, and roughen. From left to right in the bottom row, the effects are scribble and tweak, twist, and zigzag.

Find Illustrator's distortion effects under Effect ➔ Distort & Transform. Table 19.1 describes these effects.

Figure 19.6

Use distortion effects to change the shape of an object.

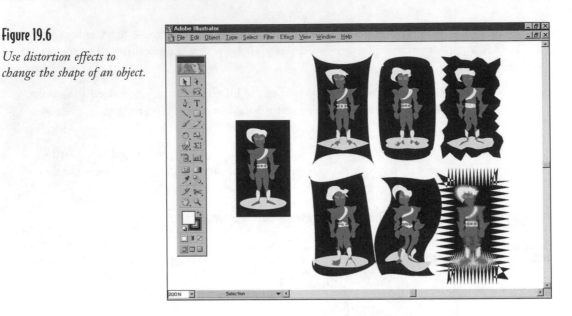

Table 19.1   What the Distortion Effects Do

Effect	Result
Pucker	Curves object inward.
Bloat	Curves object outward.
Roughen	Creates rough edges.
Scribble and Tweak	Randomly adjusts anchor points.
Twist	Rotates shape of object like a pinwheel.
Zig Zag	Converts straight lines to zigzags.
Free Distort	Enables distortion of object's bounding box.
Transform	Performs scale, move, rotate, and reflect.

Pointers

The Twist tool, which hides under the Rotate tool in the toolbox, works like the Twist effect. Select an object, and then grab the Twist tool. Drag the mouse in a clockwise direction to twist the object clockwise, or drag the mouse in a counterclockwise direction to twist it counterclockwise. The farther the mouse pointer from the object, the finer control you have over the distortion. Be warned, though! Unlike the Twist effect, the Twist tool doesn't add an appearance attribute to the object. Instead, it changes the shape of the object permanently, unless you choose Edit → Undo.

When you select an object and choose a distortion effect from the menu, the effect's dialog box appears. Check the Preview box, and specify the options that you want. I will not go through all the options here, but I will point out some of the main features.

Puckering and bloating use the same dialog box. Drag the slider to the left to pucker (or punk) the object, or drag the slider to the right for bloating. For roughening, drag the Detail slider to the right to create more rough edges. For scribbling and tweaking, the Horizontal slider controls the amount of horizontal drift in the anchor points, and the Vertical slider controls the vertical drift. For twisting, a positive value in the Angle field causes a clockwise distortion, whereas a negative value causes a counterclockwise distortion. For zigzagging, you can specify smooth points instead of corner points for a more ripple-like effect.

These effects require some practice, so by all means, experiment with the controls. Click OK to set the effect. You can modify and remove an effect with the Appearance palette. Also, don't forget that to apply a distortion effect to a group as a whole, make sure to target the group in the Layers palette.

> **Drawing Perspectives**
>
> The Free Distort effect works like the Free Transform tool when you hold down Ctrl (Windows) or Command (Mac). This effect enables you to drag the handles of the object's bounding box as if they were anchor points.

Using Photoshop Filters

Photoshop comes with a number of special image-processing commands called *filters* that make photographs look more like paintings. The full version of Illustrator borrows many of these painterly effects wholesale. Call them the *Photoshop filter effects* for obvious reasons. You can find these in the bottom half of the Effect menu. (If you're using the trial version of Illustrator, you might notice a smaller set of these effects.) Figure 19.7 provides a sampling of Photoshop filter effects. In the top row, from left to right, the effects are Cutout, Rough Pastels, and Gaussian Blur. In the middle row, they are Ink Outlines, Diffuse Glow, and Mezzotint. In the bottom row, they are Bas Relief, Chalk & Charcoal, and Mosaic Tiles.

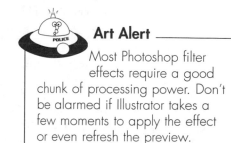

Art Alert

Most Photoshop filter effects require a good chunk of processing power. Don't be alarmed if Illustrator takes a few moments to apply the effect or even refresh the preview.

These commands work much like the others in that you select an object and then choose an effect. A dialog box appears, enabling you to set the options of the effect, and you click OK to finish.

Figure 19.7

Everyone's favorite monkey never looked so painterly.

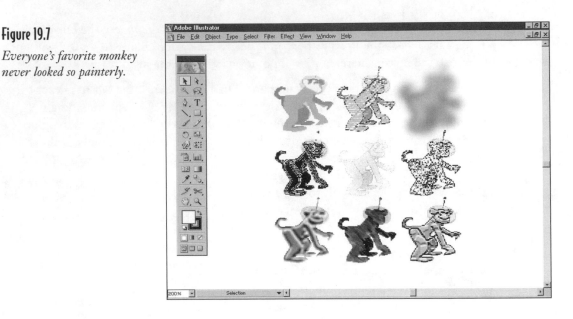

Comparing Filters and Effects

You have probably noticed that Illustrator has a separate Filter menu. When you select an object and open this menu instead of the one for effects, you see what appear to be duplicate commands, and not just in the painterly filters that Illustrator borrows from Photoshop. Filter ➜ Distort has options for Pucker & Bloat, Roughen, Twist, and the like, whereas Filter ➜ Stylize offers Drop Shadow, among others. What is going on here? Are filters and effects the same thing in Illustrator?

This calls for an experiment. Draw a simple shape, make a copy, and paste it nearby, like the circles in Figure 19.8. Select the shape on the left, choose Filter ➜ Stylize ➜ Drop Shadow, and click OK in the dialog box that appears. Then select the shape on the right and apply the same drop shadow as an effect.

Compare the shapes very closely. They look identical. It would appear that filters and effects are the same. But if you select the shape on the left and look at the Appearance palette, you will not find an entry for the drop shadow in the attributes list. When you select the shape on the right, however, the drop-shadow attribute appears. Further, the shape on the right shows up as an object on the Appearance palette, whereas the shape on the left shows up as a group.

Clearly, there is more going on with filters and effects than meets the eye. The end results may look the same, but how Illustrator achieves these results couldn't be more different.

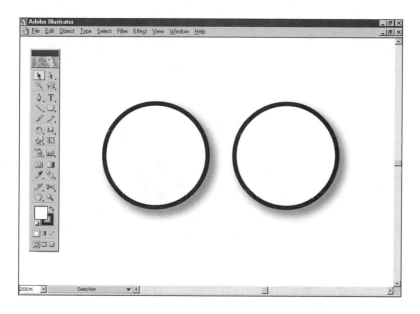

Figure 19.8

The drop shadow on the left comes from a filter. The one on the right comes from an effect. In appearance, these drop shadows are identical, but in behavior, they are quite different.

Processing an object with an *effect* keeps the original object intact. The effect shows up in the Appearance palette's attributes list, which means that you can modify the effect freely or remove it at will. By contrast, processing an object with a *filter* transforms the characteristics of the object or adds new objects to the document window.

When you created the drop shadow with the filter in your experiment, Illustrator added the shadow as a separate object and then grouped it with the original. To prove it, select the shape on the left and choose Object → Ungroup. Click an empty area of the page to deselect everything. You can now drag the shape away from its shadow, as Figure 19.9 shows. Try the same thing with the shape on the right, and you will have no luck at all. You cannot separate this drop shadow from its object, because the shadow is an attribute of the object itself. It's just as much a part of the object as the stroke and the fill.

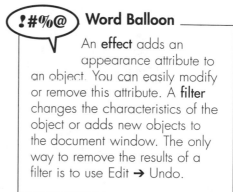

Word Balloon

An **effect** adds an appearance attribute to an object. You can easily modify or remove this attribute. A **filter** changes the characteristics of the object or adds new objects to the document window. The only way to remove the results of a filter is to use Edit → Undo.

Similarly, if you pucker an object with a filter, the shape of the object changes. Permanently. The only way to restore the original shape of the object is to call upon your old friend Edit → Undo. But if you pucker an object with an effect, only the appearance of the object changes. Remove the effect from the Appearance palette's attribute list, and the object returns to its original shape.

Figure 19.9

When you apply a drop shadow as a filter, the drop shadow becomes a separate object that you can ungroup and move.

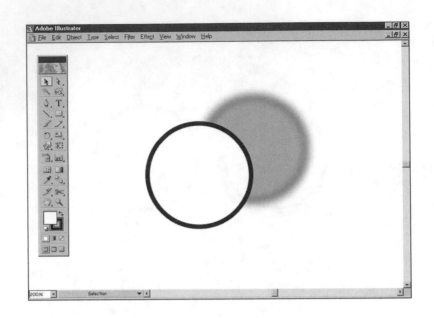

Moreover, most of the Filter commands only work on raster objects. I haven't talked about this much at all so far, but Illustrator enables you to place raster images such as JPG, GIF, and BMP files into your vector artwork. To do so, use the Place command on the File menu. When you select one of these raster objects, you can process your selection with most of the Filter commands, including the painterly Photoshop filters. Even still, the Effect commands work equally well on raster and vector objects.

Because effects offer more flexibility, you should always choose from the Effect menu instead of the Filter menu whenever possible. In a few cases, like when you want to process the colors of an object, you don't have a choice. You have to use a Filter command, because there is no corresponding Effect command. But when you do have a choice, the better choice is always the effect.

Rasterizing Vector Objects

If you insist on using a Filter command with a vector object, you may need to rasterize the object first. *Rasterizing* means transforming a vector-based image into a raster-based one. As you may recall from Chapter 2, "Of Pixels and Paths," a raster image contains pixels instead of paths, which makes it generally more difficult to edit.

To rasterize a vector object, select it and choose Object ➔ Rasterize from the menu. The Rasterize dialog box appears. Set the options as you prefer, paying particular attention to the resolution. In general, the higher the resolution, the better the image quality, but the best resolution setting isn't always the highest. For screen-based images, a resolution of

72 dpi is sufficient. See Chapter 2 to refresh your memory about this particular discussion.

Click OK to rasterize the image. Now when you click it, you can apply the bitmap-only Filter commands, but you can no longer edit the image as if it were a vector.

Art Alert

After you rasterize a vector object, the only way to change it back into a vector is to use Edit → Undo.

Managing Effects

Because effects are appearance attributes such as fill and stroke color, you can manage them using the same tools and commands as appearance attributes.

You already know that, to remove an effect, you highlight its entry on the Appearance palette and then click the trashcan icon. If you need to take more drastic measures, the Appearance palette gives you two other buttons for cleaning up appearance attributes. The second button from the left, Clear Appearance, removes all the appearance attributes of the object, leaving you with an object that has no fill, no stroke, and no effects. The third button from the left, Reduce To Basic Appearance, removes all the appearance attributes and replaces them with a white fill and a 1-point black stroke.

Sharing Effects

One way to apply an object's effects to a different object is to use the Eyedropper or Paint Bucket tool. Select the object that you want to change and click the Eyedropper on the object whose appearance attributes you want to transfer, or select the object whose attributes you want to transfer and click the Paint Bucket on the object that you want to change.

In both cases, the object that you want to change acquires all the appearance attributes of the other object, including the stroke and fill colors, stroke weight, and stroke style, along with the effects.

If you don't want all the appearance attributes, there may be a shortcut. Select the object that you want to change, and choose the first item in the Effect menu. This command applies the most recent effect to the new object.

Pointers

If you use Filter commands instead of Effect commands, don't try transferring effects with the Eyedropper and Paint Bucket, because these tools will not work. You can reapply the most recent filter to a new object, though, by selecting the object and choosing the first item in the Filter menu.

Turning Off Effects

To see your illustration without effects, choose View ➔ Outline. This command temporarily hides all the appearance attributes in the document window, including stroke and fill color and the like. Use View ➔ Preview to restore the appearance attributes.

Twinkle, Twinkle, Little Stars

A few outer glows will help you to polish off the main panel illustration for Astro Ape that you put together in Chapter 18, "Working with Masks." Remember that an outer glow appears something like a halo, which makes this effect especially useful for objects that need to shine. Or twinkle, as the case may be.

> **Drawing Perspectives**
>
> Stars seem to twinkle because the hot and cold layers of the Earth's atmosphere bend their light in different directions. If the Earth had no atmosphere, the stars would shine steadily, like the Sun.

Open up *aa_panel.ai* and grab the Group Selection tool. Hold down Shift, and click each of the stars. Choose Effect ➔ Stylize ➔ Outer Glow. If you played with the options earlier, you may need to reset them to the Illustrator defaults of the Screen blending mode, 75% opacity, and 5-point blur. For the color, use the Illustrator default, which is RGB red 250, green 250, and blue 190. Click OK, and your stars acquire subtle coronas, as you can just barely see in Figure 19.10.

Figure 19.10

The only thing better than an effect is a subtle effect, like the outer glows around the stars.

Now turn your attention at last to the rolling hills. I have been telling you to overlook them for many chapters now, and it's about time for action. An outer glow will work well here also. It will enhance the atmospheric effect that the gradient in the sky creates.

The only drawback is that the outer glow will surround the entire hill object. You only want the glow to appear above the hills—not on the sides or beneath. Fortunately, in this case, it's a nonissue, because the clipping mask you created in Chapter 18 should conceal the glow on the sides and bottom.

The first order of business is to color the hills. Click the hills object with the Group Selection tool, and then click the curved-arrow icon to the right of the fill-color square in the toolbox. This swaps the stroke and fill colors, so that the object acquires a black fill and a white stroke. I like the way this looks against the sky, so I'm leaving the black fill as is. If you prefer a different color, then apply it, by all means. Darker shades work better than lighter ones, though. A dark background helps the monkey's green space suit to *pop*, or stand out.

Now, it's a simple matter of applying the outer glow. You know what to do: Choose Effect → Stylize → Outer Glow, and use the same settings that you did for the stars. The top of the hills gives off a very pale light, and the mask takes care of the unwanted glow everywhere else, as Figure 19.11 shows.

‼#%@ Word Balloon

The foreground of an illustration **pops** when it grabs the audience's attention immediately.

Figure 19.11

Color the hills and apply an outer glow. The clipping mask conceals the glow around the sides and bottom of the object, leaving a faint haze against the sky.

There you have it: the main panel design. Save this file as *aa_panel_glow.ai*. You're ready now to bring the various Astro Ape files together and turn them into a comic strip.

The Least You Need to Know

◆ Effects are like hot peppers: Use them sparingly!

◆ Drop shadows can add depth to an illustration.

◆ Glows can help dark objects to stand out against a dark background.

◆ Distortion effects change the shape of an object.

◆ Photoshop filters create painterly effects.

◆ Effect commands add appearance attributes to an object, whereas Filter commands change the object.

◆ Rasterize vector objects to apply bitmap-only filters to them.

◆ Because effects are appearance attributes, you can manage them like other appearance attributes.

Part 6

Applying Finishing Touches

All your hard work pays off here, now, in this final part. You'll polish off the Astro Ape project with a few new vector graphics. You'll convert a digital photo into the Real World by way of Adobe Photoshop. You'll experiment with vectors in Photoshop and rasters in Illustrator, and you'll combine both types of graphics for the final comic strip. And then you'll publish your work in the medium of your choice. It doesn't get much better than this.

Putting the Pieces Together

In This Chapter

- ◆ Creating the last few vector illustrations
- ◆ Processing the photo background in Photoshop
- ◆ Combining vector and raster graphics
- ◆ Laying out the pages of the Astro Ape comic

This is it! The moment you've been waiting for! This is the chapter where you take the monkey illustrations you've been drawing since the beginning of the book and turn them into a comic strip.

You have just about all the vector art you need. There is the matter of the photorealistic panels, though, for when Astro Ape arrives in the Real World. You will recall that photographs aren't vector images at all but pixel-based rasters. Although Illustrator can work with raster images, they aren't its forte. Expect a short but pleasant detour to Photoshop in this chapter, where you will transform an ordinary urban photo into a most unpleasant postcard that no city council in its right mind would approve. Then you will lay out the panels like comic book pages, and you'll have something new for your refrigerator door.

Sticking to the Plan

Now is a good time to decide what you have and what you need to complete the Astro Ape project. To help you in this regard, refer back to your *outline*.

"Wait a minute," I can hear you saying. "You didn't mention anything about an *outline* before."

You're right, of course. I didn't tell you about the outline when you started this project, but I have been following it all along. I didn't want to bring it up while you were busy learning the tools and techniques of computer illustration. Now that you have plenty of skill in these areas, I present the outline for you to see.

Drawing Perspectives

In a professional setting, of course, you should have serious reservations about drawing anything without an outline or a project plan in front of you. I mention this because projects often don't come with outlines, and your boss or art director will ask you to overlook this minor detail. Don't do it! Create an outline yourself if you have to, but don't just start drawing. You, your boss, and the client will be much happier if you know the parameters of the project from the get-go.

The outline of a comic strip is just a panel-by-panel breakdown of the story. You know the gist of it already: Astro Ape sees a sign for the Real World, follows it, doesn't like what he finds there, and announces that reality is overrated. The outline determines which part of the story happens in what panel, as Table 20.1 shows.

Table 20.1 Outline for the Astro Ape Comic

Panel	Description
1	Logo, byline.
2	Ape walks toward arrow sign.
3	Ape activates space goggles.
4	Ape reads sign through goggles.
5	Ape follows sign.
6	Ape sees Real World.
7	Ape beats hasty retreat.
8	Ape returns, delivers punchline.

It's also never a bad idea to sketch a panel *layout* on a piece of paper or in an empty document window. This helps you to visualize the outline. After much experimentation, I'm leaning toward a two-page layout with five panels on the first page and three on the second, like in Figure 20.1. Creating a two-page comic instead of a one-pager means that your art will look better, and it gives you more freedom to try interesting panel *transitions* like the superimposed panel on page 2 of the design in the following figure.

Word Balloon

The **layout** is the arrangement of elements on a page.

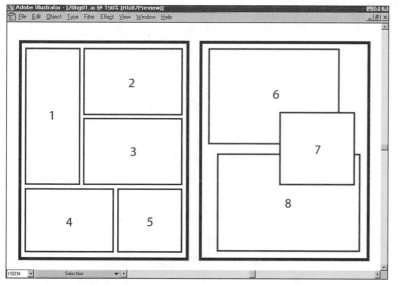

Figure 20.1

Sketching the panel layout helps you to visualize the outline for the comic strip.

Drawing Perspectives

The transition between panels is a crucial element in the medium of comics. Transitions affect the reader's perception of time and space in the story. Placing Astro Ape between panels 1 and 2 draws the reader into the story quickly while emphasizing the idea that Astro Ape has traveled far. By contrast, if you flip to "Foreboding Planet" in the color insert, note that the panel transitions slow down the pace of the story.

After you decide to make two pages, the question becomes, where should the first page end? Comic book publishers like to give their readers a reason to turn every page. Ending the first page with Astro Ape following the sign does the trick. Readers will want to see where the sign leads, so they will turn the page. Also, opening the second page with a big panel of the Real World heightens the impact of the change in scenery.

Back to business. What do you have, and what do you still need? You have the logo, and you can create a byline easily with the Type tool, so panel 1 is in good shape. Check panel 1 from the list.

You have the main panel design, which includes the hills, the sky, and the arrow sign. You could use this illustration in panels 2, 3, 5, and 8. Glancing at the layout, though, you will note that panels 2, 3, and 5 sit one on top of the other. The same image three times in a row spells monotony, and a comic strip should never be monotonous. Certainly you can come up with something clever for one of these panels, like, say, presenting Astro Ape and the sign in silhouette against a plain white background. That sounds like it would make a good panel 5. So, check panels 2, 3, and 8, and put a note next to panel 5 that you need two silhouettes.

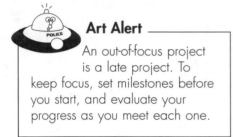

Art Alert

An out-of-focus project is a late project. To keep focus, set milestones before you start, and evaluate your progress as you meet each one.

Panel 4 is the first-person point of view that you created in Chapter 16, "Modifying Colors," so check that one from the list.

That leaves panels 6 and 7—the ones with the photographic background. To indicate that Astro Ape has vacated panel 7 in a hurry, you could add something like a cloud of dust. For panel 6, then, indicate that you need a photo background and, for panel 7, a photo and a cloud of dust. Table 20.2 presents the revised outline.

Table 20.2 Revised Outline for the Astro Ape Comic

Panel	Description	Finished?
1	Logo, byline.	✔
2	Ape walks toward arrow sign.	✔
3	Ape activates space goggles.	✔
4	Ape reads sign through goggles.	✔
5	Ape follows sign.	Need silhouettes
6	Ape sees Real World.	Need photo
7	Ape beats hasty retreat.	Need photo and dust
8	Ape returns, delivers punchline.	✔

The project comes sharply into focus. You now know exactly what you need to do to get this one out the door.

The Shadow Knows

These silhouettes are going to be a piece of cake. The idea here is to present Astro Ape and the sign as black shapes against a white background. All you have to do is change the fill color of the sign and one of the character designs to solid black, and you have silhouettes.

Start with the sign. Open up *aa_sign_type.ai*, and click the sign group with the Selection tool. Call up the Color palette, click the fill-color square, and pick black from the RGB Spectrum. If you want to mix the color instead, its components are red 0, green 0, and blue 0. (See Figure 20.2 for the finished result.) Save this file as *aa-sign-silhouette.ai*.

Figure 20.2

Simply change the fill color of this group to black to make a sign-shaped silhouette.

Close the document window, and move on to the monkey. Open *aa_side_color_t.ai*. Because creating the silhouette is so easy, why not take a few extra moments to repurpose some content and give the audience something slightly different to look at? I'm speaking here of rotating the arms and legs, much like you did in Chapter 14, "Applying Transformations," only in the opposite direction.

Last time, you rotated the foreground limbs outward. This time, rotate them inward. Using the Group Selection tool, click the foreground leg. Then grab the Rotate tool and reposition the point of origin by dragging it to the middle of the hip or so. Rotate the leg a few degrees counterclockwise. Get the Group Selection tool again

Drawing Perspectives

When you change the appearance attribute of a group, the attribute changes for all the objects in the group.

and reposition the leg slightly if the pose doesn't look right. Repeat this procedure on the foreground arm, only rotate it a few degrees clockwise. Continue with the background limbs. Rotate the background leg clockwise and the background arm counterclockwise. Reposition these paths as required to get the correct pose. When you finish, your newly repurposed Astro Ape should look something like Figure 20.3.

Figure 20.3

Rotate the limbs in the direction opposite of the one you used in Chapter 14.

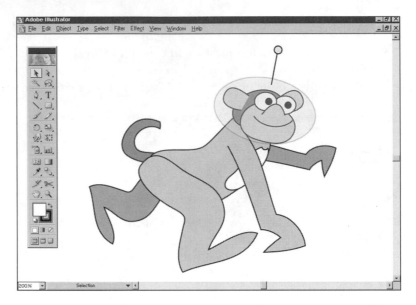

Save this as *aa_side_running3.ai*, but don't close the document window yet. You still need to create the silhouette.

Click the group with the regular Selection tool, and change the fill color to black, just like before. An incredibly cool thing happens to the helmet, as Figure 20.4 shows. The transparency you applied to the helmet survives the shift in fill color, making the helmet seem smoky gray against a white background. These kinds of added bonuses upset traditional illustrators, so don't brag too much to your noncomputer-enabled friends.

Save this file as *aa_side_silhouette.ai*. Not bad, eh? You can check off panel 5 in the outline.

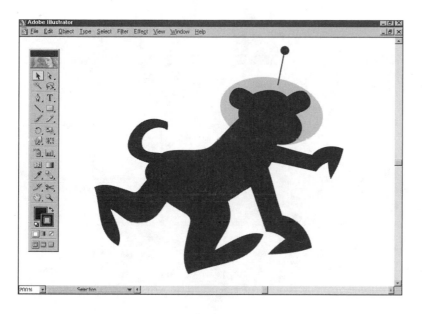

Figure 20.4

The monkey strikes a dramatic pose with a simple shift in fill color. Note the cool helmet effect, courtesy of the transparency you specified.

Mixing Photos and Fantasy

I'm going to ask you to do the unthinkable and quit out of Illustrator for the time being. You're ready now to process the photographic background for panels 6 and 7, and Illustrator isn't the tool for the job.

Illustrator's domain is vector graphics. Although it understands raster images such as photographs, it doesn't really know what to do with them. When it comes time to work with photographs in almost any computer graphics project, there is really only one choice: the venerable Adobe Photoshop.

If you have the full version of Photoshop already, then allow me to compliment you on a wise investment. If you haven't bit the bullet and gone out and bought it, you can find a trial version on the CD-ROM that comes with this book. The Photoshop trial doesn't enable you to save or print, but you can use it to do everything else in these examples, and you can find my saved versions of the art on the CD-ROM.

Go ahead and launch Photoshop. The interface in Figure 20.5 should look familiar to you. Photoshop has a toolbar and palettes, much like Illustrator. If you glance at the Filter menu, you will find the painterly effects that Illustrator borrows. Notice, though, that Photoshop doesn't have an Effect menu. Instead, Photoshop offers *layer styles* for things such as glows and shadows. Access layer styles from the Layer menu.

> **Drawing Perspectives**
>
> Photoshop's layer styles fill in for Illustrator's Effect menu.

Figure 20.5

The Photoshop interface has many familiar elements, including a toolbar and movable palettes.

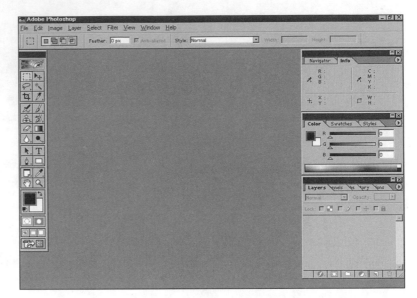

Be warned, though, that Undo is *not* your friend in Photoshop. Unlike Illustrator, Photoshop can only undo the most recent action. To compensate for this, Photoshop provides the History palette, which opens after you choose Window → Show History. As you can see in Figure 20.6, the History palette lists the actions that you performed on an image. By clicking an action in the list, you can roll back your work to an earlier time. For instance, if you decide that you don't like a change that you made four actions ago, click the action immediately above the undesired change in the History palette, and start again from that point.

Figure 20.6

Use the History palette instead of Edit → Undo to correct old mistakes.

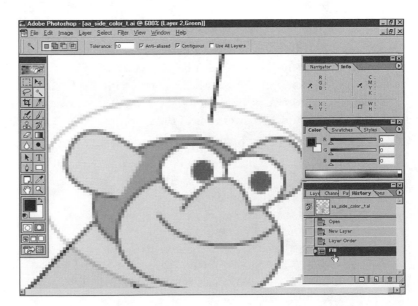

Now, for a photographic background, you need a photograph. I went out and took one of Chestnut Street in my adopted home of Philadelphia. You can find it on the CD-ROM in the Chapter 20 subfolder of the Art folder. The filename is *photo.jpg*. Have a look at it in Figure 20.7. You can use your own photograph if you like.

Figure 20.7

Choose File → Open in Photoshop to load the background photograph.

To bring this picture into Photoshop, go to the File menu and choose Open. Navigate to the *photo.jpg* file on the CD-ROM and click the Open button. Then choose View → Fit On Screen to make the photo as large as possible, so that you can see what you're doing.

This photo is a raster image, which means that it is a series of pixels, or very small, colored squares. There are no paths in this image. There are no objects. There are no anchor points or segments of any kind. There are only rows and rows of colored squares.

To get the vital statistics for this image, choose Image → Image Size from the menu. The Image Size dialog box appears, like in Figure 20.8. According to Photoshop, this city photo is 1,800 pixels wide and 1,200 pixels tall. Its print size is 6 inches by 4 inches, which means that 300 pixels are crammed into every inch of space. This value, 300 pixels per inch, is the *resolution* of the photo.

Art Alert

Avoid taking photos on Chestnut Street in Philadelphia. Passers-by look at you strangely.

As far as resolutions go, 300 dpi (dots per inch) isn't too bad. It's a good working resolution. If you print out the photo, it will not look too grainy. As a matter of fact, this resolution is about three times too high for use on screen, but that's all right. Going from high resolution to low resolution is never a problem. I step you through the procedure for optimizing your work in Chapter 21, "Getting It Out There."

Figure 20.8

Photoshop's Image Size dialog box provides the vital statistics of the current photo.

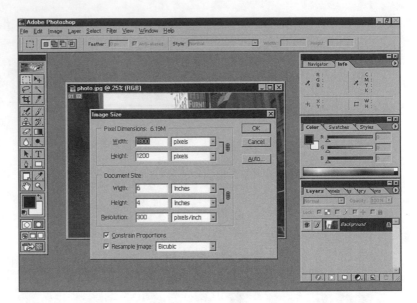

Click OK or Cancel to close the Image Size dialog box, and take a good, hard, critical look at the photograph before you. It's the Real World, all right, but it doesn't appear to be quite as menacing as it needs to be for the comic strip. Fortunately, Photoshop provides.

Choose Image → Adjust → Hue/Saturation from the menu to get the Hue/Saturation dialog box, as in Figure 20.9. You will recall from Chapter 16, "Modifying Colors," that saturating colors in Illustrator makes them more vivid, and desaturating them washes them out. The same holds true in Photoshop. Photoshop also enables you to *colorize* an image, which converts the image's color information into shades of some other color. The effect is like a black-and-white photo, only the picture is red and white, periwinkle and white, chartreuse and white, or what have you.

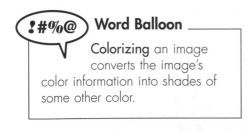

Word Balloon

Colorizing an image converts the image's color information into shades of some other color.

Check the Colorize option on the Hue/Saturation dialog box, and drag the Hue slider to see what I mean. As the hue of the image changes, Photoshop colorizes the image differently. You will note that Photoshop also automatically sets the saturation to 25%. This washes out the colors of the photo just enough for the colorization effect.

Hue 36 creates an especially polluted, bilious shade of brown that helps to cast the right pall upon the Real World. Drag the Hue slider to 36, or type **36** directly into the field. Keep the saturation at 25% and click OK.

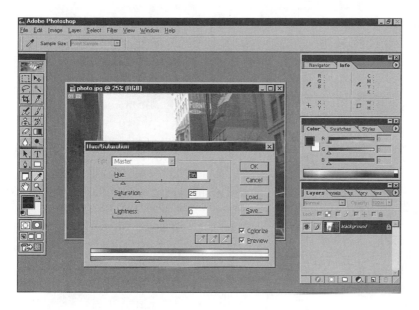

Figure 20.9

Adjust the saturation and colorize a photo with the Hue/Saturation dialog box.

Already you're getting somewhere. Now, how about making the lighting a bit harsher? Choose Image ➔ Adjust ➔ Brightness/Contrast, and the Brightness/Contrast dialog box appears, as in Figure 20.10.

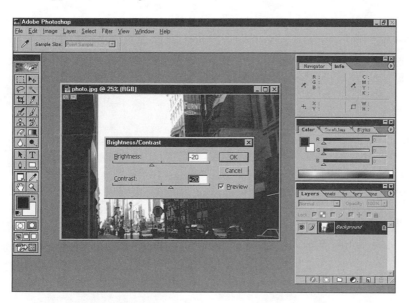

Figure 20.10

Use the Brightness/Contrast dialog box to modify the lights and shadows of an image.

Brightness and contrast control the levels of light and shadow in the image. Set the brightness at –20 to darken the image, and then bump up the contrast to +20 to accentuate the light and dark areas. Click OK. Philadelphia now looks very unpleasant indeed.

For the last step, create a black panel border around the photograph. You could use Photoshop's drawing tools, but there is a quicker and better way: changing the size of the canvas.

Photoshop's canvas is something like Illustrator's artboard. The canvas is inside the document window, and the photograph sits on top of it. When you open a raster image, Photoshop automatically adjusts the canvas to match the image size, which is why you cannot see the canvas right now. The image covers it completely. But you can easily set the size of the canvas to anything you want.

Before you do that, though, set the canvas color to black. Take a look at the Photoshop toolbar, and you will see what appear to be fill-color and stroke-color squares. These are actually the foreground and background color, and the background color is the color of the canvas. By default, the foreground color is black, and the canvas is white, but I'll bet you can figure out how to switch them. Click the curved-arrow icon that sits between the squares, just like in Illustrator. When you do, the square on the left turns white, and the square on the right turns black.

Pointers

Double-clicking the color square for the foreground or background enables you to set the foreground or background color. You can also use Photoshop's Color palette, which opens with Window → Show Color. Click the color square for the foreground or background on the Color palette, and then choose from the RGB Spectrum at the bottom of the palette or mix the color by hand with the sliders, just like in Illustrator.

Now choose Image → Canvas Size from the menu. This brings up the Canvas Size dialog box, like in Figure 20.11. To change the size of the canvas, type values for the width and the height in the appropriate fields, and then set the anchor by clicking one of the squares in the diagram. The anchor determines where the photo sits on the canvas. If you want the photo to be in the lower left corner, for instance, you click the lower left square in the Anchor diagram.

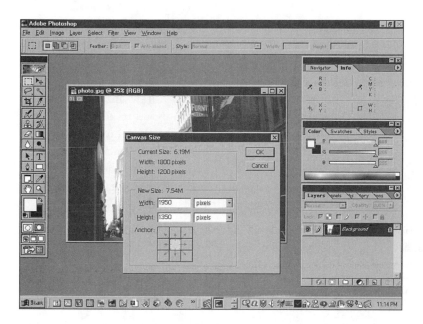

Figure 20.11

Change the size of the canvas with Image → Canvas Size.

For now, you want to create a border around the photo on all four sides, so leave the anchor in the middle of the diagram. Type **1950** for the width and **1350** for the height, and click OK. The image appears in the middle of a black canvas, as Figure 20.12 shows. Now you have a black border.

Figure 20.12

It's no fun being a Philadelphian, at least not after you colorize, desaturate, adjust the brightness and contrast, and resize the canvas.

It's time to bring the monkey into the scene, which means that it's time to add a new layer to the image.

Layers in Photoshop work just like layers in Illustrator. They're like transparent sheets of plastic that you pull over the artboard or, in this case, the canvas. Although layers in Illustrator are handy organizational tools, they are far more important in the Photoshop environment, where adding new layers is the best way to combine different images. In Illustrator, all you have to do is draw, and Illustrator's stacking order decides what appears on top of what. Not so in Photoshop. If you take the Pencil tool and draw something on top of the photo, the Pencil pixels completely replace the photo pixels. Draw the Pencil pixels in a new layer, though, and the photo pixels in the previous layer remain safe and sound.

> **Drawing Perspectives**
>
> Photoshop's Pencil tool doesn't create freeform paths. Instead, it puts down a continuous series of pixels.

Choose Window ➔ Show Layers to get the Layers palette, and click the new-layer icon at the bottom of the palette. Photoshop creates a new layer and inserts it above the current one. This will be the home for the rear view of Astro Ape.

The next step is to bring the rear view into Photoshop. You will recall that this illustration is vector-based, and I have only mentioned about five hundred times in this chapter alone that Photoshop likes pixels, not paths. True enough. But, just like Illustrator can deal with raster images, Photoshop can deal with vectors.

To prove it, choose File ➔ Open, and set the Files Of Type list to All Formats. Locate your copy of *aa_rear_color_t.ai*, and click Open. The Rasterize Generic PDF Format dialog box comes up. In essence, Photoshop is telling you that it wants to convert the paths of the file into pixels, and it's giving you the opportunity to determine the resolution and size.

Type **300** into the Resolution field, because the photo background is also 300 dpi. Then, for the height, type **500** pixels. Photoshop calculates the proportionate width. Leave the rest of the controls on their default settings, and click OK to proceed.

> **Pointers**
>
> The Move tool moves the layer itself, not the individual pixels. This is why you don't have to put the mouse pointer directly on top of the monkey pixels. However, you will find that it's easier to position Astro Ape if you bring the mouse pointer into his vicinity before you start dragging.

Photoshop does as promised. It rasterizes the vector image and places it in its own document window against a transparent canvas. The checkerboard pattern in the background represents transparency.

Now choose Select ➔ All. A flashing marquee appears around all the pixels in the image. Choose Edit ➔ Copy. Then click the document window of the photograph. Look at the Layers palette, and click the new layer to highlight it. Then choose Edit ➔ Paste from the menu. The pixels that you copied from the Astro Ape image transfer to the new layer in the photograph.

Grab the Move tool from the toolbox. This is the first tool on the right. Position the mouse pointer anywhere in the image, hold down the mouse button, and drag. The monkey follows. Bring Astro Ape to the lower left corner of the canvas.

Now add an effect, or a *style*, to this layer. Choose Layer → Layer Style → Inner Shadow, and drag the Distance slider in the Inner Shadow dialog box to 10 pixels or so. Astro Ape acquires a pleasing, if subtle, lighting effect, as in Figure 20.13.

Figure 20.13

Copy the pixels from the rasterized Astro Ape image and paste them into a new layer in the photograph. Then, with the Move tool, position Astro Ape in the lower left corner and apply a layer style to create the lighting effect.

Good job! That takes care of panel 6. If you're using the full version of Photoshop, choose File → Save As from the menu. Type the filename *aa_photo.jpg* into the field, and make sure the Save As Type list shows the JPEG format. When you click the Save button, the JPEG Options dialog box appears. These options enable you to control how Photoshop saves the image. Notice that you can reduce the quality of the photo, which creates a smaller file at the expense of some picture clarity. For now, leave the values at their default settings and click OK.

Before you tackle panel 7, close the document window for the rasterized rear-view illustration. You don't need it anymore. Make sure to click No when Photoshop asks whether you want to save the changes.

Panel 7 is easy. It's just a smaller version of panel 6, without Astro Ape, of course. He has departed in a cloud of dust. You can add the cloud of dust in Illustrator. For now, just make the image smaller.

First things first. To get rid of Astro Ape, highlight the ape layer in the Layers palette, click the

Drawing Perspectives

By default, Photoshop saves in the PSD format. PSD is Photoshop's native format, much like the AI format in Illustrator.

trashcan icon at the bottom of the palette, and click Yes to confirm. The layer and its monkey pixels disappear.

Now, when I say "resize the image," I need to define my terms, because there are two possible ways to go. You can scale the image, in which case the entire image becomes smaller, as if you were dragging bounding-box handles in Illustrator. You can also crop the image. Cropping is like cutting the image with a pair of scissors. You keep the part that you want and throw away the rest.

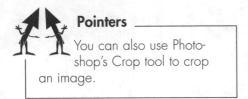

Pointers

You can also use Photo-shop's Crop tool to crop an image.

If you wanted to scale the image, you would use Image ➔ Image Size and enter new values in the Width and Height fields. But to create panel 7, cropping is the better choice. Panel 7 should direct the reader's atten-tion to the place where Astro Ape used to be. This space would be too small if you scaled the entire image. With cropping, you can trim the full-sized image to exactly the dimensions you need.

Remember that, in Photoshop, the image sits on top of a canvas. Making the canvas larger than the image creates a border, as you saw earlier in this chapter. Making the canvas smaller than the image causes cropping, which means that Image ➔ Canvas Size is the command to use.

Choose Image ➔ Canvas Size from the menu. In the Canvas Size dialog box, type **900** pixels for both the width and the height, and set the anchor in the lower left corner by clicking the corresponding square in the diagram. When you use the Canvas Size dialog box to crop, the anchor determines which part of the image that you keep. Click OK, and Photoshop crops the image, like in Figure 20.14.

Figure 20.14

Use Image ➔ Canvas Size to crop the image, creating the smaller photo background for panel 7.

Done! If you have the full version of Photoshop, choose File ➔ Save As. Give this one the file name *aa_photo2.jpg*, and pull JPEG from the Save As Type list if it isn't there already. Click Save, and then click OK in the JPEG Options dialog box.

Spitting and Polishing

Quit out of Photoshop for now, and fire up Illustrator again. You just played with vector graphics in Photoshop, and it's only fair that you play with some rasters in Illustrator.

Choose File ➔ Open, and select *aa_photo.jpg*. (If you weren't able to save this file from Photoshop, you can use my copy on the CD-ROM.) Illustrator creates a new document window and places the photograph inside it. If you click the photo with the Selection tool, you find that you can drag it around the screen, just like a path, a group, or any other object. That's because the photograph *is* an object—a *bitmap object*. Right now, it's sitting at the bottom of the stacking order, just waiting for you to enhance it with some vector art.

You can oblige by adding some sound effects. I'm thinking of some honking horns and sirens, maybe also a jackhammer. Not only will this improve the panel, it will also give you an excuse to test out distortion effects on type. Have a look at what I did in Figure 20.15.

‼#%@ Word Balloon

A **bitmap object** in Illustrator is a raster image. You can move it around the document window freely, but you cannot use the drawing tools to edit its appearance.

Figure 20.15

Distorting type creates the sound effects for this panel.

To create the first sound effect, open the Character palette under Window ➔ Type ➔ Character. Set the font to Myriad, which is the Illustrator default. Choose Bold Italic for the style, and make the font size 48 points. Now grab the Type tool, and click an empty area of the document window to bring up the flashing cursor. Type **HONK** in all capital letters. I used 14-point Myriad Bold for the sound effect in panel 3.

Clicking the Selection tool in the toolbox should automatically select the type object. If it doesn't for some reason, just click the type with the Selection tool. Then open the Color palette. Set the fill color to web-safe RGB red 204, green 153, and blue 0, and set the stroke color to web-safe RGB red 255, green 204, and blue 0. Make the stroke weight 2 points on the Stroke palette.

For the distortion, go to Effect ➔ Distort & Transform ➔ Scribble and Tweak, select the Relative option, check all the check boxes, and drag the Horizontal and Vertical sliders to 10% each. Click OK to make the change, and position the sound effect on top of the photograph.

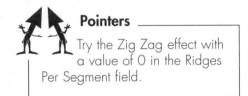

Pointers

Try the Zig Zag effect with a value of 0 in the Ridges Per Segment field.

Following the same basic procedure, create as many sound effects as you like. Experiment with different colors, different fonts, different styles, different sizes, and different distortion effects. I like Scribble and Tweak because it uses a random function, so the results are always different, but all the distortion commands create interesting type effects.

When you finish, group everything together and save the file as *aa_panel6.ai*.

Close the document window and open *aa_photo2.jpg*. (Again, find my copy of this file on the CD-ROM if Photoshop didn't let you save your own.) If you look back at the outline, you see that you need to create a cloud of dust for this one.

No problem. Set the fill color to white, the stroke color to black, and get out the Pencil. Draw a cloud directly on top of the photo. Don't forget to hold down Alt (Windows) or Option (Mac) to close the path. Then pull up the Transparency palette, and set the opacity of the cloud to 75% so that a portion of the background shows through. Deselect everything, and complete the panel by using the Pen to create a 1-point white motion line with no fill color. (In comics, a *motion line* is a thin rule that represents the movement of a character or an object.) See my design in Figure 20.16.

Now reset the stroke color to black and the fill color to white, and make the stroke weight 4 points. Grab the Rectangle tool, and draw a panel around the entire photograph. Use Object ➔ Arrange ➔ Send To Back to position the panel behind the photo in the stacking order. Then add a drop shadow with Effect ➔ Stylize ➔ Drop Shadow, like in Figure 20.17. This helps panel 7 to stand out when it sits on top of panels 6 and 8.

Group everything together, and you can check another panel off the list. Save this file as *aa_panel7.ai*.

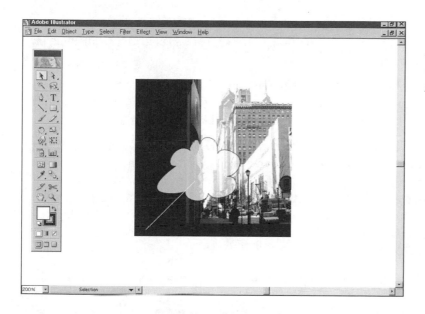

Figure 20.16

A little vector graphics action creates a cloud of dust for panel 7.

Figure 20.17

Draw a rectangle, send it to the back of the stacking order, and add a drop shadow to complete panel 7.

Assembling the Comic

Now comes the fun part, and I mean that in the truest, most nonsarcastic way possible. Your adrenaline is going to kick into high gear when you see the pieces of this comic strip come together.

Close any remaining document windows and open a new one. Instead of zooming in like usual, keep it so that you can see the entire imageable area at a glance. This will come in handy for laying out the page.

Before you get down to business, double-click the Scale tool to open the Scale dialog box. Check the option for scaling strokes and effects, and click OK. This prevents the outlines from appearing too thick if you need to scale down your illustrations to fit on the page.

Start by inserting the main panel design. Open *aa_panel_glow.ai*, click the group with the Selection tool, and choose Edit → Copy. Close this document window without saving the changes, and paste the main panel into the document window that you just created. Referring to the layout guide that you made, position this object in the space for panel 2. Resize the panel to fit as you need. Don't forget to hold down Shift to constrain the proportions correctly. Afterward, make a copy of this object and position it directly below for panel 3, as Figure 20.18 shows.

Figure 20.18

In an empty document window, arrange two copies of the main panel design to create panels 2 and 3 of the comic strip.

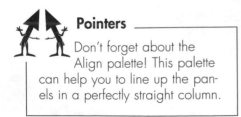

Pointers

Don't forget about the Align palette! This palette can help you to line up the panels in a perfectly straight column.

Now grab the Rectangle tool and draw panel 1. Set the stroke color to black, the stroke weight to 4 points, and the fill color to red 255, green 255, and blue 204, which is a very pale yellow. This is the panel for the logo, so open up *aa_logo_blends.ai*, copy its contents, close its document window, and paste the logo onto the page. Position the logo toward the top of panel 1.

The panel has a good deal of empty space at this point, but you can easily fill it with one of your Astro Ape illustrations. Paste the contents of *aa_side_color_t.ai* into the new document window. Position the monkey at the bottom of panel 1, but leave some space for your byline—you know, the line where the author's or artist's name goes.

Open up the Character palette under Window ➜ Type ➜ Character, and set it to 16-point Myriad Roman. Then get out the Type tool, and click in the vicinity of Astro Ape's foot. Type the word **by**, press Enter or Return, and type your name. Fine-tune the position of the byline with the Selection tool. Figure 20.19 shows the completed design.

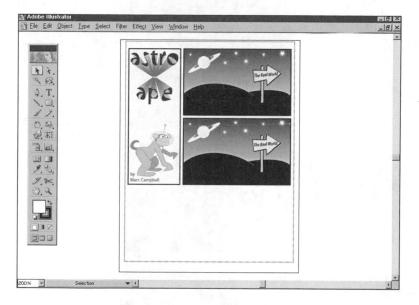

Figure 20.19

Combine the logo and the side view of Astro Ape with a rectangle and a byline, and you have panel 1. Don't use my byline! Put your own name in there.

Panel 4 is ready to go. Copy and paste the contents of *aa_sign_pov.ai* into the document window and resize as needed. For panel 5, paste *aa_sign_silhouette.ai* and *aa_side_silhouette.ai*. Don't draw a rectangle for a panel border around the silhouettes. They will look better without, as Figure 20.20 shows.

The only thing this page needs now is a couple of apes. Supply them from *aa_side_running1_t.ai* and *aa_side_goggles_t.ai*. The running pose technically belongs in panel 2, but you don't have to follow the outline *that* closely. Have the monkey straddling panels 1 and 2 to inject some dynamism into the page. Position the goggles pose squarely in panel 2. You might also want to add a sound effect with the Type tool to reinforce what is happening in the panel, as in Figure 20.21.

Figure 20.20

The first-person point of view and the silhouettes form panels 4 and 5.

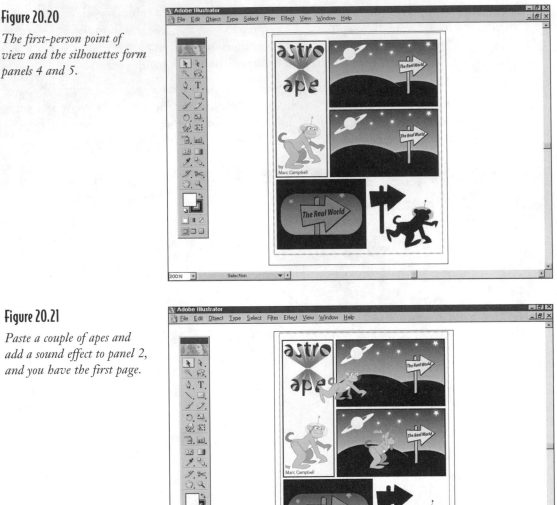

Figure 20.21

Paste a couple of apes and add a sound effect to panel 2, and you have the first page.

You have just finished page 1! You're doing great so far. Save your work as *aa_page1.ai*. Close this document window, and create a new one for page 2.

To start, paste *aa_panel6.ai* into place. Then open *aa_panel_glow.ai* again, and paste a new copy into the document window for panel 8, as Figure 20.22 shows.

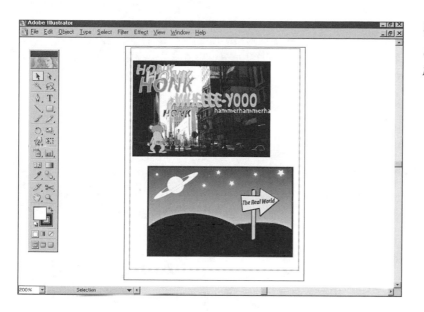

Figure 20.22

Start off page 2 by placing panels 6 and 8.

Add *aa_panel7.ai*, and pat yourself on the back for the coolness of the drop shadow that you applied. Finish off the page with *aa_side_running2.ai* and *aa_wordballoon.ai*, positioning them like you see in Figure 20.23. Save this file as *aa_page2.ai*.

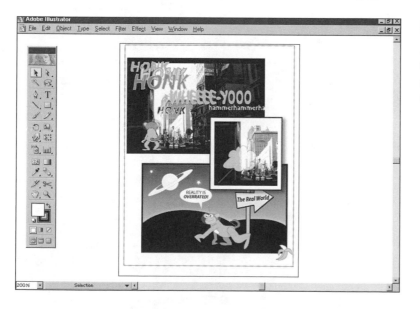

Figure 20.23

Finish by placing panel 7, the monkey, the word balloon, and an optional banana.

Don't look now, but you just created a comic strip. Let me be the first to commend you on a job very well done.

You might notice that I added a banana to the bottom of the page as a marker for "The End." The CD-ROM includes this file as *aa_banana.ai*, but I'm not going to take you through creating it step by step. I don't need to. Computer illustrators like you know what they're doing.

The Least You Need to Know

- Use planning materials like outlines and layouts to manage an illustration project.
- Photoshop works best with raster images like photographs.
- Use the History palette instead of Edit → Undo to correct mistakes in Photoshop.
- You can adjust the hue, saturation, brightness, and contrast of an image in Photoshop.
- Use Image → Canvas Size to crop an image or add a border.
- Use Image → Image Size to scale an image or change the resolution.
- Loading a raster image into Illustrator creates a bitmap object.
- Apply distortion effects to type for stylized, dramatic lettering.
- When designing a layout, make sure that you can see the entire imageable area in the document window.

Getting It Out There

In This Chapter

- Printing your comic strip
- Creating Astro Ape desktop wallpaper
- Preparing the comic for the web

You created a comic strip. Now what are you going to do with it?

As a computer illustrator, you have all kinds of options. You can print out your work, turn it into desktop wallpaper or post it on the web. The choice is yours.

This final chapter steps you through the procedures for printing, wallpapering, and web-readying the Astro Ape comic for your adoring public.

Preparing for the Printer

If your goal is to print each page of the comic on its own sheet of paper, then your job couldn't be easier. Simply open *aa_page1.ai*, choose File → Print, and click OK in the Print dialog box that appears. Follow the same procedure for *aa_page2.ai*.

You can also print smaller versions of both pages on the same sheet of paper, side by side. The process is slightly more involved, and that's what this section covers.

Getting Ready

To print both pages of the comic on the same sheet of paper, you need to make a few adjustments to Illustrator's print settings. By default, Illustrator prints in *portrait mode*, which means that the page is taller than it is wide. In portrait mode, the $8^1/_2$-inch side is the top of the page on a standard $8^1/_2$-by-11-inch piece of paper.

> **!#%@) Word Balloon**
>
> In **portrait** mode, the page is taller than it is wide. In **landscape** mode, the page is wider than it is tall.

To get both pages to fit on the same piece of paper, switch to *landscape mode*, where the page is wider than it is tall. The 11-inch side is the top of the page in landscape mode.

Begin by loading *aa_page1.ai*. Choose Edit ➔ Select All and then Object ➔ Group, because you will need to scale down the page and reposition it. To switch to landscape mode, choose File ➔ Document Setup. Look in the dialog box for the Orientation buttons, and click the one on the right. Now click the Print Setup button, and set your printer for landscape mode also. Click OK to close the Print Setup dialog box, and click OK again to close the Document Setup dialog box. When you look at the document window, you see that Illustrator has reconfigured the artboard for landscape printing.

Select the group, and then double-click the Scale tool. After the dialog box appears, check the option for scaling strokes and effects. Type **60** in the Scale field and click OK. Your artwork shrinks to a little more than half its size, leaving plenty of room for the second page.

Speaking of which, go ahead and open *aa_page2.ai* now. Select everything, make a group, copy the art, and close the document window without saving your changes. Paste the second page next to the first. Then call up the Scale dialog box again and reduce the art to 60%, just like before. Use the Selection tool to adjust the position of the second page, and you get something like Figure 21.1. Save this file as *aa_landscape.ai*. You're ready to print.

Printing

Look no further than File ➔ Print to send your work to your printer. Feel free to ignore most of the options on the Print dialog box—these are for more sophisticated print jobs. If you have more than one printer, though, make sure that the one that you want to use appears in the Name list. Otherwise, just click the OK button to print, or click Cancel to return to Illustrator.

Illustrator prints razor-sharp vectors; the 300-dpi raster images of the city look pretty good, too.

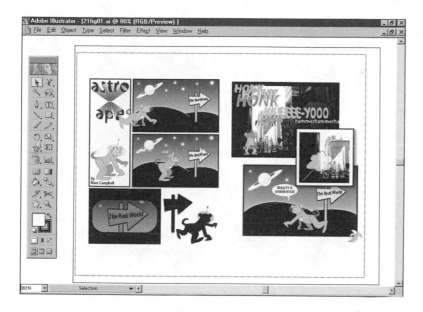

Figure 21.1

Using landscape mode, you can print both pages on the same piece of paper.

Preparing for the Screen

But print is so twentieth-century (says the guy who writes books for a living). Computers open the door for electronic delivery. You can publish your work in novel ways, none of which involve the death of trees.

For instance, you can use your cartoon as desktop wallpaper for your home PC. But why stop there? Take Astro Ape to work with you, and put it on your work PC. You will be the envy of the office. You'll probably earn a raise. All you have to do is follow these steps. (Unfortunately, you also need the full version of Photoshop, because the procedure involves saving.)

Pointers

If you plan to e-mail your cartoon to friends and family, skip to the section on preparing for the web. The procedure here creates a large file.

Getting Ready

To create desktop wallpaper, you need a raster image, and raster images mean Photoshop. Quit out of Illustrator if you have it running, and open Photoshop.

The trick to making desktop wallpaper is knowing the dimensions of the screen in pixels. The most common settings are 1024 by 768 or 800 by 600. If you aren't sure what you're using, pull up your screen settings and check. Windows users can find this information in the Control panel under Display. Mac users can use the Display button on the control strip (OS 9.x) or check under systems preferences (OS X).

In Photoshop, choose File ➔ New to create a new canvas. Type the dimensions of your screen in the Width and Height fields of the dialog box. Assuming that you have an 800-by-600 pixel screen, type **800** pixels for the width and **600** pixels for the height.

In the Resolution field, specify 72 pixels per inch. I mentioned elsewhere that 72 dpi (dots per inch) is the standard resolution for screen-based images. Set the Mode list to RGB Color, and click the White option below Contents. Click OK to create the canvas.

Now bring the first page into Photoshop. Choose File ➔ Open, and set the Files Of Type list to All Formats if it shows something else. Navigate to *aa_page1.ai*.

Before the file opens, Photoshop presents you with the Rasterize Generic PDF Format dialog box. Before you proceed, you should figure out how you want Photoshop to rasterize the vector art.

The first thing to do is to set the resolution. The canvas is 72 dpi, and if the art isn't the same resolution, you will have problems, so type **72** into the Resolution field.

Drawing Perspectives

If Windows is your operating system, you can make the resolution 96 dpi, because Windows displays screen images at a slightly higher resolution than the Macintosh.

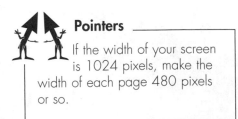

Pointers

If the width of your screen is 1024 pixels, make the width of each page 480 pixels or so.

What about the dimensions of the art? This requires some simple arithmetic. If the canvas is 800 pixels wide, then each page of Astro Ape should be no more than 400 pixels wide. Leave yourself a little room for margins, and make the width 380. Type this value into the Width field, and Photoshop calculates the corresponding height. Click OK.

In a moment, page 1 of the comic appears in a new document window. Go back to File ➔ Open, and bring in *aa_page2.ai*, using the same width and rasterization settings.

Click the blank document window, and choose Window ➔ Show Layers to call up the Layers palette. Click the new-layer icon at the bottom of the palette twice to create two new layers. Then click Layer 1 to highlight it in the list.

Go now to the first page's document window and click anywhere inside it. Choose Select ➔ All to select all the pixels in the image. Copy them with Edit ➔ Copy. Click the blank document window, and choose Edit ➔ Paste. This transfers the page-1 pixels to Layer 1. Grab the Move tool from the toolbox, and drag the page to the left side of the document window. Return to the Layers palette, and click Layer 2.

I'll bet you can guess what happens next. Copy the pixels from page 2 into Layer 2, and use the Move tool to position them on the right side of the document window. To fine-tune the layout, you can nudge the pixels with the arrow keys. Don't forget to highlight the appropriate layer on the Layers palette. To adjust page 1, highlight Layer 1. To adjust page 2, highlight Layer 2.

When you finish, close the individual document windows for the first and second pages without saving your changes. Your combined document window should look something like Figure 21.2.

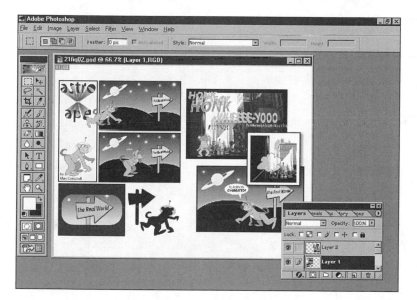

Figure 21.2

To prepare Astro Ape for wallpapering your desktop, paste each rasterized page of the comic into a separate Photoshop layer.

If you have the full version of Photoshop, choose File ➔ Save As. Pull BMP from the Format list and type **aa_wallpaper.bmp** in the File Name field. *BMP* is the *Windows Bitmap* format. It's not a very compact format in terms of file size, but it retains the quality and color depth of your image, which makes it a good choice for desktop wallpaper.

Click Save, and then click OK in the File Format dialog box to create the BMP. You can close the document window and quit out of Photoshop now, because it's wallpaper time.

‼#%@ Word Balloon

BMP (Windows Bitmap) is a raster format that creates a sharp image but a rather large file.

Desktop Wallpaper, Anyone?

The procedure for creating wallpaper depends on your operating system. Windows users should follow these steps:

1. Click the Start button and choose Settings ➔ Control Panel.
2. Double-click the Display icon.
3. Click the Background tab, and then click the Browse button.
4. Navigate to *aa_wallpaper.bmp*. Double-click this file.
5. Click OK in the Display Properties dialog box.

If you use Mac OS X, follow these steps:

1. Select Preferences from the Finder menu.
2. Click the Select Picture button.
3. Navigate to *aa_wallpaper.bmp* and select this file.
4. Click the Choose button.

If you use Mac OS 9, follow these steps:

1. Select Control Panel from the Apple menu.
2. Choose Appearance and select the Desktop tab.
3. Click the Place Picture button.
4. Navigate to *aa_wallpaper.bmp* and select this file.
5. Click the Set Desktop button.

Preparing for the Web

These days, it's practically illegal to bring up the web in polite conversation. Blame it on the dot-com industry. There have been some very public demises of some very popular websites in the last couple of years, and the hype implosion has bruised some egos. Be that as it may, the web is far from dead, and it's still the best way for computer illustrators to present their work to a worldwide audience.

To publish Astro Ape on the web, you need to rent some space on a web server. Chances are, you already have this but may not realize it. If you subscribe to a service such as America Online or the Microsoft Network, you get a fair amount of web space as part of your membership. Even if your Internet service provider doesn't throw in virtual real estate, plenty of companies offer it for free or for a minimal monthly charge. Load up www.google.com in your favorite browser and search for web hosting. Be sure to read the fine print! Almost always, the free services make their money by selling advertising space on your site.

After you find the server space, you need to create and upload your website. Again, the larger ISPs offer web-building tools at no additional charge. You can also build your site with one of many excellent software packages. I will not go into the procedure for creating a site, at least not in this book, because you will never get me to shut up. Needless to say, there are many fine books on the subject by many respectable authors, and there are all kinds of tutorials on the web to help get you started.

Getting Ready

Assuming that you have the server space, the website, and the full version of Photoshop, you can post the Astro Ape comic as a single graphic. Fire up Photoshop and follow the procedure that I described in the preceding section for creating a new canvas and pasting each page into its own layer. Instead of making the dimensions of the canvas 800 pixels by 600, make it 760 by 500 or so. This allows room for the scrollbar and the margins of the page in the browser window. If you use 760 pixels as the canvas width, the width of each page should be about 370 pixels. Figure 21.3 shows you what I'm talking about.

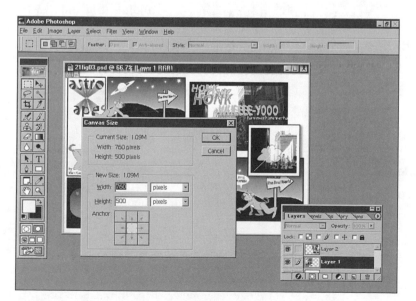

Figure 21.3

If you want to publish your comic to the web, make the dimensions of the Photoshop canvas 760 by 500 pixel.

Stop when you get to the part about saving the file in BMP format. BMPs are great for wallpaper, but they are terrible for the web because of their large file size. The larger the file size, the longer the download time. I'm sure the frustration of waiting for a heavy graphic to load is not unknown to you. Fortunately, Photoshop makes it easy to optimize graphics for the web. This process crunches a multimegabyte image like the Astro Ape comic into a smaller, more manageable size.

Optimizing and Web-Readying

To *optimize the image* for online consumption, choose File ➔ Save For Web. (If you don't have the full version of Photoshop, skip to the next section, "Using Illustrator Instead of Photoshop.")

The Save For Web dialog box provides a large window for viewing the quality of the image. Keep your eye on this window as you adjust the settings on the right side of the dialog box.

The Settings list controls the format for the web image. There are three formats: GIF, JPEG, and PNG. Normally, GIF makes a good choice for computer illustrations, because GIFs work best with large areas of flat color. But if you choose GIF Web Palette from the Settings list, notice that the gradients in the sky take a serious quality hit. This makes sense if you think about it: The gradients are closer to photographs in terms of color depth. The best GIF option is GIF 128 Dithered, although even this format causes some banding in the sky. Look in the lower left corner of the dialog box, just under the image window. Photoshop reports that this image is about 70KB in size and that it will take about 30 seconds to download on a slow modem connection.

Make a note of it, and try a different setting. JPEGs work better for photographs and images with subtle changes in color, so see what the JPEG options have to offer.

JPEG Low cuts the image size and download time roughly in half, but look at that image quality! It isn't great. JPEG Medium improves the quality considerably, but the image size jumps to about 60KB. JPEG High looks the best of all. Then again, the image is 100KB, and it will take 40 seconds to download on a slow connection.

Image quality versus download time: This is the choice that web designers everywhere have to make all the

!#%@ **Word Balloon**

Optimizing an image for the web means compressing the graphic file into a manageable size while retaining as much image quality as possible.

Drawing Perspectives

GIF images work best for art with large areas of flat color. JPEG images work best for art with subtle changes in color, such as photographs.

time. You should rule out JPEG Low as an option, because the image quality is so poor. People don't want to wait even two seconds for an awful image to load.

If you know for a fact that almost everyone in your audience always uses the best equipment and the fastest Internet connections, go with JPEG High. Most web designers cannot make so bold a claim, however. Clunkers appear on every highway, and the Information Superhighway is no exception. If you can avoid it, you don't want to penalize your audience for preferring to drive jalopies instead of sports cars.

That leaves you with JPEG Medium or GIF 128 Dithered. The JPEG file is smaller, and it looks better to these eyes, but if you prefer the GIF, then go for it!

Make your final selection in the Settings list and click OK. The Save Optimized As dialog box appears. Supply **aa_web.jpg** or **aa_web.gif** as the filename, depending on your choice of format. If you just want to save the image, keep the Save As Type list on Images Only. If you want Photoshop to create a blank web page that contains the image, choose HTML And Images. Click Save to finish. Upload the image to your site, and you're online.

Using Illustrator Instead of Photoshop

The trial version of Photoshop doesn't allow you to save, but don't let that stop you. Your Illustrator trial software also has a Save For Web command. Open *aa_page1.ai* and *aa_page2.ai* in Illustrator, combine the pages into a single landscape-oriented document like you did in the "Preparing for the Printer" section earlier in this chapter, and choose File ➜ Save For Web.

The Save For Web command in Illustrator works identically to the one in Photoshop, so follow the same procedures and observe the same guidelines that I presented in the previous section, "Optimizing and Web-Readying."

What Happens Next?

The best advice you can get as a writer is to write all the time. Write like crazy, they say. Keep those muscles in shape.

The same holds true for computer illustrators. Practice is the key. The more you computer-illustrate, the better you get. Don't be discouraged if your work doesn't meet your standards at first. Keep plugging away. You will have a breakthrough sooner than you think.

If you're professional minded, in addition to practicing, practicing, practicing, you will want to start putting together a portfolio of your very best work. You don't need dozens of pieces to make a respectable showing. At the same time, you want your portfolio to convey the full range of what you can do. There's no sense in showing an art director 20 pieces if they are all very similar in tone, style, and subject matter. Pick two or three of the best in that category, and then move on to something else.

Art directors look for more than talent. They look for professionalism. For a computer illustrator, this boils down to the ability to meet deadlines and the willingness to accept criticism and make changes. Making changes isn't fun, but it's part of the racket. It says nothing about your skill as an illustrator, and you should never infer that it does.

The illustration game can be the proverbial tough nut to crack. If you're just starting out, you can make your own opportunities happen. By all means, enter contests and the like.

Pointers

The philosopher Immanuel Kant argued that developing one's talents isn't just a good idea—it's a moral duty. So never stop practicing, even after you master computer illustration. Use your practice time to experiment with new techniques. Challenge yourself! Expand your skills. Make Manny Kant happy.

Awards are great, but greater still is that professional or quasi-professional experience. Illustrate for the office newsletter. Design for your friends in the rock band. Work for free. You have to practice anyway, right? Any experience that resembles the service-provider/client relationship pays off in the end.

Finally, always reserve time in your schedule for your personal artistic interests. Never fill this time with extra paying work. Keep that beautiful flame bright, burning, and hot.

I ask again: What happens next? You're the computer illustrator. Go illustrate something!

The Least You Need to Know

- Print in landscape mode to fit both comic pages on the same piece of paper.
- Use Photoshop to prepare your work for onscreen or online distribution.
- Optimize images for the web in Photoshop with File → Save For Web.
- In computer illustration, practice makes perfect.

An Illustrator's Guide to Software

This book presents computer illustration by way of Adobe Illustrator and Adobe Photoshop. From an industry standpoint, these are the best tools for the job. They are also my personal preferences. They aren't the only tools for the job, however. There are many others, each with a loyal user base of talented computer illustrators. In this appendix, I say a few words about some of the best software alternatives.

Table A.1 gives a quick comparison between these packages and the Adobe products.

Table A.1 Computer Illustration Software at a Glance

Software	Specialty	Home Use	ProUse	Price
Adobe Illustrator 10	Vector		✔	$399
Adobe Photoshop 6	Raster		✔	$609
Adobe Photoshop Elements	Raster	✔		$99
CorelDRAW 10	Vector	✔		$549*
CorelPHOTO-PAINT 10	Raster	✔		$549*
Deneba Canvas	Both		✔	$399
Jasc Paint Shop Pro 7	Raster	✔	✔	$109
Macromedia Fireworks	Raster		✔	$299
Macromedia FreeHand	Vector		✔	$399

CorelDRAW 10 and CorelPHOTO-PAINT 10 ship together as a software suite with Corel R.A.V.E.

CorelDRAW and CorelPHOTO-PAINT

CorelDRAW's reputation is that it is a great vector graphics package for home users but not powerful enough for working pros. Corel doesn't quite shake this image but gives it a good rattling with CorelDRAW 10 Graphic Suite. The suite includes three applications: CorelDRAW 10 for respectable vectors, CorelPHOTO-PAINT 10 for respectable rasters, and Corel R.A.V.E. for beginning web graphics and Flash animation.

Many people find Corel products easier to learn and use than Adobe products. Even still, at $549 U.S., the suite doesn't have the same price advantage that it once enjoyed over the big boys. Feature-for-feature, Illustrator and Photoshop remain the better bargains.

CorelDRAW 10 Graphics Suite is available for Windows and Mac platforms. For more information, see www.corel.com.

Deneba Canvas

Deneba Canvas combines vector graphics, raster graphics, and web design features into a single software application that has received some very good reviews. Canvas doesn't provide the same level of advanced control that comes with the Adobe products, but it comes close enough to encourage many graphics people to make the switch. The reasonable price point of $399 U.S. doesn't hurt, either, considering that the similarly priced Illustrator 10 and FreeHand 10 are primarily vector applications.

Canvas 8 is available for Windows and Mac platforms. For more information, see www.deneba.com.

Jasc Paint Shop Pro

Many graphics people cut their teeth on this remarkable raster graphics program, and many never looked further. It's powerful, versatile, easy to use, and at $109 U.S., inexpensive to a fault. If the price tag of Photoshop is the problem, then Paint Shop Pro is the answer.

Paint Shop Pro 7 is available for Windows platforms only. For more information, see www.jasc.com.

Macromedia Fireworks and FreeHand

Macromedia Fireworks is a strange bird to classify. In essence, it does rasters. But what goes in is a hybrid of vector and raster objects, and what comes out are great web graphics. As a standalone raster application, it is very capable. It works best, though, with its traveling companion and comrade in arms, Macromedia Dreamweaver, the best web design and site management software around.

Fireworks 4 is available for Windows and Mac platforms for $299 U.S. Bundled with Dreamweaver 4, the cost is $399 U.S.

Macromedia FreeHand is a vector graphics program that offers exceptional integration with Macromedia Flash. The Flash format is fast becoming the animation standard on the web. Many designers use FreeHand as a kind of extended Flash toolset, but it provides very capable vector graphics for print media as well.

FreeHand 10 is available for Windows and Mac platforms. You can buy it separately or bundled with Flash 5. By itself, FreeHand 10 retails for $399 U.S. The Flash 5 FreeHand 10 Studio goes for $499 U.S. For more information on FreeHand and Fireworks, see www.macromedia.com.

What's on the CD-ROM

The CD-ROM that comes with this book makes an excellent coaster for soft drinks, but it also has another use. It contains all kinds of software tools and sample files to enhance your computer illustration experience. Marketing people call such things *value-added materials*, but you can think of them as *free goodies*. To access them, all you have to do is pop the CD into the tray of your Windows or Macintosh machine. This appendix shows you what to do next.

Exploring the Contents

The CD-ROM is organized into folders and files, just like the hard drive of your computer. The Examples folder on the CD-ROM contains the following subfolders:

◆ **Color Insert.** Here are files for the eight-page color insert in the middle of this book. Open these files in Adobe Illustrator to see how I set up the artwork.

◆ **Extra Art.** This folder has character designs for Astro Ostrich and Astro Kangaroo as well as a set of Astro Ape paintbrushes. Open these files in Adobe Illustrator.

◆ **Project Files.** This folder contains the completed practice exercises for each chapter.

The Software Library folder offers the following pieces of trial-ware and free samples:

◆ **Adobe.** Here are trial versions of Adobe Illustrator 10 and Adobe Photoshop 6.

◆ **CValley.** This folder contains the trial version of FILTERiT 4.1, which is a popular plug-in for Adobe Illustrator.

◆ **HotDoor.** Find the trial version of Hot Door 1.0 for Illustrator 8 or 9 and Perspective 1.0.1 for Illustrator 10, an Illustrator plug-in for creating three-dimensional art, in this folder.

◆ **Sapphire.** This folder contains several sample Illustrator plug-ins and paintbrush sets from Sapphire Innovations.

Launching the CD

Turn on your computer, place the disc in the CD-ROM tray, and then close the tray. On a Windows system, the main menu of the CD should appear momentarily. If it doesn't, choose Start ➔ Run from the Windows desktop and type *x:* in the field (where *x* is the drive letter of your CD-ROM drive), then Index.html. Click OK or press Enter to launch the CD.

On a Macintosh system, the CD-ROM doesn't launch automatically. If you use a Macintosh, follow the instructions in the next section, "Browsing the CD."

Browsing the CD

You can also easily view and explore the directory structure of the CD. On a Windows system, double-click the My Computer icon. Left-click the icon for the CD-ROM drive that appears, and choose Explore from the context menu. Double-click the **QUE** icon to launch the CD, or double-click the folder icons to see what's inside.

On a Macintosh system, an icon representing the CD should appear on your desktop shortly after you insert the disc. Double-click this icon to see the CD contents. The **CIGCI** icon launches the disc. Browse the disc yourself by double-clicking the folders.

Installing Illustrator

Adobe Illustrator is the industry-standard drawing and illustration program. Install this software when you're ready to begin the practice exercises in Chapter 3, "Illustrating Illustrator."

Find the free trial version of Adobe Illustrator 10 in the **SoftwareLibrary/Adobe/Illustrator** folder of the CD-ROM. This folder contains two icons: the Installer folder and a readme text file. The readme file gives you important information about the trial software, as well as step-by-step installation instructions for Windows and Mac systems, so double-click the readme file and look over it carefully before you continue. You may even want to print it out and keep it handy during the installation.

The procedure itself goes much like any other installation you've performed. A series of dialog boxes appears on the screen, giving you different installation options. Feel free to customize the installation if you prefer; when in doubt, choose the default settings. The entire installation takes about 10 minutes.

Keep in mind that, once you install the Illustrator trial, you have 30 days to use it. After the 30 days, the trial-ware expires. Your 30 days doesn't start until you successfully complete an installation.

Installing Photoshop

Adobe Photoshop is the industry-standard image-editing program. Install this software before you get to Chapter 20, "Putting the Pieces Together."

The **SoftwareLibrary/Adobe/Photoshop** folder contains a trial version of Adobe Photoshop 6. Again, open and read the readme file that sits in this folder for important information and complete installation instructions.

The Photoshop trial version never expires, so you don't have to worry about a 30-day time limit. However, the trial-ware doesn't allow you to save or print your work.

Installing FILTERiT

Cvalley FILTERiT is optional plug-in software that enhances Adobe Illustrator with special filter commands for advanced effects.

Find the folder for the trial version of FILTERiT 4.1 in the **CValley** directory on the CD-ROM.

Please note that the FILTERiT trial partially expires after 30 uses or 15 days, after which most of the features stop working. See the readme file for more details.

Installing Hot Door Perspective

Hot Door Perspective is a plug-in package for Adobe Illustrator that helps you to create three-dimensional illustrations.

The Hot Door Perspective trial version is in the **HotDoor** folder on the CD-ROM. Open and read the Perspective Read Me.wri file in this folder for important information and step-by-step installation instructions.

This trial version has no time limit, but it purposely distorts three-point perspective. The full version of this plug-in correctly displays three-point perspective.

Installing Sapphire Plug-Ins

The CD-ROM contains a number of Illustrator plug-ins from Sapphire Innovations, including special-effects filters and paintbrushes.

Find the sample Sapphire plug-ins in the **Sapphire** folder on the CD-ROM. Be sure to open and read the readme.pdf file in this folder for important information.

You can install as many or as few of the samples as you like. To install, copy the plug-in files from the CD-ROM and paste them inside the **Plug-ins** folder in Illustrator 10. Likewise, copy the brush files from the CD-ROM and paste them inside the **Brushes** folder. On a Windows system, the Illustrator 10 **Plug-ins** folder is typically under *C:\Program Files\Adobe\Illustrator 10 Tryout\Plug-ins*. The **Brushes** folder is under *C:\Program Files\Adobe\Illustrator 10 Tryout\Presets\Brushes*.

The filters and brushes that you install become available the next time you launch Illustrator. Find the filters, appropriately enough, in the Filter menu. The brushes appear under Window ➔ Brush Libraries.

Installing the Astro Ape Paintbrushes

I include a set of my own specially created Astro Ape paintbrushes for your drawing pleasure. These brushes come as an Illustrator plug-in. They are Campbell-ware. They never expire, and they're yours to use however you like. Enjoy!

To install them, copy the Astro Ape Brushes file from the **Examples/Extra Art** folder on the CD-ROM and paste it inside the **Brushes** folder in Illustrator 10. On a Windows system, the **Brushes** folder is usually located at *C:\Program Files\Adobe\Illustrator 10 Tryout\Presets\Brushes*.

After you install the paintbrushes, you'll be able to use them the next time you launch Illustrator. Find them under Window ➔ Brush Libraries.

Glossary

align   To arrange objects in a straight line.

anchor point   The part of a path that tells the path which way to go.

appearance attributes   The visible characteristics of a path, including the fill color, stroke color, stroke weight and style, and effects.

archive   To store finished projects on external media such as CD-ROMs or zip disks.

area type   Text that occupies the fill of a path.

art brush   A brush style that places a separate illustration along the entire shape of the path.

artboard   The area representing the paper to which you will print in Illustrator's document window.

back   The starting object of a blend object.

baseline   The line—like the rule on a sheet of notebook paper—upon which most typographical characters sit. Some characters, such as the lowercase letter *p*, have descenders that drop below the baseline.

bitmap fonts   Character sets that describe the shapes of their letters with pixels, very much like raster graphics. Bitmap fonts are resolution-dependent. They scale poorly.

bitmap graphics   Another name for pixel-based raster graphics.

bitmap object   In Illustrator, a raster image. You can move a bitmap object around the document window freely, but you cannot use the drawing tools to edit its appearance.

Blend commands   Illustrator commands for filling a series of objects with in-between shades of two colors.

blend object   An object derived from the gradual shift in characteristics between two or more other objects.

blending modes   Mathematical operations that process two overlapping colors for interesting color effects.

BMP (Windows Bitmap)   A raster format that creates a sharp image but a rather large file.

bounding box   The transformation control that appears around the rectangular area of an object.

brushed path   A path that has the additional appearance attribute of a brush style, which makes the stroke more visually interesting.

C-shaped curve   A curve that maintains its original direction from start to finish.

calligraphic brush   A brush style that follows the shape of the path closely.

canvas   The rectangular field on which a raster image sits in Photoshop.

cap   The part of an open path that appears at either end.

clipping mask   An object that determines which portions of its underlying objects are visible.

clipping path   Another name for the mask in a clipping mask.

closed path   A path that doesn't have obvious start and end points, such as a rectangle or a triangle.

CMYK   A color model that reproduces color by mixing different levels of cyan, magenta, yellow, and black ink. CMYK is common in print media.

color mode   The setting of the document window that prepares your art for a particular color model.

color model   A method for reproducing color. RGB and CMYK are common color models.

color separation   The division of a color image into four separate color plates—one for each of the four CMYK inks.

colorize   To convert an image's color information into shades of some other color.

complement   A color's inverse shade in the RGB color model. The original and its complement often match.

compound path   An object that contains two or more ordinary paths. By default, the areas where these paths overlap become perfectly transparent.

compression   The process of making an image file smaller in terms of file size.

computer animation   A method related to computer illustration that lets you bring static drawings to life.

computer illustration   A method for creating art using computer equipment instead of traditional tools.

constrain the proportions   To preserve the width-to-height ratio of a graphic.

corner point   An anchor point whose segments come out at angles.

descender   The portion of a typographical character that extends below the baseline in a line of type. The lowercase letter *p* has a descender. The lowercase letter *b* doesn't.

desktop publishing   The process of creating page layouts on the computer.

digital photography   The process of capturing and manipulating photographic information with computer equipment.

direction handle   The round bulge at the end of a direction line. Drag the direction handle to change the position of the direction line.

direction line   The part of an anchor point that determines the slope and depth of a curved segment.

distortion   An effect that changes the shape of an object.

distribute   To space objects evenly within a given area.

drop shadow   An effect that can help to create the illusion of depth in an illustration.

effect   A command that adds a special appearance attribute to an object. You can easily modify or remove this attribute.

extraneous anchor points   Anchor points that a path doesn't need in order to define its shape.

feathering   The process by which the edges of an object become gradually more transparent.

fill   The part of a path that describes the interior area.

filter   In Illustrator, a command that changes the characteristics of the object or adds new objects to the document window. The only way to remove the results of a filter is to use Edit ➔ Undo. In Photoshop, a command that changes the characteristics of the selected pixels.

freeform drawing   The process of creating vector graphics by dragging the mouse instead of explicitly plotting anchor points. The computer calculates the positions and directions of the anchor points as you go.

front   The ending object of a blend object.

GIF (Graphical Interchange Format)   A raster file format that works well with line art containing large areas of flat color.

glow   An effect that can help a dark object to stand out against a dark background.

gradient   A gradual blend of two or more colors.

graphics   The generic name for computer images.

group   An object that contains other objects.

handle   The part of a bounding box that you can drag to change the object's shape.

hanging punctuation   Punctuation that sits outside the margin of the type area.

hidden tools   Related tools that sit underneath another tool on the Illustrator toolbar.

hyphenation   Breaking lines of type in the middle of words to fit more type on a page.

illustration program   Vector graphics software for creating drawings from scratch. Examples include Adobe Illustrator and Macromedia FreeHand.

image editor   Raster graphics software that enables you to modify graphics files. Its strong suite isn't creating new art. Examples include Adobe Photoshop and CorelPHOTO-PAINT.

imageable area   The area that represents the printable region of Illustrator's document window.

inner glow   A glow effect by which the light appears to be inside the object, like a neon sign.

inverse   The opposite shade of a color.

join   The part of a path that appears at the connection point of two segments.

JPEG (Joint Photography Experts Group)   A raster file format that works well with images that contain subtle changes in color, such as photographs.

justification   A typographical technique that creates lines of type of equal length by inserting space between words and individual characters.

kerning   The amount of space between two characters in a line of type.

landscape mode   A printing mode in which the page is wider than it is tall.

layer   An object—much like a clear sheet of plastic—that you superimpose upon the artboard in Illustrator or the canvas in Photoshop.

layer styles   Photoshop commands that are similar to Illustrator's Effect menu.

layout   The arrangement of elements on a page.

leading   The amount of space between two lines of type.

linear gradient   A gradient that blends colors in a straight line.

loss   The amount of picture information that an image-compression process discards.

marquee   A rectangular selection zone.

mask   In a clipping mask, the object that acts like a window. In an opacity mask, the object whose colors determine the level of transparency.

masked object   An object that a mask affects.

mix   To define a color by manually setting the values of the component colors.

mockup   An illustration or design that an artist creates for sample purposes only.

native format   The default file format of a software application, such as AI for Illustrator and PSD for Photoshop. The native format is usually proprietary and not suitable for external use.

nonimageable area   The area representing your printer's built-in margins in Illustrator's document window.

object   In computer illustration, a distinct element. Paths, groups, and masks are all objects.

object-oriented graphics   A graphics environment, such as Adobe Illustrator, in which each path is its own, independent object that you can change without affecting any other object in the drawing.

opacity   The opposite of *transparency*.

opacity mask   An object that creates different levels of transparency on another object.

open path   A path that has obvious start and end points, such as a zigzag or the letter z.

optimize   To compress a graphics file into a manageable size while retaining as much image quality as possible, especially when preparing images for the web.

out of gamut   The state of an RGB color when the CMYK color model cannot reproduce it.

outer glow   A glow effect by which the light appears to be outside the object, such as a halo.

outline fonts   Character sets that describe the shapes of their letters with mathematical relationships, very much like vector graphics. Outline fonts scale easily.

palettes   The floating windows in Illustrator and Photoshop that give you access to commands and options.

path   A mathematical description of a shape. The path is the most fundamental element in a vector graphic.

path type   Type that runs along the stroke of a path.

pattern   A separate piece of artwork that tiles throughout a path.

pattern brush   A brush style that tiles a series of separate illustrations across the shape of the path.

perspective   An illustration technique that creates the illusion of depth by shortening and lengthening the lines of a drawing in a uniform way.

Photoshop filter effects   Painterly effect commands that Illustrator borrows from Photoshop.

pixel   A very small, colored rectangle. The pixel is the most fundamental element in a raster graphic.

plug-in   A piece of software that adds new tools, functions, or menu commands to another piece of software.

point of origin   A transformation control that determines the reference point of a transformation.

polygon   A shape with more than four sides. In Illustrator, three-sided shapes (triangles) are also polygons.

portrait mode   A printing mode in which the page is taller than it is wide.

primitive   A simple geometric shape in vector graphics.

proof   To print samples of your art before making final adjustments.

radial gradient   A gradient that blends colors in concentric circles.

ragged text   A block of text that lines up on one margin only.

raster graphics   Computer images composed of pixels. BMP, GIF, and JPEG are raster graphics formats.

rasterize   To change a vector image into a raster.

reference point   The point at which a transformation occurs.

reflow   To reposition text after a change in the size or shape of a type area.

repurpose content   To reuse existing material, perhaps with minor changes, instead of developing something new.

resolution   The number of pixels per inch in a raster graphic. In general, the higher the resolution, the better the image quality and the larger the file size.

reverse the spine   To switch the front and back objects of a blend.

RGB   A color model that reproduces color by mixing different levels of red, green, and blue light. RGB is common in onscreen graphics.

S-shaped curve   A curve that changes direction in the middle.

scale   To change size.

scatter brush   A brush style that takes a separate illustration and places copies of it outside the boundaries of the path.

scratch area   The space outside the margin of the page in Illustrator.

segment   A section of a path that falls between two anchor points.

shape tools   Tools in Illustrator that draw simple shapes, such as ellipses and rectangles.

smooth color blend   A blend object with so many intermediate steps that it appears to be a continuous shape.

smooth point   An anchor point whose segments come out as curves.

spine   The path along which the intermediate shapes of a blend object fall.

stacking order   The internal list in Illustrator that determines which paths appear in front of other paths in the document window. By default, the most recently drawn path sits at the top of the stack.

stroke   The part of a path that describes the outline or contour.

swatch   A small square that represents a color, gradient, or pattern.

tile   To repeat an image at regular space intervals.

trace   To change a raster image into a vector.

tracking   The amount of space between all the characters in a line of type.

transformation   Any kind of modification to a path, especially when the modification comes from a transformation tool or command.

transparency   The appearance attribute that makes its object partially invisible.

type area   A predefined container for text.

type layer   A separate layer that contains all the text in an illustration.

vector graphics   Computer images composed of paths. EPS (Encapsulated PostScript) and SWF (Flash) are vector graphics formats.

vertical type   Text that flows from top to bottom instead of left to right.

web-safe color   One of the 216 most common RGB colors. Nearly every Windows and Mac computer can display these colors, so you can use them with confidence in web graphics.

weight   The thickness of a stroke.

Index